SOCIAL JUSTICE, EQUALITY AND EMPOWERMENT

SOCIOECONOMIC STATUS AND HEALTH IMPLICATIONS

Social Justice, Equality and Empowerment

Additional books in this series can be found on Nova's website
under the Series tab.

Additional E-books in this series can be found on Nova's website
under the E-book tab.

Health Care Issues, Costs and Access

Additional books in this series can be found on Nova's website
under the Series tab.

Additional E-books in this series can be found on Nova's website
under the E-book tab.

SOCIAL JUSTICE, EQUALITY AND EMPOWERMENT

SOCIOECONOMIC STATUS AND HEALTH IMPLICATIONS

SARAH REIBERT
AND
ALICE JANNINGS
EDITORS

Nova Science Publishers, Inc.
New York

Library of Congress Cataloging-in-Publication Data

Socioeconomic status and health implications / editors, Sarah Reibert and Alice Jannings.
p. ; cm.
Includes bibliographical references and index.
ISBN 978-1-62100-675-6 (hardcover)
I. Reibert, Sarah. II. Jannings, Alice.
[DNLM: 1. Health Status Disparities. 2. Healthcare Disparities--economics. 3. Socioeconomic Factors. WA 300.1]

362.1086'2--dc23

2011037430

Published by Nova Science Publishers, Inc. † New York

CONTENTS

PREFACE

The relation between socioeconomic status and population health is evident in epidemiological studies. Socioeconomic status is typically measured using income and financial resources, occupation type, and educational attainment. In this book, the authors present topical research in the study of socioeconomic status and its health implications. Topics discussed include diabetes, marginality, and gender identity; the socioeconomic aspects of health services in Israel; low socioeconomic status and child mental health disparities; adolescent health risk behavior from a migrant population in the United Arab Emirates; Japanese women's health related to job stress and the hidden costs incurred by families and friends of patients with low health literacy.

Chapter 1 – In this chapter, it is explored how men's illness experiences interplay with notions of male gender identity in a context of urban poverty. It draws on empirical findings from an anthropological fieldwork in Northeast Brazil among men and women with low-income, living in the city of Salvador, and afflicted with type 2 diabetes, which has become a common illness among urban poor in Brazil. Brazil is the country in Latin America with the highest number of people afflicted with diabetes and while it used to afflict the more affluent members of society, it is now increasingly afflicting people with low socioeconomic status. This high diabetes prevalence is part of a global trend in which chronic and non-communicable diseases have become the major disease burden in many low and middle-income countries. Diabetes is a chronic disease that affects people in their social and gendered lives and it often does so in a disruptive manner. In this chapter it is argued that the conditions of poverty and privation shape and limit peoples' ability to take care of their chronic illness, but the ethnographic data from Brazil also demonstrates that gender can be a determining factor. This is due to the challenges diabetes poses to male gender identity, which is central to understanding the resistance to being ill that was observed among the male interlocutors. In illuminating this matter, the analysis also touches upon how diabetic disruptions are experienced differently among men and women. Inspired by Kleinman's notion of asking what is at stake for people in a given situation (2001), it is concluded that what really is at stake for men with diabetes is – more than their health – their male gender identity. This is what they respond to as they try to resist being ill and put their health at risk, which have dire and even fatal consequences.

Chapter 2 – The southern peripheral area of Israel is characterized by a widely dispersed, culturally-diverse and polarized socio-economic population creating special needs in the healthcare delivery system. This chapter explores quantitatively the main issues influencing the delivery and use of the central health specialty clinics in Beer-Sheva (the main city in the southern-periphery). The findings were complemented by qualitative research that analyzed issues considered important by the population in regard to health-service delivery. The quantitative study population consisted of patients that visited specialist clinics in a central medical care facility in Beer-Sheva between 2000-2005. The number of patient visits was analyzed (parametric and non-parametric) according to independent variables – population size, age-distribution, gender, family size, cars/household, socio-economic-level and distance from Beer-Sheva. The findings show that the distance from Beer-Sheva and socio-economical-level have a negative correlation to the number of patient visits to the specialist clinics. The qualitative study consisted of interviews with public administrators, health-service deliverers, and local residents (Jews and Bedouin). Using Extracting-Field-Theory and Content-Analysis, three main topics that represent "Socio-economic Aspects of Health Service in the Southern-Periphery of Israel", were identified: (1) Distance, an objective aspect measured in kilometers, includes other elements revealed in the interviews, such as the direct cost of travel to the clinics in Beer-Sheva, car availability, public transportation availability, distance from home to bus stop, time wasted in traveling, and affect on work and domestic routines. Residents living in different areas of the region relate differently to the travel issue to health clinics: A mother with a developmentally disabled child living in a rural town, thinks that "*it is hard work*" to get to the clinic; a family from kibbutz says that "*Every time we needed follow-up, we made the visit into a fun outing in the big city*". The Bedouin population living outside the recognized towns surrounding Beer-Sheva encounters the hardest difficulties and barriers in accessing health care in the main city. Public transportation is often not accessible and the low socio-economic level prevents private transportation. One interviewee explained: "*I have to walk 4 kilometers with my child in my arms to the main road and then wait for someone to do me a favor and stop to give me a ride*". These interviews indicate that distance does have impact on the use of health services, however economic level, accessibility and availability of transportation are just as important. (2) Level of social identification with the community is based on the individuals' sense of belonging to their local place of residence, the geographical area, and to the state. A virtual scale divides the population according to the variety of culture, and level of foreignness and belonging. At the high extreme are the Kibbutz-members: "*The kibbutz-community is in many ways the highest level in Israel*". The middle section contains Jewish and Bedouin communities, a woman from a recognized Bedouin town says: "*If a woman has self-confidence she should have no problem doing anything she wants. I drive a car and can go easily to the market, medical care or anywhere I want*". The low-extreme is the Bedouin from outside the recognized towns. One man says "*It is a disgrace to ask a neighbor for help. I alone have to take care of my issues. Everything – alone*". (3) The inequality of health services in the periphery in comparison with the center is an issue the interviewees included even though it was not in the scope of the interview. One mayor stated the general feeling of frustration of the population: "*If I would sum all the budget promises given to me by the government, they would total the budget of the USA*". On the other hand, many have a good personal feeling: "*When we lived in the center it was good but here, we have a good life here...different attitude, better ...we feel we are in a good place*". It is clear that a fitting health system in the periphery has to build programs that take into consideration the needs of specific communities, such as distance to health services, the socio-economic level, and culture.

Chapter 3 – The link between low socioeconomic status (SES) and child mental health problems is well established. Nevertheless, the mechanisms underlying this relationship are multi-faceted and complex, involving factors at the child, parent, community, and system levels. For children living in low-income families, disparities in mental health are further accentuated by limited access to care, fragmented care, and poor quality of care. Thus, in this chapter we review the influential role of social determinants of mental health for children living in poverty. Next, we review disparities in mental health services access and utilization. Finally, we discuss strategies for reducing disparities among low SES children through interventions targeted to prevent, detect, and treat mental health problems within and across community-based care sectors serving low-income children.

Chapter 4 – This chapter will explore the relationship between socioeconomic status and health in fast developing nations. Using new data from the United Arab Emirates (UAE), the health status of the expatriate population that resides in the UAE is examined. The UAE is a federation of seven emirates that has experienced unprecedented growth in the past forty years. The federation is situated in the southeast of the Arabian Peninsula in Southwest Asia on the Persian Gulf. The largest emirate, Abu Dhabi is the nation's capital. The remaining six emirates (Dubai, Sharjah, Ajman, Umm al-Quwain (UAQ), Ras al-Khaimah (RAK), Fujairah) form the Northern Emirates. Using oil revenue, the UAE continues to reduce reliance on oil and to diversify its economy from a conventional, labour-intensive economy to one based on knowledge, technology and tourism. In doing so, the UAE relies on a large expatriate population to transfer their skills and to build these sectors. These expatriates seeking financial gains are usually allowed into the country on a work permit. Although their socioeconomic status varies, many face challenges related to access to healthcare, proper housing, and various environmental changes. This chapter will report on data collected under the *National Study of Population Health in the UAE (NSPHUAE)* (2007 – 2009). A comprehensive large-scale cross-sectional survey was administered on expatriate families with children that attend public and private schools in the seven emirates. The survey collected data related to the general health status of this sub-population, exposures to a range of health determinants, demographics, as well as medical diagnoses.

Chapter 5 – The socioeconomic status (SES) is considered a well-established risk factor for poor health, the poorer the SES the worse prospects for health outcomes. SES gradients in disease's risk are partially explained by bad health related behaviors, and partially by environmental conditions that people at lower SES are exposed to. Stressors whether they were physical or psychological, activate several neural pathways including the hypothalamus-pituitary-adrenal axis and the autonomic nervous system. The stress response aimed to create resilience and guarantee survival may then turn in mal-adaptation, increasing vulnerability to illnesses. One of the consequences is the increase in the cortisol plasma levels that superimpose to the endogenous corticosteroids circadian rhythm which might be altered by the low SES, as well as by an adverse work or domestic environment, conditions that determine chronic psychosocial stress, and contribute to the prevalence of severe illnesses. Indeed, negative correlations between monthly income wage and salivary cortisol levels were reported. When the SES is accompanied by additional stressors, the risk for diseases is accentuated and, in some cases, stress is characterized by hypocortisolism rather than hypercortisolism. High levels of epinephrine were also associated with low SES. These stress hormones effects on the brain and peripheral organs may trigger diseases to which the individual presents some genetic predisposition. Therefore, public policies that give social support to people living in low SES may impact positively on their health.

Chapter 6 – Socioeconomic status (SES) has been shown to play an important role in socialization. In the present study three indicators of socioeconomic status were examined in terms of their relations with each other and three areas of social adjustment. The three measures of SES were: father occupation, Family Affluence Scale, and a single question regarding the individual's subjective evaluation of the family's SES. The social adjustment measures included school adjustment, parental support, psychosocial well-being, and two related behaviors health habits (physical activity, and dietary habits). The sample was composed of 3,168 Italian middle school students (47.3% girls). Bivariate correlations among the three measures of SES were weak, and only one of those measures (the subjective evaluation) was consistently correlated with adjustment. Using Structural Equation Models, however, showed that the different measures of SES could be used to create a latent construct of SES, which demonstrated a reliable relation with four of the five social adjustment constructs (school adjustment, parental support, and two health habits). Our results suggest that, in the study of social inequalities during adolescence, we need to consider indicators that could have a strong effect during the rest of the life. Moreover, comparing different type of analysis, the study offered a rationale for use SES in terms of a latent construct.

Chapter 7 – This paper intends to investigate how some elements of material and social deprivation affect standard of living and life expectancy in the Italian and French regions. Literature suggests that forty indicators from Eurostat databases have a significant influence on them; thus a study with a set of comparable data on deprivation in Italy and France (a couple of quite similar countries according to their social and economic structure) is likely to yield interesting results. Our analysis aims at highlighting the difference between the two countries and also the different parts of them. The research has been carried out following the factorial analysis methodology on those database collections. The factorial analysis has been used to choose the deprivation variables, which were utilised to create two distinct condition indexes referring to material and social, respectively. The index of the social and material condition (SMCI) consists of the sum of the two indices. Both indexes are positively correlated with life expectancy; the material index, however, correlates more highly than the social index. Our choice of putting together Italy and France is due to the comparable history, culture, institutions of both countries and the structure of their economies, as several authors maintain and the Governor of the Bank of Italy has remarked recently (May 2011) in his report on the Italian economy, citing social and economic indicators.

Chapter 8 – The Japanese average life expectancy has continued to increase during the periods of high economic growth in Japan after World War II. Indeed, it is widely acknowledged that economic growth has an impact on health inequality. However, these changes occur alongside the facts that Japanese women have unstable job statuses, and encounter large wage differences compared with men, low promotion rates, low access to child-rearing services and high burdens of aged people's care. Despite this, their life expectancy is longer than those in other countries. Gender differences in physical health should be clarified with consideration of not only biological and physical factors, but also social, psychological and cultural factors. In this chapter, Japanese women's physical health related to socioeconomic factors, specifically job stress, will be discussed with data from Japanese cohort studies, to indicate how the study gender not only contributes to, but is central to, a wider social analysis.

Chapter 9 – *Introduction:* Low written and numerical literacy significantly impact patient outcomes. However, no research has focused on the impact of low health literacy on a patient's friends and family. Moreover, the costs of health literacy have not addressed the extended costs to family and friends. We prospectively conducted a cross-sectional study using validated instruments and structured patient interviews to assess the impact of this guidance. *Methods:* This cross-sectional study consisted of face-to-face interviews of 356 patients. Patients were asked questions assessing their demographics and socioeconomic status and the status of a possible companion to the visit. Finally, patients were asked how many times per month they required accompaniment to the physician. In addition to this interview, patient literacy, numeracy, and educational status were assessed. Frequency analysis and descriptive statistics were performed to examine the distribution of demographic and clinical characteristics of these groups. Univariate analysis was conducted to compare patients with and without accompaniment. Chi-squared analysis and Whitney-Mann U-test was used for categorical variables and the t-test for continuous variables. *Results:* Of the cohort, 199 patients (56%) were accompanied by a friend or relative. Patients with accompaniment tended to be more likely female ($p=0.001$), have a lower educational attainment ($p<0.001$), and have lower health literacy ($p=0.048$). Patients with accompaniment reported on average (SD) 1.3 (1.7) doctor appointments per month, which was significantly higher than the 0.9 (0.9) visits reported by patients without accompaniment ($p=0.031$). According to the patient, these appointments lasted an average (SD) of 1.5 (1.5) hours, though some lasted up to four hours. Of the variables examined, only educational attainment and health literacy were significant predictors. *Conclusions:* Navigation of the US healthcare system often requires accompaniment. This accompaniment incurs significant expense and dramatically increases the costs of low socioeconomic status.

Chapter 10 – Although the undernourished still outnumber the over-fed, global rates of obesity are increasing, especially among older adults. While overweight and obesity is inversely proportional to socioeconomic status in the developed world, the reverse has historically been true for the developing world. Labeled the "nutrition transition" by (Popkin 1994, 2004) and initially described in Latin American urban populations, this phenomenon appears to be spreading rapidly across the developing world. As overweight and obesity increase, a concomitant increase in prevalence of chronic diseases (e.g., cardiovascular disease and diabetes) is likely. Recent epidemiological studies report rates of overweight and obesity exceeding 70% for U.S. and South African older adults (National Social Life Health and Aging Project; WHO Study of Global Aging and Adult Health), and near 15% for the aged in India (WHO/SAGE). However, less is known about the cultural and socioeconomic context of this nutritional transition. This paper combines in-depth anthropological data from field work in western Kenya and India with population-level data, to demonstrate the importance of cultural and socioeconomic context for understanding global trends in overweight and obesity among older adults. The Indian data demonstrate the importance of social position in shaping dietary patterns and physical activity. Increasing medicalization has led to the belief that health problems associated with overweight are easily addressed with medication. As the prevalence of overweight and obesity increases in India so does chronic disease prevalence. In Kenya, overweight and obesity are closely tied with higher socioeconomic status and perceived as a sign of wealth and health. Data from western Kenya suggest that, at least for some health problems overweight are associated with better health. The complex relationships between socioeconomic status, cultural context and body size present considerable challenges for public health efforts towards curbing the growing obesity pandemic.

In: Socioeconomic Status and Health Implications
Editors: Sarah Reibert and Alice Jannings, pp. 1-27
ISBN: 978-1-62100-675-6

Chapter 1

DIABETES, MARGINALITY AND GENDER IDENTITY: CHALLENGES AND CONTRADICTIONS IN MEN'S DIABETES CARE IN NORTHEAST BRAZIL

Marie Kolling
University of Copenhagen

ABSTRACT

In this chapter, it is explored how men's illness experiences interplay with notions of male gender identity in a context of urban poverty. It draws on empirical findings from an anthropological fieldwork in Northeast Brazil among men and women with low-income, living in the city of Salvador, and afflicted with type 2 diabetes, which has become a common illness among urban poor in Brazil. Brazil is the country in Latin America with the highest number of people afflicted with diabetes and while it used to afflict the more affluent members of society, it is now increasingly afflicting people with low socioeconomic status. This high diabetes prevalence is part of a global trend in which chronic and non-communicable diseases have become the major disease burden in many low and middle-income countries. Diabetes is a chronic disease that affects people in their social and gendered lives and it often does so in a disruptive manner. In this chapter it is argued that the conditions of poverty and privation shape and limit peoples' ability to take care of their chronic illness, but the ethnographic data from Brazil also demonstrates that gender can be a determining factor. This is due to the challenges diabetes poses to male gender identity, which is central to understanding the resistance to being ill that was observed among the male interlocutors. In illuminating this matter, the analysis also touches upon how diabetic disruptions are experienced differently among men and women. Inspired by Kleinman's notion of asking what is at stake for people in a given situation (2001), it is concluded that what really is at stake for men with diabetes is – more than their health – their male gender identity. This is what they respond to as they try to resist being ill and put their health at risk, which have dire and even fatal consequences.

INTRODUCTION

Brazil is undergoing tremendous changes and today it has become the leading economic power in Latin America and among the 10 largest economies in the world. With the changes in living standards and life style that many Brazilians are experiencing (Pearlman 2004) new challenges are emerging. The chronic disease burden facing low and middle-income countries worldwide is arising as a result of an increase in life expectancies combined with urbanization, modernization and economical development (Meyrowitsch and Bygbjerg 2007:32). It is estimated that on a global scale, 80 percent of the burden of diabetes and other non-communicable diseases (NCDs) falls on developing countries (Silink 2009:2). This is evident in Brazil that is the country in Latin America with the highest number of people with diabetes and it has also become the fourth main cause of death preceded by stroke, heart attack/ ischemic heart disease and assaults (WHO 2004:8; MoH/WHO 2006:37). Diabetes prevalence is higher in urban areas than in rural areas and this is also the case in Brazil where 87 percent of the population today live in urban areas (IDF Diabetes Atlas 2006:82-83, CIA World Factbook). The global epidemiological transition from communicable to non-communicable diseases has not only been geographic but also demographic and diseases like diabetes are now increasingly afflicting people with low socioeconomic status (Unwin and Marlin 2004:27, IDF Atlas 2006:3). This chapter thus provides a much needed insight into local responses of men and women with T2D living in urban poverty to this global epidemiological transition.

T2D accounts for 85 to 95 percent of all diabetes worldwide and perhaps an even higher percentage in developing countries (IDF Atlas 2006:8). People with T2D are therefore the object of investigation here. The study presented is based on five months of ethnographic fieldwork, conducted in 2009 among men and also women with T2D living in low-income communities in the city of Salvador, Northeast Brazil. The illness experiences are examined with regard to the challenges of being poor and being ill, but also, and what came to be more important, how male gender identity affects men's diabetes care. The ethnographic study will be referred to as the Bahia study.

In the state of Bahia where the ethnographic fieldwork was carried out, diabetes prevalence has doubled in less than a decade. It went up from 7.6 percent in 1999 to 15.7 percent in 2008 and is thus higher than the national prevalence of 11 per cent (da Cruz Silva 2008:314). Bahia is located in the northeast of Brazil, which continues to be the region in Brazil with the highest mortality rates of NCDs, according to the latest surveys, and it is also among the poorest (Schmidt et al. 2011:1950-51). Many scholars have pointed to the correlation between low socioeconomic status and poor health and the pervasive structural inequalities that destine poor populations to disease and ill health (Biehl 2007:9 see also Farmer 1999, Wilkinson 1996). Poverty has, however, been under-recognized as a contributory factor to diabetes prevalence (Congdon 2006:73). It is now estimated that on a global scale, poor people are more likely to develop chronic diseases and more likely to die from them (IDF Diabetes Atlas 2006:3). This means that the risk of becoming ill when poor is high and once afflicted, taking proper care of the illness is difficult, which colleagues and I have discussed elsewhere, based on ethnographic data from Tanzania (see Kolling, Winkley and von Deden 2010; Kolling et al. 2008). Some of the same dynamics pertain to the situation in Brazil. Taking a closer look at the diabetes prevalence in Brazil fewer men than women are afflicted with diabetes and yet more men die from diabetes (IDF Atlas 2006:81,231, Ministry of Health/Vigitel 2007), which raises questions about the way that men take care of their diabetes. In this chapter men's illness experiences will therefore be explored and the interplay between male gender identity, chronic illness and socioeconomic poverty. I found that diabetes affects arenas for the enactment of masculinity and thereby contests male gender identity. This becomes an obstacle for their diabetes care that is characterized by challenges and contradictions.

T2D manifests itself much later in life than type 1 diabetes and when it does, it causes bodily disruption that often is so comprehensive that it reshapes the sufferer's circumstances and social relationships.

I propose the term *diabetic disruptions* to capture this process. It draws on the term *biographical disruption* coined by Bury (1982) to describe the disruptive nature of chronic illness and the dual process for the individuals afflicted who, on the one hand, have to deal with the physical symptoms and impairments and on the other hand, have to (re)negotiate social roles and responsibilities (de-Graft Aikins 2006:428).

Diabetes is an individual and complex disease that affects people differently both in terms of the physical complications and their social consequences. '*Diabetic disruptions'* thus encompasses the diversity of individual bodily experiences that have shared social consequences.

Chapter Outline

I begin the chapter by presenting the interlocutors of the study, the setting, and the methodology in order to contextualize the obstacles people experienced in taking care of their diabetes.

These obstacles will be examined with regard to access to public health care and the health care services provided. I then pursue a more gendered analysis and look into the interplay between illness experiences and male gender identity. I explore various types of diabetic disruptions and how they interfere with arenas for enacting male gender identity. The two arenas in focus here are; the arena of sexuality, since a common complication of diabetes is impotence, and the arena of employment as it becomes difficult for men to uphold employment due to ill-health. Both issues are closely connected to notions of masculinity (Kimmel 2007; Parker 1991; Kulick 1997; Morgan 2005; Scott 1996; Silberschmidt 2001, 2005, Barker 2005).

Having established that diabetes poses challenges to male gender identity, ethnographic accounts are provided of the ways that the male interlocutors tried to do away with diabetes that this in turn posed challenges to their diabetes care. The ethnographic data show that diabetic disruptions were experienced differently among men and women and this gendered difference in illness experiences is analysed.

Finally, I discuss the implications of these findings, in particular, the risks and contradictions in the male interlocutors' ways of dealing with diabetes and its potentially fatal consequences.

The Interlocutors

In Brazil, it is documented that health problems and their severity are distributed unevenly according to gender, ethnic origin, age and economic status and due to inequality in access to health services and other social interventions (Barradas Barata 2008:174; MoH/WHO 2006:36).

Given their structural position in Brazilian society in terms of these intersecting parameters as well as urban living, it is not surprising that the interlocutors had developed diabetes although many looked for explanations as to why *they* had been afflicted.

The primary interlocutors were between 40 and 67 years old and had been diagnosed with diabetes from 2 and up to 28 years ago. All interlocutors had developed common complications of diabetes such as kidney problems, nerve damage, hypertension, or severe visual impairment and some were retired due to their illnesses. Their educational level was generally low. They had all attended *ensino fundamental* (from 6 to 14 years of age), but not necessarily completed it. All interlocutors earned a low income in the area of a minimum salary, some a little more, others far less. An interlocutor, Francisco, who received a pension at the age of 43 that was equivalent to the minimum salary, explained the insufficiencies of the amount and concluded: "*Minimum salary is not enough for anything, it's not nearly enough to survive on!*". The interlocutors often pointed to their socioeconomic status when I was with them such as when I was invited for home visits and several would comment, apologetically, that: "*This is a poor people's house*".

Colour and class is interconnected in Brazil and although Brazil has the largest concentration of people of African descent outside of Africa this social group is disproportionately unrepresented in positions of power and, from the economic and social point of view, has a lower income and educational background than the rest of the Brazilian population (Aruajo et al. 2010:550-51). Compared to other major cities in Brazil, the population in Salvador has the highest percentage at 82 percent of people of Afro-Brazilian descent (IBGE September 2006). Throughout Brazilian history, whiteness in and of itself has been an important attribute of social status and is still a major line of demarcation between elites and the lower classes (Rebhun 1999:101). In an interview, a female interlocutor, Veronica 54, complained about being old, not finding employment and feeling overlooked. She then added: "*We are no different no, by being black, by being poor, we're not. We just don't have opportunities*". The majority of interlocutors were black, as were the vast majority of patients in the public hospital. In contrast, the health care professionals were white, which reflects that colour has a major bearing on education and class in Brazil.

The Setting

Salvador is the capital of the federal state of Bahia, located in the Northeast. The Northeast was once among the richest regions of the Americas and Salvador, which was founded in 1549 as the first capital of colonial Brazil, was at the heart of the economic fortunes (Rebhun 1999:38; Andrade and Brandão 2006:16). For three centuries, the trans-Atlantic slave trade made the port of Salvador the most important in the Americas. The abolition of slavery in 1888 and strong competition from the sugarcane and tobacco production in the Caribbean marked the economic decline at the end of the 19th century (Andrade and Brandão 2006:63-64; Shepher-Hughes 1992:41). Today the Northeast is poorer and less developed than the South of Brazil in terms of infrastructure, industries, universities, health services etc. (Rebhun 1999:38; Santos and Silveira 2008:231-34,275). The economic and also political shift from the Northeast to the Southeast combined with years of inequitable investment by the national government intensified differences among the regions of Brazil, favouring the South (Rebhun 1999:38,52). A period of industrialization and urbanization was sparked by the discovery of petrol near Salvador and between the 1950s and 1980s Salvador more than tripled its number of inhabitants. The uncontrolled migration to the city was accompanied by a lack of urban planning. This contributed to the marginalization of many of its inhabitants and a socio-spatial segregation that characterizes Salvador today and reflects the persistent, glaring and racialized socioeconomic inequalities of its population (Andrade and Brandão 2006:105-107,141; Biehl 2007:14; Gledhill and Hita 2009:11).

The interlocutors lived scattered all over the city, but common to them was that they lived in the deprived areas of the city, referred to in Brazil as the *periferia* (periphery). This emic term no longer merely reflects the geographical location of a neighbourhood on the resource-deprived outskirts of the city, but is used as a contrast to the centre in a centre-periphery hierarchy of those who are included in society and those who are excluded (DaMatta 1997b:32). *Periferia* covers a variety of neighbourhoods and likewise, there was diversity in the type of neighbourhoods as well as the particular type of housing (and their precariousness) where the interlocutors lived. Some of the districts of the city were among the poorest in Salvador based on income (Gordilho Souza 2008:238).

Overview of the Fieldwork and Its Methodologies

The fieldwork was conducted through March to July 2009. The methodological entry point was the Federal University Hospital where specialized diabetes treatment is offered for free, serving mainly patients of low-income backgrounds. From there I visited and interviewed interlocutors in their homes or at work and conducted participant observation in their daily lives that geographically extended itself to the entire municipality of Salvador and yet was restricted to its resource deprived areas. Through the network of these interlocutors, I met other interlocutors and hence used a snowball sampling method (Bernard 2006:192-93). By spending time with people in their daily lives, I also got to know their families, neighbours or friends from church or colleagues at work. A variety of complementary methods were employed to investigate the objectives of the study and to understand the lifeworlds of the interlocutors, predominantly individual interviews and participant observation.

I obtained informed consent from the primary interlocutors (men and women with T2D) prior to the interviews. Informed consent means that the researcher asks interlocutors for permission to include them in the study after information about the research objectives has been provided (Hardon et al. 2001:282). Interlocutors were assured that their participation was voluntary and that the data would be handled in a confidential manner and that their names would not be used in any publication or presentation. Hence, the names that appear in this paper are pseudonyms.

I was required by the University Hospital's Ethical Research Committee to use written consent forms. Many interlocutors seemed uneasy signing the document although we went through it before we both signed it. Among the interlocutors I met through my own or other networks, I therefore used verbal consent, which I found more useful in building an atmosphere of trust and confidentiality also because many interlocutors were not fully literate. It is stated in the Code of Ethics of the American Anthropological Association that informed consent does not necessarily imply or require a particular written or signed form. It is the quality of the consent, not the format that is relevant (2009:3). In a similar vein, Oxlund (2009) argues that following the formalized procedures for ethical research praxis does not in itself insure a responsible ethical engagement in the field. That is created through continuous critical reflection upon one's own engagement in relation to the analytical objective of the research and the insights gained throughout the research on local moral experiences.

That my investigation was carried out, in part, among men, demanded continuous critical reflection given the difference in my young age compared to the interlocutors as well as my sex, whiteness and foreign status. I attempted to position myself not only as a friend of the male interlocutors but also of their families. Befriending male interlocutors was not as simple and straightforward as building friendships with female interlocutors nor was establishing mutual trust and comfortable presence, which was probably due to some of – or a combination of – these differences. One interlocutor merely seemed to tolerate my presence and particularly, all my questions, while another interlocutor, on the other hand, appeared a little too fond of my company. Home visits were therefore repeated more among some interlocutors than others as I had to adapt to the possibilities and challenges the field presented.

The access I gained to the University Hospital was among the possibilities that emerged. I had originally intended to start the fieldwork at the ambulatory merely for the purpose of gaining access to people with low socioeconomic status diagnosed with diabetes, but since I was allowed to attend consultations and talk to staff, the hospital became a site for regular visits. So did a diabetes association in Salvador, ADISA, which provides: "Assistance to the deprived diabetic" as the sign at the entrance read.

Poverty and Illness

Urban poverty can be characterized as a number of material insecurities that translates into vulnerabilities and with that social uncertainty (Kolling et al. 2008; Meikle 2002; Whyte 1997). To spend time with interlocutors over a period of time was crucial in gaining insights into their life situations as they changed over time both due to the unpredictability of external conditions as well as the internal physical condition of their unstable health. Uncertainty and insecurity generally characterized the interlocutors' situations with regard to vital matters such as income, housing, safety, or the future of their children and/ or grandchildren. A deteriorating unstable health added further insecurity and vulnerability to their situation. Given the chronic nature of the disease, the health condition of the person with diabetes is subject to change as the chronic disease sometimes is in remission and at other times in recurrence (Kleinman, 1980:74). Such instability and with that unpredictability was also evident on a day-to-day basis as their health made them unable to follow through with the plans for the day or they would do so, but with discomfort and suffering from headache, exhaustion or pain. As pointed out by an interlocutor, Roberto, with regard to his health he never knew what the day was going to bring.

It requires a great variety of measures to take proper care of diabetes, which often necessitates profound lifestyle changes such as changes in diet, weight and exercise patterns. Various types of regular checkups are usually also necessary when afflicted with diabetes and many require one or more types of pharmacological therapy. To be able to take the necessary measures entail continuous access to such. All the primary interlocutors in the Bahia study had access to free public health care at local health posts. A national health service, *Sistema Ùnico de Saúde*, was put in place in 1988, entitling all Brazilians access to free public health services (Carvalho de Noronha et. al. 2008:436-538). Eight interlocutors were enrolled at the diabetes ambulatory at the university hospital where they had access to free specialized diabetes care and they were also entitled to certain benefits in accordance with Brazilian legislation, Lei N°11.347, that was passed on September 27, 2006. The benefits included free oral medication and/or insulin and other materials necessary for monitoring the blood sugar such as syringes, which were otherwise a huge expense for a low income family. Patients are only entitled to a limited range of medicines, which diminished the individualized medical treatment available. In addition, some interlocutors were granted free access to public transport and some with the right of an accompanying person, for example those with impaired vision.

For one interlocutor, Silvia, free consultations at the local health post was not sufficient for her to be able to attend treatment. She had not attended treatment for some time and she was hesitant about returning because she anticipated that she would be sent all over town for medical examinations and paying the bus fare was something she could not afford. She would also be prescribed medication that was unaffordable to her even at the subsidized prices at the public pharmacies, *Farmácia Popular*.[1] She was thus currently not attending any type of treatment due to financial constraints.

Curiously, the interlocutors received different benefits. Finding out why was time consuming, as well as why I gained contradicting information from the interlocutors about their illness and their options for treating it. The differences were not only due to interlocutors' lack of knowledge or lack of information provided by their health care professionals. It was also a result of the complexities of the system and not least because of the irregularities of the system, further exacerbated by people's abilities to bend the rules of the system. An interlocutor, Edilson, had for instance been able to enrol at the diabetes ambulatory in spite of the fact that the enrolment desk had been closed down because the system was overloaded. The interlocutor had a friend who was enrolled at the ambulatory, who had a good relationship with his physician and by mobilizing his personal connections he managed to enrol in the programme. Another interlocutor had managed to enrol in free

[1] *Farmácia Popular,* or the People's Pharmacy Programme, was launched in 2004. The programme aims to increase people's access to essential medicines. 107 items can be purchased at the *Farmacia Popular* at lower prices than the commercial pharmacies for the most common diseases in the Brazilian population such as drugs for diabetes, cholesterol, hypertension and gastritis. Today there are 530 public pharmacies in 408 municipalities that are implemented through a partnership of the Ministry of Health, federal governments, municipal government and charities (Ministry of Health).

specialized diabetes care both at the federal hospital and at the state hospital, which was officially not allowed. This is also called a *jeitinho,* which is an emic term that means to find a way or to find a solution to a problem, typically by managing to bend the rules of the system to one's advantage, using one's informal, often personal connections. It is a tactical practice that is made use of in all aspects of Brazilian life – necessary in dealing with an overburdened health system (see da Matta 1997a:232-238; Shepher-Hughes 1992:472-474; Rebhun 1999:69-76; de Certeau 1984:37). Mobilization of resources was enacted by all interlocutors in order to better their situation whether through *jeitinhos* or receiving help from their family or social network.

Structural Challenges to Effective Diabetes Care

The closing of the enrolment desk was a result of the great burden on the public health system that the drastic rise in diabetes prevalence has caused and allures to the much needed political response to the epidemiological reality of Brazilian society. In Brazil, it is generally only people who cannot afford private health care or do not otherwise have access to such who make use of public health care. Research shows that Brazilians of African descent live in areas which are less equipped with basic infrastructure services, and have more restricted access to health services, or these services have worse quality and are less efficient (Aruajo et al. 2010: 550-51). This is also evident from the Bahia study.

The health services provided generally appeared inefficient, ineffective and in some regards even counter-productive. To be granted free public health care was not necessarily the same as being granted access to quality care. An interlocutor, Sandro, had several toes amputated during the course of my fieldwork due to a huge wound on his foot. The wound was caused by a visit to a local health post because of a lump on his foot. He was attended to by a nurse who decided to cut off the lump. Given his diabetic condition, the wound did (of course) not heal. On the contrary it worsened, resulting in the deformation of the whole foot even as it started healing. He could barely even walk when I first met him and by the time I left Bahia, he had been on sick leave for six months.

As this story about Sandro's disabled foot shows, the limitations to the quality of the services provided affected the interlocutors' diabetes care. This also pertains to the doctor-patient relations at the diabetes ambulatory and standardized and rigid counseling that was not necessarily adapted to the local context and specific situations of the patients. In an article about diabetes self-management, Vallis (2009) writes that for people with a chronic disease, the relationship with health care providers is crucial and should be based on open and supportive interactions in which people can feel free to discuss the struggles as well as the positive changes they have attempted (2009:8). The lack of open and supportive dialogue that I found at the ambulatory can be exemplified by the case of an older patient. He had not been taking insulin for a month at the time of the consultation that I observed. The reason he had stopped taking insulin was that his wife who used to apply the insulin injections had died. The doctor told the patient off because he had not been taking his medication and all that was discussed in the consultation, that took about five minutes, was his medicine intake that had to be resumed. The patient was in a wheelchair, he had had both legs amputated and because his condition had worsened he faced having some of his fingers amputated as well. He was accompanied by his daughter who was concerned but unable to care for him because her own daughter was in the hospital, close to passing away. No sympathy was expressed towards the patient's situation or that of his daughter, only discontent that he was not complying. As they were leaving the room, the daughter turned to me with an apologizing look and said timidly "*coitada doutora*" (poor doctor) as if they were a bother to the doctor. At the diabetes ambulatory, the doctor-patient relation was characterized by differences in class, race and educational level, and it seemed evident that these differences influenced the interaction between staff and patients, which I believe the "*coitada doutora*" revealed. The whole scenario revealed an obvious lack of open and supportive dialogue and lack of consideration towards the social problems affecting their difficult situation. This example also allots to the concern expressed by interlocutors that there was an over-emphasis on medication during the consultations. Biehl has criticized the Brazilian public health system for having undergone: "an incremental change in the concept of public health, now understood less as prevention and clinical care and more as access to medicines" (2007:12). Biehl has labled this process the *pharmaceuticalization of public health* (ibid). Likewise, Shepher-Hughes (1992) argues that the interlocutors in her study in Northeast Brazil were met with a medicalization of their needs. Suffering from chronic hunger and undernourishment they were treated with tranquilizers, vitamins and sleeping pills and their condition was seen as an individual psychological problem detached from the social problems at stake (1992:169). This resembles a well-known critique of biomedical care famously raised by Kleinman et al. (2006). Kleinman claims that biomedical clinical care has banished the illness experience as a legitimate object of clinical concern. The primary interest is in diagnosing and treating diseases while clinical care should be directed at both the disease itself (abnormalities in the function of body organs and systems), and the illness that is the patient's experience of the problem (2006:140-141).

The Time and Efforts Put into Diabetes Care

For the interlocutors, attending consultations, other regular medical checkups or collecting the free medication or syringes would easily take up, all in all, most of their day. This was both due to the interlocutors' spatial and social location in the city and poor infrastructure, but also the structure of the health care services and problems of shortages of supplies. Some interlocutors noted that the public state hospital had a pharmacy where patient could collect their medication, which had been closed down at the federal hospital. This meant that interlocutors would spend a considerable amount of time every month doing "illness work" (Corbin and Strauss cited in Hardon et al. 2001:93).[2]

At the ambulatory, to be attended to was strenuous and to get an appointment in the first place was complicated. Patients could not set up appointments over the phone because there was no phone at the secretary's desk and she did not have readily access to their medical records either. Patients therefore not only had to go to the ambulatory to set up a new appointment, but they usually had to spend hours there, waiting to be attended to. That was the reason an interlocutor, Edilson, was at the diabetes ambulatory the first day I met him in the waiting room. It took him two hours by public transport to get to the ambulatory. That day

[2] For people holding employment this would be a problem, which several interlocutors commented on, but the interlocutors who held a job were largely self-employed and did therefore not run the risk of being laid off.

he had arrived at seven in the morning because people were attended to according to their time of arrival so the earlier the patients got there; the faster they would be attended to. Most of the interlocutors therefore left their home at about five in the morning when they had to go to the diabetes ambulatory. Once they got there, they could wait up to five hours for their (five minute) consultation or for the rescheduling of an appointment.

While patients were waiting, many often started feeling unwell. It seemed that it was not allowed to bring refreshments to the waiting room and since their name potentially could be called anytime they could not leave the waiting room to have refreshments elsewhere. I learned that several interlocutors would not have breakfast given that they would rise early and therefore did not take their medication either because it has to be taken in connection with food. It happened several times when I was in the nurses' office that patients who were waiting for an appointment would come in to have their glycemia measured because they worried that they were going into the hypoglycaemic condition, which is a critical condition that occurs when there is too little sugar in the bloodstream from not eating anything for too long.[3] Towards noon some of the patients still waiting to be attended to would start dozing off and one day when I was in the waiting room a woman did in fact go into hypoglycaemia.

It seemed paradoxical that patients would go for too long without food intake, which made them unwell, when attending consultations was supposed to better their condition. Given the increase in patients at the ambulatory, the frequency of appointments was reduced, lowering the quality of the treatment offered to patients. Some health care professionals also experienced a pressure to attend to more patients at higher pace in order to tackle the increased level of demand. One day I met an interlocutor, Maristela, who complained that she had spent the whole morning at the ambulatory to set up an appointment and was given one in four months time: "*If we die in the mean time – we die*!" she commented.

This exclamation gained a quite literal significance when I accompanied an interlocutor, Fabio, for his routine blood test. It was an early Tuesday morning in June. While an assistant nurse was drawing his blood, we heard shouts from outside and suddenly medical staff and patients burst into the laboratory and quickly locked the door. A robbery was taking place at the entrance hall of the hospital, where a bank was located. When we left the laboratory after some time, the hospital was in a complete state of chaos. Rumours had it that robbers had tried to rob the money transport and that one of them was still hiding somewhere in the building. The hospital had therefore been closed off by the police and police officers were running around the corridors armed with loaded guns, looking for the assaulter. When we finally managed to leave the hospital a crowd of people had gathered outside and local media crews were on the spot, broadcasting the event for the news at noon. Violence and crime affected the interlocutors in their daily lives – also in their diabetes care and at times in very direct ways.

Violent crime has increased in Brazil over the last three decades (Caldeira and Holston 1999:697; Caldeira 2006:106-115). Goldstein shows in her book on race, class, violence, and sexuality in Brazil, how violence is experienced in profoundly different intensities according to socioeconomic class (2003:202). It is also documented that the risk of suffering violence in its extreme form – homicide – is higher for residents of poor neighborhoods compared to the risk for residents of more wealthy neighborhoods (ibid; MoH/WHO 2006:42). At the time of

[3] Hypoglycaemia can cause dizziness, hunger, weakness and confusion and may lead to coma and death (Weiss & Funnell 2007:248).

my fieldwork, Salvador had the third highest homicide rate in Brazil (ranked by number of homicides per year) after Rio de Janeiro and São Paulo (*Último Segundo* 26/4/2010). One day while I was in the nurse's office, a patient asked to be attended by the nurse although she did not have a scheduled appointment. Her grandson had been shot dead by intruders in the night and she was now suffering such emotional stress that her blood pressure and blood sugar levels were out of control. There were many imperfections to the health care provided and even the severity of the security situation in Salvador intervened in peoples' attempts to do their illness work. Finances, geography and infrastructure also played a role in limiting access to the measures necessary to take care of their diabetes. Making use of *jeitinhos* was necessary in dealing with these challenges and mobilizing resources, which all interlocutors did. Poverty and privation were, however, not the only obstacles. The men in the Bahia study all had access to diabetes health care so although it was of questionable quality, access was not a problem in itself. Sandro's foot sheds light on this issue. The fact that he became unable to uphold employment due to his ill foot was not entirely the fault of the nurse at the health post. He had been told not to go to work, but only when his health deteriorated to the point that he had no other choice but to stay at home, he finally did. He then ended up on sick leave for a much longer period than would have been necessary. Problems to the men's diabetes care was about being poor and becoming ill, but as the following analysis suggests, in addition, the ways that male interlocutors dealt with the variety of diabetic disruptions they experienced also challenged their diabetes care profoundly.

Diabetic Disruptions to Male Gender Identity

The men's illness experiences were shaped by the challenges diabetes posed with regard to living up to the prevailing socio-cultural notions of masculinity. In suggesting so, I draw on the work of Carrigan, Connel and Lee. They have argued that there is a distance, and a tension, between the collective ideal of masculinity and actual lives of men. One should distinguish between the expectations made of people and what they in fact do since most men's lives reveal some departure from what the "male sex role" is supposed to prescribe (2002:106). It is this 'tension', or 'discrepancy' as I prefer to label it, between collective expectations of certain gendered behaviour and individual attempts to live up to these expectations that is intensified in the interplay between diabetes and enactment of gender identity. I posit that this discrepancy is central to understanding the illness experiences of the male interlocutors in the Bahia study. This is evident in relation to the arena of employment and sexuality in which interlocutors' experienced diabetic disruptions that will now be unfolded.

Challenges to the Arena of Employment

The notion that men should hold the position as providers of families was expressed by both male and female interlocutors and their children as well. Attempts of renegotiating this role in the wake of chronic illness was a challenge for many interlocutors as their health deteriorated. Roberto was an interlocutor whose health deteriorated dramatically, while I was on fieldwork. He came down with the flue after spending two days participating in a religious afro-Brazilian event. His condition worsened, he was then hospitalized for weeks and while in the hospital he came close to passing away. I visited him after he returned from the hospital and was shocked to see such a drastic change in his health. His foot was in a bad condition and had nearly been amputated and he was very weak and looked a lot older than last time I had seen him.[4] When I returned two weeks later he was better but still weak and severely walk-impaired. Yet he wanted to go back to work the following day. This seemed unwise given his condition and even a little absurd so I asked him if it could not wait a little bit to which he answered: "*You have to understand that although I'm sick, the bills don't stop coming.*" Roberto insisted on his responsibility to pay the bills, ignoring his wife's assistance in this matter. Although she probably earned a low income as a domestic worker, they did, nevertheless, share the burden of paying bills. This was perhaps because going to work was not only about the pride he took in earning money and paying bills like many of the interlocutors did, which was probably also connected to their working class background (cf. Morgan 2005). For Roberto, it was also a matter of maintaining his social potion as the provider and the male gender identity that was enacted in this capacity.

In Silberschmidt's work on masculinity and male sexuality in East Africa, she argues that men who are challenged in one arena of constructing gender identity will compensate for the loss of social roles and social value in other arenas (2001:667). Roberto was already challenged in the arena of sexuality because of his vulnerable health that made him suffer a loss of potency and reproductive ability. In view of Silberschmidt's argument, Roberto wanted to go to work in order to live up to the social position as the provider and thereby compensate in one arena for the enactment of masculinity because he was 'failing' in others. Roberto's wife was aware that he had to take good care of his health in order for his condition to improve and was deeply concerned that he insisted on going to work. I think Roberto knew as well, but he was determined to ignore the compliance of the good patient and stay committed to the responsibilities of the good husband. To choose between these two conflicting positions was a key dilemma for the male interlocutors in the Bahia study and a source of concern for their wives.

For interlocutors, whose wives went to work while they were confined to stay at home due to illness, this did not only mean that the male obligation of providing for the family was now undertaken by the wife; it also meant that the husband and wives' engagement in the male and female spheres had been reversed. In the analytical framework of the Brazilian anthropologist Da Matta (1997a, 1997b), the spheres of the street (*rua*) versus home (*casa*) form a dichotomy that is tied to the public world of men and domestic world of women, respectively, which was originally proposed by Rosaldo and Lamphere in 1974 (Lamphere 2001:100). If the home is considered a feminine space, then being confined to the home may be emasculating as staying 'at home' is not assertive to the preservation of male gender identity.[5] Ethnographic studies from low-income neighbourhoods in Recife, Northeast Brazil have shown that for a man, the ability to control his home and provide for it financially is

---

[4] Foot problems and amputations are very common among people with diabetes who are at risk of nerve damage and problems with blood supply to their feet that slow down the process of wound healing which can lead to ulceration (Bakker et. all 2009:15). A wounded diabetic foot is therefore a very serious problem.

[5] The men confined to the domestic sphere did not necessarily take on domestic chores that they would not otherwise take care of, but invested their time in other activities. To take on other domestic chores might have been even further emasculating.

essential in order for a man to establish his gender identity successfully (Dalsgaard 2000:162, Dalsgaard and Gough 2004:99; Scott 1996:289-90). Labour is therefore not only about generating an income; it is also about constructing a male gender identity (Morgan 2005, Scott 1996, Silberschmidt 2005). In a context of widespread poverty, the discrepancy between men's individual lives and the collective cultural expectations for men to be the providers is already severely challenged, and as the data from the Bahia study shows this discrepancy is likely to be further intensified in the wake of chronic illness.

Extramarital Relations

I was told by several interlocutors that the expectations for husbands were not only to provide for the family, but also to satisfy the wife's sexual needs. The husbands of Maristela and Ana Paula, two female interlocutors, did not provide anything at home neither sexually nor emotionally, but invested their affection in their mistresses. Hence, they were frequently referred to as "*he who pays bills*" rather than 'my' or 'her' husband because their relation had reduced him to the role of the financial provider. Further underscoring the importance of provision and the obligation to satisfy his wife sexually, one interlocutor, Lucas, explained how he would make sure to "eat in" before "eating out". This was also a matter of making sure nothing lacked at home as he later elaborated:

> "If I buy a kilo of flour for you, I'll have to give two kilos to my house. My house has to be supplied so that nothing is missing. That's my theory. First I have to provide for my family to then take care of others. Not the other way round."

This was likely to be because wives were on guard, watching for small signs of infidelity such as if the provision for the household diminished or if the husband stayed out all night, which female interlocutors mentioned as infidelity indicators (cf. Dalsgaard 2000:163). To be engaged in multiple relations and extramarital relations seemed to be a norm for masculine behaviour shared by many in Bahia and for some interlocutors a good sex life was tantamount to having multiple sexual partners. Several male interlocutors had had extramarital relations or still had at the time of my fieldwork. Concomitantly, the female interlocutors complained extensively about their ex-husbands' infidelities. Francisco mentioned that engaging in extramarital relations was an expensive endeavour that he could not afford. It was unclear if it was because of his financial inability to have such a need that his needs had changed:

> "I do not see the need today to have an extra [-marital relation] because it involves financial costs, right? For you to go out, to date, you have to have money, you know?"

Employment did not only enable men to provide for their families, but also enabled them to engage in extramarital relations in the sense that money is a condition for such relations. Both employment and extramarital relations were generally activities that were connected with the social sphere of the street, which can be exemplified in the manner an interlocutor talked about his adultery in an interview: "*I'm no saint, I already have a kid in the street*". Diabetic disruptions to male engagement in income generating activities as well as social activities connected to the social life in the street changed their life situations and at the core of this issue was also the change in their sexuality due to impotence.

Masculinity and Impotence

Sexuality is an arena that has been singled out by many masculinity scholars to be crucial to the enactment of masculinity (Kimmel 2007; Parker 1991; Kulick 1997; Silberschmidt 2001, 2005). Masculinity is closely associated with notions of virility, fertility, and potency (Parker 1991:43; Silberschmidt 2001:667), and the importance of virility therefore also makes male sexualities "signs of weakness and vulnerability" (Plummer 2005:179). Diabetes may affect male sexuality and expose such vulnerabilities because of the high correlation between diabetes and impotence[6] (Ekoé et. al. 2001:8; Sexual Health and Medicine August 2006:6). According to statistics, impotence affects more than 50 percent of men with diabetes (de Brito Cunha 2005:69; Tamler 2009:5; Hatzimouratidis and Hatzichristou 2009:115; Hopper 1981:14), and urologists I spoke with in Salvador believed this percentage to be much higher and more likely at 75 percent, which is also suggested by other researchers (Rendell et. al. 1999:422). Diabetes is a progressive condition for which there is no cure, which thereby also applies to impotence caused by diabetes although glycemic control is key to avoiding complications of diabetes (interview urologist June 4 2009 and endocrinologist April 1 2009, de Brito Cunha 2005:69). Impotence may also be caused by a complex relationship between physical complications and psychological factors and a large study conducted in Brazil about impotence concluded that apart from depression, low self-esteem from unemployment was also an important risk factor (Abdo et al. 2006:8).

In the interlocutors' narratives of impotence, some said directly that it was a problem while others spoke specifically of reduced frequency in sexual activity rather than reduced quality in sexual performance. Furthermore, these experiences were normalized through explanatory idioms such as age and monogamy rather than diabetes. For some it was normalized through both age and monogamy like Lucas, who said that: "*You have to accept the things by the age that you come around*" and spoke of a natural reduction in one's sexual needs when in the 30es compared to the 50es. He continued his account saying that, if he used to have sex three times a day he now had sex three times a week and implied that reduced sexual activity was naturally something that came with age. Meanwhile, this did not entail changes in the quality of his sexual performance as he was: "*until now still doing things normally*". He hereby indicated that he was not experiencing sexual dysfunction as such. It was rather his sexual desire for his partner that had diminished after many years of marriage, which resulted in less sexual activity: "*when you go on being with the same person you get used to that person, so you don't stay with that fire.*" He then added that this was not an issue when he was with other women.

---

[6] Impotence refers to a complexity of problems with ejaculation and erectile dysfunction such as the inability to attain or maintain an erection that is sufficient for sexual intercourse (Sexual Health & Medicine August 2006:6). I have chosen to use the term *impotence* rather than the much used term *erectile dysfunction* (ED) because I find that ED narrows down the many different causes of male sexual dysfunction. It is a term that has become increasingly popular with the expansion of pharmaceutical treatments of ED such as the introduction of the oral medicine Viagra in 1998 (Johnson 2008:38). The major causes of impotence in men with diabetes are due to problems with blood flow and nerve damage because of the affects diabetes has on both the vascular and nervous systems (IDF Atlas 2007:351, interview urologist June 4 2009).

In accounts about sexuality, male interlocutors expressed an emphasis on the importance of erection. Such phallocentric understanding of male sexuality matches the conclusions reached by Parker (1991, 1998) and Kulick (1997) in their ethnographic works about sexuality in Brazil. Both describe that men must be understood in part through their opposition to women, but also other men such as the homosexual. In this manner, the gender hierarchy in Brazil can be structured along the distinction between homosexuality and heterosexuality (Parker 1991:44, 1998:256). The patriarchal tradition still provides an ideal for men with the father and the *machão* being positively valued figures, who embody values of force and power, aggression, virility and sexual potency (Parker 1991:44). The distinction between those who take the *active* role during sexual intercourse and those who *passively* offer themselves to be penetrated by their partners presents a system of classification and it is the first of these two groups that Brazilian culture defines – in view of their active, phallic domination – as men (Parker 1998:256). Gender identity is hereby thought to be determined by one's sexual behaviour and as Kulick writes: "The locus of gender difference is the act of penetration. If one only penetrates, one is a man..." (1997:579-80). Hence, the determinative criterion in the enactment of male and female identities is not so much the biology (genitals), but the role the genitals perform in sexual encounters. This underscores the gravity of impotence problems and may also explain why some of the interlocutors spoke of reduced frequency in sexual activity rather than erectile difficulty. Reduced sexual activity was not as threatening to their masculinity.

That gender identity is enacted through one's sexual behaviour links up with Judith Butler's argument that gender is not a fixed attribute but something that is constantly enacted and performed (1999).[7] My theoretical approach to understanding gender identity is social constructivist, drawing particularly on the theories of Connel and Butler. In Connel's classic work on masculinity, she discusses a dynamic approach to masculinity and moves towards a definition of masculinity as simultaneously a place in gender relations, the practices through which men and women engage that place in gender, and the effects of these practices in bodily experience, personality and culture (Connel 1995:71). Connel argues that gender is social practice which ties in with the work of Butler on the construction of gender identity that is performatively produced:

> "Gender is always a doing, though not a doing by a subject who might be said to pre-exist the deed. [...] There is no gender identity behind the expressions of gender; that identity is performatively constituted by the very "expressions" that are said to be the results" (1990:25).

That gender is socially constructed does not make gender illusory or artificial but it makes the process of *doing gender* an ongoing bodily as well as discursive practice (ibid). When Roberto displayed his intentions of going back to work as described above, perhaps this was not only a wish to resume a "bodily practice" of working and paying bills but also an expression of a discursive practice to affirm his position as the provider of the household. In the arena of sexuality male interlocutors experienced reduced frequency of sexual activity and

[7] The enactment of gender identity through sexual behaviour applies to women as well. In the interview with Maristela she said that she felt like a woman in her sexual relation with her boyfriend: *I felt like a woman, I felt great [...] With him I felt fulfilled."* She felt gendered though her sex life which illustrates that not only men perform their gender through sexual relations, but so do women.

a few also mentioned erectile difficulty and an explanation will now be offered as to why none of these experiences were attributed to diabetes.

Diabetes, Impotence and Stigma

When I went to visit the diabetes association, ADISA, I had hoped to meet men with T2D. When I got there I learned that the association had 70 female members and only two male members and these two men did not take part in the daily activities. They only participated in special events from time to time, accompanying their wives who were also members of the association. There had been a maximum of five male members throughout ADISA's existence. When I asked how come there were so few male members, the secretary pulled me aside and said in a low voice:

> "Let me tell you a secret". "Men with diabetes become impotent. Everybody knows that and therefore they don't like to show that they have diabetes because it is a big blow to them to lose their potency. Potency means everything. Without it they are no man."

While this was not the explanation I had expected, the secretary's explanation did confirm my assumption that the correlation between diabetes and impotence was commonly known in Brazil. People would instantly connect 'men' and 'diabetes' with impotence, which were the two key words I would mention when asked about the purpose of my fieldwork. This has not been my experience in Europe and Africa and it therefore surprised me that this issue was commonly known and often spoken of in a low and even secretive whisper.

If potency is crucial to a man's sense of masculinity, as discussed above, and if it is commonly known that men with diabetes experience impotence problems in a socio-cultural context where potency is particularly prevalent to enacting and performing masculinity, then surely men would not want to be associated with diabetes. This specific complication of diabetes can hereby create a *disease stigma* for men with diabetes. *Disease stigma* constitutes a "negative social 'baggage' associated with a disease" (Parker and Aggleton 2003:19), but stigma is a dynamic social process rather than a fixed attribute that people associated with a certain disease may try to resist (ibid:14). This may explain why some interlocutors largely attributed their reduced frequency in sexual activity to ageing and monogamy rather than diabetes although it was likely to have been diabetes related.[8] This may also explain why the diabetes association had almost no male members, since being a member would be a clear statement of being diabetic, which was not a statement that was in the men's interest to make. The link between diabetes, impotence and stigma is likely to have made the diabetes association a stigma producing site for men to go to. None of the male interlocutors expressed any interest in joining ADISA or seeking any of the services and activities offered there.

In an article about stigma and secrecy, Reid and Walker write that secrecy entails a selective denial of uncomfortable truths and denial is self-deception, which is a way to keep secret from ourselves the truths we cannot face (Reid and Walker 2003:85). I believe there is an aspect of denial in the interlocutors' accounts. However, Reid and Walker also write that

[8] While impotence problems are likely to happen as a man becomes older, age in itself does not cause impotence. Rather, it is the more frequent occurrence of certain health issues in older men, such as diabetes, that account for the increase in impotence with age (Sexual Medicine Society 2009).

secrets do not only operate to repress and dominate, but can also be a resource used by marginal individuals and groups to claim power (ibid). If stigma should be understood in relation to broader notions of power then the male interlocutors, in negotiating the loss of status that illness and loss of potency cause, were possibly resisting this social process by attempting to conceal it to avoid stigma and a general loss of power. One of the interlocutors even talked about getting rid of "*the stigma of the diabetic*" when talking about going off insulin.

DOING AWAY WITH DIABETES

None of the male interlocutors liked to take insulin and some even refused to take it. Sandro was one of the interlocutors who so far had avoided it as he explained in an interview:

> *Sandro:* "The doctor prescribed it for me, but I have only taken it once. I thought: 'I've never taken insulin and will never take insulin'. Instead I take the oral medication and drink a [herbal] tea. It lowered my blood sugar so I am waiting to see how it goes. Only if it gets really high I will take insulin."
>
> *Interviewer:* "Why do you prefer not to use it?"
>
> *Sandro:* "It leaves this spot, this black spot. People think that... horrible things! It leaves these spots on the legs, on the arms [visible body parts]."

The head doctor at the diabetes ambulatory confirmed that if applied incorrectly, insulin injections may leave black spots on the skin of people with dark skin. Here it seems relevant to point to stigma in the original sense of the word in which it refers to discrediting visible marks on the body (Goffman 1963:11). That insulin was experienced as a marker of disease was also expressed explicitly by Marcio in an interview who stated: "*Insulin, it marks you as diabetic*". Marcio had managed to replace insulin with oral tablets by undertaking lifestyle changes such as significantly decreasing his alcohol intake and he had stopped smoking, which had improved his condition. The commitments to changes in lifestyle or the consumption of herbs were measures by which Marcio and Sandro attempted to avoid insulin and thereby the visible marker of diabetes and of (disease) stigma. Marcio said it had made his life a lot easier and pointed to the problem of the dependency on insulin not only in terms of the impracticalities of taking insulin, that has to be stored in a cool place which is complicated when away from home, but also with regard to the burden of being dependent on insulin to stay well. He now felt much more "*free*", he said, and I asked if that was important to him to which he answered:

> "I think it's very important because you get rid of the stigma of the diabetic, that you are a person who has to take insulin, carry it with you and so on... I think it is an enormous burden..."

Edilson was another interlocutor who found that insulin created dependency and that this made people live in function of the disease. He thought that the dependency on medication made people weak and live as if they were even more sick. He therefore chose not to think of himself as someone living with an illness and in his effort to do away with insulin and his diabetes in general, he redefined what controlling diabetes means. A common approach promoted in guides for a good diabetes life such as *The Little Diabetes Book You Need to Read* (Weiss and Funnell 2007) is that: 'by controlling diabetes it will not control you'. Edilson's interpretation of this approach was, however, that he should do exactly what he wanted to. As a consequence, for nearly three weeks during carnival Edilson did not take his oral medication; he did not eat properly and he drank excessively. When he returned to the diabetes ambulatory for his consultation the following month, he had lost 10 kilos and his blood sugar was high. He was told that he had to start taking his medication properly; otherwise they would change his medication to include insulin, but for Edilson, taking insulin was a trait of weakness:

> "...it's no good to go around thinking: 'Oh I'm diabetic, so I shouldn't do this or that'[...] you cannot be a weak person, you have to be a strong person and that person who depends only on medication is weak, he will live as if he was sicker. If the doctor says so to me: 'Edilson, you will have to take insulin' I think, I'd tell her: 'I will not take it, I will not take it!'"

The pressure to be put on insulin was used deliberately by doctors at the diabetes ambulatory because insulin was associated with something bad, with being severely ill as one doctor put it, and the prospect of having to take insulin was therefore considered an incentive for patients to start complying. Edilson, however, continued not to make the advised life style changes because being strong was about resisting giving in to the illness and resisting insulin.

Francisco was an interlocutor who was insulin dependent and in poor health and when I learned that he would skip his insulin from time to time I assumed it was because he did not always have access to insulin. He had another severe condition for which he took daily medication and his wife and daughter also suffered serious chronic conditions for which they needed medication so his family had plenty of medical expenses and was in a critical financial situation.

Francisco had, however, never failed to obtain insulin, he explained, he just did not always take it because he did not like it. When I asked him why, he answered that it hurts. Health care professionals and interlocutors alike alerted me to the discomforts of insulin injections, but I found it hard to believe that Francisco did not take his insulin only because he found it uncomfortable – particularly as the discomfort followed by not taking it ought to be worse. I later learned that Francisco sometimes worked as a day-labourer in construction although he was retired due to his ill-health. He had to take the insulin an hour after breakfast at which time he was already on his way to work so the impracticality of having to inject insulin *in the street* (*na rua*) offered yet another explanation.

I believe, however, that there was more to the avoidance of insulin than impracticalities and discomfort. One evening, I stayed at Francisco's house until the point in the evening when the neighbours returned from work.

A few neighbours passed by and one of them was a young man who came over to ask Francisco to help him inject hormones into his biceps. The neighbour came to Francisco's house once a week because

Francisco was the 'syringe expert'. Injecting hormones to facilitate a well trained body was common among young men in Salvador and so was walking around in public without shirts on and show off their muscular bodies.[9] The young man wanted to look big and buff because he worked at a naval base north of the city as Francisco explained. The injection was taken care of in the living room where Francisco's family was gathered. This scenario demonstrated that injections were not problematic per se. It was more likely the type of injection that constituted the problem. The young man received an injection to enhance a masculine body image and thus perhaps an injection due to vanity was easier to accept than one, representing vulnerability.

Pursuing a gender identity through the active enhancement of a muscular body resonates with Butler's theory that gender is performatively produced (1990:25). If insulin was perceived as a marker of disease, representing weakness and dependency on medicine to stay well, then injecting insulin necessary for survival may be counter-productive to performing gender. I found it intriguing that Francisco was ascribed the status as 'syringe expert' because he had diabetes and yet he did not like to take insulin although it was vital to his health, but perhaps it was because using it was emasculating and contested the notion of men being the strong gender, which was a dilemma other interlocutors also struggled to come to terms with.

In the social constructivist approach, masculinities are constructed in a context of class, race, ethnicity, age, region of the country and location in the global economy and are embedded in historical processes and power dynamics (Silberschmidt 2003:142; Connel and Messerschmidt 2005:846). The context of the male interlocutors in the Bahia study was one of marginality within Brazilian society given their class, race, socio-spacial location within the city of Salvador and in the country as previously described.[10] They were also undergoing a process of aging that was exacerbated due to illness and thus there was undoubtedly a lot at stake for the men in the Bahia study as their gendered understanding of self and in relation to others was challenged, which further challenged their already marginalized position both inside and outside the home.

Gender Differences in Illness Experiences

The male interlocutors' attempts of doing away with diabetes undermined their diabetes care, which was due to the challenges the illness posed to their male gender identity as it affected arenas for enacting masculinity. Examples of doing away with diabetes have been illustrated by Edilson who redefined controlling diabetes to mean that he should not change his lifestyle or be compelled to take insulin because that would make diabetes control him – and staying in control was about staying masculine. Or Sandro who had ignored his wounded foot and kept going to work. This had worsened his condition, eventually rendering him unable to work, and at the time of my fieldwork, he had been on sick leave for more than six months and uncertain of when he would be able to return. Roberto was in the process of doing

[9] Hormonal injections seemed to be a common measure for young men to build up a muscular body along with exercise and powdered forms of protein. Hormonal injections can be purchased over-the-counter at pharmacies in Salvador and at a relatively cheap price. Likewise, Kulick describes in his article about transvestites in Salvador how they used hormones to achieve female figures to look more attractive and they were much valued (over silicone injections or implants) because hormones were inexpensive, easy to obtain and fast working (1997:392-93).

[10] I found people in Salvador to be quite conscious of this regional difference, expressed as a sense of inferiority towards the South, and it came up in many of my interviews, particularly with those interlocutors who had previously migrated to the South, namely São Paulo and Rio de Janeiro, to find employment.

the same. Or Francisco who helped a neighbour inject hormones to enhance a masculine body image while he did not like to inject his own insulin regularly although it was vital to his already unstable health.

These male responses to diabetic disruptions differed from the illness experiences of the female interlocutors perhaps because the social consequences differed. The men experienced diabetes as confining to them in their everyday life as they became unable to go to work or otherwise participate in social activities in the street like taking lovers or hanging out with male friends, drinking in the street or participate in carnival as some lamented. On the contrary, diabetes was experienced as enabling for the women as they engaged in formal and informal diabetes networks that provided them with new opportunities to socialize and participate in the public sphere. Apart from attending ADISA regularly, Maristela also attended a support group for people with diabetes at the university hospital run by a nurse. Likewise, Silvia had been attending a diabetes group at the local health post and Veronica interacted on a daily basis with 'sisters' from the church in her neighbourhood who had diabetes and other chronic illnesses. Their participation in these networks also presented opportunities to receive support in their diabetes care whereas male interlocutors received support from their wives at home. During my participant observation in the interlocutors' daily lives another common difference between male and female interlocutors was that the women constantly talked about their diabetes with me and with each other, which I came to realize was never the case among the men unless I brought up the topic (see Kolling 2010). I would attribute the women's engagement in formal and informal diabetes networks and constant diabetes talk to a social process whereby they internalized and appropriated a diabetes identity. This process was a contrast to male interlocutors for whom it was a matter of doing away with diabetes.

The concept of *biological citizenship* formulated by Rose and Novas (2005) is useful here because it accounts for this internalization and appropriation of a diabetes identity. *Biological citizenship* can embody a demand for particular protections, policies or actions and create access to special resources such as to a form of social welfare based on medical, scientific and legal criteria that both acknowledge biological injury and compensate for it (2005:441). Biological citizenship is both individualizing and collectivizing in the sense that individuals shape their relations with themselves in terms of knowledge of their somatic individuality. Expressions like: "*I'm diabetic*" or "*we diabetics*" are manifestations of somatic individualities, which were frequently used among female interlocutors and curiously absent among male interlocutors. Biological citizenship is also collectivizing in that new forms of *biosociality* are assembled around categories of corporeal vulnerability, somatic suffering and genetic risk and susceptibility (2005:442, 446). It can lead to *biosocial groupings* such as support groups that are collectivities formed around a biological conception of a shared identity and ADISA is an example of such a *biosocial grouping*. Its members received both emotional and technical support and were encouraged to claim their rights to free medication or pension and explained how to do so. Other topics relevant for their diabetes care were discussed formally by the association secretary and health care professionals affiliated with the association and informally among the members. ADISA also organized social activities and festivities at the association as well as excursions. When attending any type of ADISA activity, members were expected to wear blue ADISA t-shirts. Both the individualizing and collectivizing aspects of biocitizenship, as described by Rose and Novas, demand an acknowledgment of the illness and the vulnerability that the illness presents. This is likely to have made the participation in biosocial groupings and the appropriation of a diabetes identity less attractive to men than women as this was not advantageous to the performing of their gender identity. I also posited previously that the diabetes association could be seen as a stigma producing site for the male interlocutors, which may also explain male and female interlocutors' different engagement in diabetes care and biosocial groupings. Perhaps the requirement to wear special ADISA t-shirts was not favouring for the recruitment of men either.

RISKS AND CONTRADICTIONS

The ways in which the male interlocutors dealt with their diabetes can be characterized by resistance since they resisted staying at home and recovering, or resisted taking insulin, or refused to adapt to the lifestyle changes necessary for postponing or perhaps even avoiding some of the many complications derived from diabetes. In this resistance there was an inherent contradiction in choosing to stay committed to masculine ideals, and the ideals of the good husband and not committing to the compliance of the good patient, which entailed clear health risks. Gender theory underscores that men's health risks are shaped by social norms and cultural expectations of masculinity and the commitment to risk-taking practices as a means to establish masculine reputation and live up to masculine ideals (Bates et al. 2009:1003; Connell and Messerschmidt, 2005:851; Chant 2003:120; Barker 2005:2). Risk-taking is considered a major health risk for men in Latin America where male morbidity and mortality are more likely than for women to occur as a result of risk-taking practices (Chant 2003:120). The Bahia study thus shows that older men in Brazil also engage in risky conduct to perform their masculinity and not only young men, as typically have been the focus of studies on risky male behaviour (e.g. Barker 2005; 2006 Dalsgaard 2007; Goldstein 2003). Linking the risky behaviour of the male interlocutors to the mortality rates among men with diabetes in Brazil indicates that masculine ideals can be pervasive and even deadly matters. In Brazil, the number of deaths attributable to diabetes is higher among men than women in most age groups (from 20-49 and 70-79) although diabetes prevalence is higher among women than men (IDF Atlas 2006:81,231, Ministry of Health/Vigitel 2007). This matches the general mortality rates in Brazil that are much higher among men than women, which is especially attributed to violent deaths among young men (IBGE demographic survey 2000). Considering that diabetes is the fourth main cause of mortality in Brazil (MoH/WHO 2006:37) the extent of this issue is concerning.

All the male interlocutors spoke of accepting diabetes or that one had to "respect" the illness, but accepting diabetes encompassed more than adapting to lifestyle changes such as cutting down on sugar, alcohol or fatty foods, which some had mastered. It also entailed accepting the social consequences that followed as the illness progressed, which made the respect of diabetes something that was easier said than done – depending on what was at stake. For the male interlocutors to fully accept diabetes would therefore have required an adjustment of the ideals of what a respectable masculine identity encompassed in order to re-negotiate their social roles and responsibilities in the wake of their illness. During a conversation with Roberto he mentioned that diabetes complicates everything and said: "*When a guy acquires diabetes, he stops living*". He then explained the things he could no longer do that had meant a great deal to him, as well as things he could not eat that he really liked, and continued: *"Diabetes has diminished everything in life. Like the sex as well... Diminished the potency*". This underscores what has been examined throughout this chapter that what really is at stake for men with diabetes as their health worsen is their male gender identity.

CONCLUSIONS

There is a knowledge gap within research about how people with a low socioeconomic status in low- and middle-income countries cope with diabetes and the social implications of the disease that they are in fact coping with, which I have shed light on here. The interlocutors were dependent on public health care and, thus, had to live with its imperfections and make the most of the benefits they were able to mobilize. To refuse to take insulin or not attend scheduled consultations calls for further explanation and here I have argued that the gendered aspects of illness experiences, related to socio-cultural ideals of masculinity and male interlocutors' attempts to live up to them, were the reasons for their attempt to do away with diabetes and their resistance to being ill. Diabetes challenged male gender identity by limiting the ways in which men could enact their masculinity and exposing them to emasculization and stigma. In trying to resist and negotiate these social processes, the male interlocutors dealt with diabetes differently compared to the female interlocutors whose social positions were not similarly threatened. With the various challenges and contractions in men's diabetes care, they put their health at risk that in return was further weakened and their masculinity further contested.

REFERENCES

Araujo, E. M., Nascimento Costa, M., Fernandes de Oliveira, N., Santos Santana, F., Barreto, M.L; Hogan, V., Araújo, T.M. (2010). "Spatial distribution of mortality by homicide and social inequalities according to race/skin color in an intra-urban Brazilian space". *Revista Brasileira de Epidemiologia.* [online]. Vol.13 (4): 549-560.

Abdo, C. H. N., Oliveira Jr, W. M. de, Scanvino, M. de T., Martins, F. G. (20069. "Erectile dysfunction: results of the Brazilian sexual life study". *Revista da Associação Médica Brasileira.* Vol.52 (6): 424-429.

American Anthropological Association. (2009). "Code of Ethics of the American Anthropological Association. Approved February 2009". [cited March 8th 2010]; Available from: http://www.aaanet.org/_cs_upload/issues/policy-advocacy/27668_1.pdf

Andrade A. B. and Brandão P. R. B. (2006). *Geografia de Salvador*. Salvador: Editora da Universidade Federal da Bahia

Bakker, K. van acker, K. Morbach, S. and Perry, A. (2009). "Promoting foot care education in developing countries: the Carribean Diabetic Foot Care Programme". *Diabetes Voice.* Vol 54 (3): 15- 21.

Banerji, M.A. and Lebovitz, H. (2001). "Non-Caucasian North American Populations: African Americans". In: *The Epidemiology of Diabetes Mellitus: An International*

Perspective. Ekoé, J.-M., Zimmet, P. and Williams, R. (eds), pp. 157-180. New York: Wiley.

Barker, G. T. (2005). *Dying to be men. Youth, Masculinity and Social Exclusion.* London and New York: Routledge.

Barker, G. T. (2006). "Growing up Poor and Male in the Americas. Reflections from Research and Practice with Young Men in Low-income communities in Rio de Janeiro". In: *The Other Half of Gender. Men's Issuues in Development.* Correia and Bannon (eds), pp. 111-135.Washington: Washington: World Bank Publications.

Barradas Barata, R. (2008). "Condições de Saude da População Brasileira". In: *Políticas e Sistema de Saúde no Brasil.* Giovanella, L. (org.), pp. 167-213. Rio de Janeiro: Editora Fiocruz.

Bates, L. M, Hankivsky, O. and Springer, K. W. (2009). "Gender and health inequities: A comment on the Final Report of the WHO Commission on the Social Determinants of Health". In: *Social Science and Medicine.* Vol. 69: 1002-1004.

Bernard, R. (2006). Research Methods in Anthropology: Qualitative and Quantative Approaches. 4th ed. Lanham: AltaMira Press, pp. 169-195

Biehl, J. (2007). *Will to Live: AIDS Therapies and the Politics of Survival.* Princeton: Princeton University Press.

Bordieu, P. (1998). Den maskuline dominans. 2nd edition. Copenhagen: Tiderne Skifter, pp. 1-50.

Bury, M. (1982). "Chronic illness as bibliographical disruption." *Sociology of Health and Illness.* Vol. 4 (2):167-180.

Butler, J. (1990). *Gender trouble: feminism and the subversion of identity.*_London: Routledge, pp. 1-35.

Bygbjerg, I. C. and Meyrowitsch, D. W. (2007). "Global burden of disease – a race against time". *Danish Medical Bulletin.* Vol. 54: 32-34.

Caldeira, T. P. R. (2000). *City of Walls. Crime, Segregation, and Citizenship in São Paulo.* Berkeley and Los Angeles: University of California Press, pp. 1-52, 105-222, 317-322.

Caldeira, T. (2006). "I came to sabotage your reasoning!": Violence and Resignifications of Justice in Brazil pp. 102-149. In: Comaroff, J. and Comaroff, J. (eds.) *Law and Disorder in the Postcolony.* Chicago: University of Chicago Press.

Caldeira, T. and Holston, J. (1999). "Democracy and violence in Brazil". In: Comparative Studies in Society and History. Vol. 41 (4).

Carrigan, T., Connel, B., and Lee, J. (2002). "Toward a New Sociology of Maculinity" [1987]. In: *The Masculinity Studies Reader.* Adams, R. and Savran, D. (eds), pp. 99-118. Massachusetts: Blackwell Publisher.

Carvalho de Noronha, J., Dias de Lima, L., Viera Machado, C. (2008). "O Sistema Único de Saúde - SUS".In: *Políticas e Sistema de Saúde no Brasil* (Giovanella, L. org.), pp. 435-472. Rio de Janeiro: Editora Fiocruz.

Chant, S. (2003). "Gender and Health" In: *Gender in Latin America.* Chant, S. and Nikki, C. (eds), pp. 98-128. London: Latin American Bureau.

CIA World Factbook [cited June 30, 2011]; Available from: https://www.cia.gov/library/publications/the-world-factbook/geos/br.html

Congdon, P. (2006). "Estimating diabetes prevalence by small area in England". *Journal of Public Health.* Vol. 28 (1): 71-81.

Connel, R. W. (1995). *Masculinities*. Cambrigde: Polity Press, pp. 67-81

Connell, R. W. and Messerschmidt J. W. (2005). Hegemonic Masculinity: Rethinking the Concept. *Gender and Society*. Vol. 19: 829-858.

Da Cruz Silva, N. (2006). "Acepção da dieta pelos diabéticos de Serrunha (Sertão da Bahia)". In: *Escritas e narrativas sobre alimentacao e cultura.* Soares de Freitas, M. C., Fontes, G.A: V. and Oliveira, N. (eds), pp. 313-335. Salvador: EDUFBA.

Dalsgaard, A. L. (2000). *Matters of Life and Longing. Female sterilisation in Northeast Brazil.* PhD Thesis, Department of Anthropology, Faculty of Social Science, University of Copenhagen.

Dalsgaard, A. L. (2005). "Birth control, life control: female sterilization in Northeast Brazil" In: *Managing Uncertianty. Ethnographic Studies of Illness, Risk and Struggle for Control.* Steffen, V., Jenkins, R. and Jessen, H. (eds.), pp. 53-70. Copenhagen: Museum Tusculanums Forlag.

Dalsgaard, A. L. (2007). "Aids i periferien: ungdom, nydelse og social ulighed i Brasilien" In: *Unge Liv i Syd -Beretninger om børn og unge i udviklingslande.* Valentin, K. and Christiansen, C. (eds.), pp. 61-76. Copenhagen: Danmarks Pædagoiske Universitetsforlag.

Dalsgaard, A. L. and Gough, K. (2004). Et spørgsmål om forskel : Ungdom, vold og overlevelse i Recife. [A question of difference: Youth, violence and survival in Recife] In: *Ny Verden*, Vol. 37 (3)

DaMatta, R. (1997)a. *Carnavais, Malandros e Heróis: Para uma Sociologia do Dilema Brasileiro.* 6th ed. Rio de Janeiro: Rocco, pp. 85-136

DaMatta, R. (1997)b. *A casa and a rua. Espaço, cidadania, mulher e morte no Brasil.* 5th ed. Rio de Janeiro: Rocco, pp. 29-63.

Davies, M. (2007). "Should diabetes services routinely screen for psychological distress?" *Practical Diabetes International.* Vol.24 (9): 483-486.

Deacon, H., Stephney, I., Prosalendis, S. (2005). *Understanding HIV/AIDS stigma. A theoretical and methodological analysis.* Cape Town: HSRC Press, pp. 15-19.

de Brito Cunha, P. R. (2005). *Disfunção Erétil e o Endotélio. Diagnóstico e Tratamento.* Rio de Janeiro: Guanabara Koogan, pp. 21-81.

De Certeau, M. (1984). *The Practice of Everyday Life.* Berkeley: University of California Press.

de-Graft Aikins, A. (2006). "Reframing Applied Disease Stigma Research: A Multilevel Analysis of Diabetes Stigma in Ghana". *Journal of Community and Applied Social Psychology.* Vol. 16: 426-441.

Ekoé, J.-M. and Zimmet, P. (2001). "The Clinical Syndrome and the Biochemical Definition" pp.7-10. "Diabetes Mellitus: Diagnosis and Classification" pp. 11-31. In: *The Epidemiology of Diabetes Mellitus: An International Perspective.* Ekoé, J.-M., Zimmet, P. and Williams, R. (eds). New York: Wiley.

Farmer, P. (1999). *Infections and Inequalities. The Modern Plagues.* Berkeley: University of California Press, pp. 1-59

Gledhill, J. and Hita, M. G. (2009). "New Actors, new political spaces, same divided city? Reflections on poverty and the politics of urban development in Salvador, Bahia". Paper for the Congress of the Latin American Studies Association, Rio de Janeiro, Brazil.

Goffman E. (1990) [1963]. Stigma. Notes on the Management of Spoiled Identity. New Jersey: Prentince-Hall, pp. 11-75.

Goldstein, D. (2003). *Laughter Out of Place. Race, Class, Violence, and Sexuality in a Rio Shantytown.* Berkeley and Los Angeles: University of California Press.

Gordilho Souza, A. (2008). *Limites do Habitar. Segrecação e exculção na conficuração urbana contemporânea de Salvador e perspectivas no final do Século XX.* 2nd edition. Salvador: EDUFBA.

Hardon, A., et al. (2001). *Health Systems in Applied Health Research Manual - Anthropology of Health and Health Care.* Amsterdam: Het Spinhuis Publishers.

Hatzimouratidis, K. and Hatzichristou, D. (2009). "Erectile Dysfunction and Diabetes Mellitus". *Insulin.* Vol. 4 (2): 114-122.

Hopper, S. (1981). Diabetes as a Stigmatized Condition: The Case of Low-income Clinic Patients in the United States. *Social Science and Medicine.* Vol. 15: 11-19.

IBGE (Brazilian Census Bureau) (2000). "Características da população" [demographic survey]. [cited October 10, 2009]; Available from: http://www.ibge.gov.br/ibgeteen/pesquisas/demograficas.html

IBGE (2006). [cited October 6, 2009]; Available from: http://www.ibge.gov.br/home/presidencia/noticias/noticia_impressao.php?id_noticia=737

IDF Diabetes Atlas (2006). 3rd edition. Brussels: International Diabetes Federation.

Johnson, E. (2008). Chemistries of love. Impotence, erectile dysfunction and Viagra in Läkartidningen. *Nordic Journal for Masculinity Studies.* Vol. 3, (1): 31-47.

Kimmel, M. (2007). The sexual self: the construction of sexual scripts. Nashville: Vanderbilt University Press.

Kleinman, A. (1980). *Patients and Healers in the Context of Culture: An Exploration of the Borderland between Anthropology, Medicine, and Psychiatry.* Berkeley: University of California Press, pp. 24-119.

Kleinman, A and Kleinman, J. (1991). Suffering and its professional transformation: toward an ethnography of interpersonal experience. *Culture, Medicine and Psychiatry.* Vol. 15 (3): 275-301.

Kleinman, A., Eisenberg, L. Good, B. (2006) [1978]. "Culture, Illness, and Care: Clinical Lessons From Anthropologic and Cross-Cultural Research". *Focus. The Journal of Lifelong Learning in Psychiatry.* Vol. 4 (1): 140-149.

Kolling, M., von Deden, M., Kudahl, N. , Svalgaard Nielsen, S., Nisansala Schmidt, N. (2008). "What will tomorrow bring? An anthropological investigation of characters of and conditions for illness action among people with diabetes in Dar es Salaam, Tanzania". Available from: http://www.psych.lse.ac.uk/socialpsychology/research/hcd/events/2007-08/partnershiponchronicdis/10_kolling_deden.html

Kolling, M., Winkley, K. and von Deden, M. (2010). '"For someone who's rich, it's not a problem". Insights from Tanzania on diabetes health-seeking and medical pluralism among Dar es Salaam's urban poor'. *Globalization and Health.* Vol. 6 (8).

Kolling, M. (2010). *Diabetic Disruptions to Male Gender Identity. An Anthropological Investigation of Chronic Illness among Men in the City of Salvador, Northeast Brazil.* Copenhagen: University of Copenhagen. MSc thesis.

Kulick, D. (1997). "The Gender of Brazilian Transgendered Prostitutes". *American Anthropologist.* Vol. 99 (3): 574-585.

Law no. 11.347. Lei N°11.347, de 27 de Septembro de 2006. Approved by the National Congress. Brasília. [cited April 20, 2010]; Available from: http://www.planalto.gov.br/ccivil_03/_Ato2004-2006/2006/Lei/L11347.htm

Lamphere, L. (2001). "The domestic sphere of women and the Public World of Men: The strength and Limitations of an Anthropological Dichotomy". In: *Gender in Cross-cultural Perspective*. Brettell, C. B. and Sargent, C.F. (eds.), pp. 100-109. Upper Saddle River, New Jersey: Prentice Hall.

Meikle, S. (2002). "The Urban Context and Poor people". In: *Urban Livelihoods. A people-centred approach to reducing poverty.* Rakodi, Carol and Lloyd-Jones, Tony (eds), pp. 37-52. London and Sterlin, VA: Earthscan Publications Limited.

Ministry of Health/ Vigitel (2007). "Dia Mundial do Diabetes: dados estatísticos". [cited March 29, 2010]. Available from: http://portal.saude.gov.br/portal/saude/ visualizar_texto.cfm?idtxt=29793andjanela=1

Ministry of Health. "Farmácia Popular". [cited March 26, 2010]. Available from: http://portal.saude.gov.br/portal/saude/visualizar_texto.cfm?idtxt=30269

Ministry of Health and World Health Organization (2006). *Painel de Indicadores do SUS.* SEGEP/MS and OPAS/WHO (eds). Brasília.

Morgan, D. (2005). "Class and Masculinity". In: *Handbook of Studies on Men and Masculinities,* pp. 165-177. Thousand Oaks: Sage publications.

Oxlund, B. (2009). "Kærlighedens topografi. Forskning som en rejse i et moralsk landskab". In: *Mellem mennesker. En grundbog i antropologisk forskningsetik.* K. Hastrup (ed.), pp. 95-113. Copenhagen: Hans Reitzels Forlag.

Parker, R. (1991). *Bodies, Pleasure and Passions. Sexual Culture in Contemporary Brazil.* Boston: Beacon Press, pp. 1-7, 30-67.

Parker, R. (1998). "'Within Four Walls': Brazilian Sexual Culture and HIV/AIDSCulture". In: *Society and Sexuality. A Reader*, pp. 253-266. London: Routledge.

Parker, R. and Aggleton, P. (2003). "HIV and AIDS-related stigma and discrimination: a conceptual framework and implications for action". *Social Science and Medicine.* Vol. 57: 13-24.

Perlman, J. (2004). "Marginality. From Myth to Reality in the *Favelas* of Rio de Janeiro, 1969 – 2000" pp. 105-146. In: Roy, A. and Alsayyad, N. (eds.) *Urban Informality: Transnational Perspectives from the Middle East, Latin America and South Asia.* Lanham, Maryland: Lexington Books.

Plummer, K. (2005). "Male Sexualities" In: *Handbook of Studies on Men and Masculinities*, pp. 178-195. Thousand Oaks: Sage Publications.

Rebhun, L.A. (1999). *The Heart Is Unknown Country. Love in the Changing Economy of Northeast Brazil.* Stanford: Stanford University Press.

Reid, G. and Walker, L. (2003). "Secrecy, stigma and HIV/AIDS: An introduction". *African Journal of AIDS research*, vol. 2 (2): 85-88.

Rendell, M., Rajfer, J., Wicker, P., and Smith, M. (1999). "Sildenafil for Treatment of Erectile Dysfunction in Men With Diabetes". *Journal of the American Medical Association*, vol. 281 (5): 421-426.

Rose, N. and Novas, C. (2005). "Biological citizenship". In: *Global Assemblages: Technology, Politics and Ethics as anthropological Problems.* Aihwa Ong and Stephen Collier (eds.) Oxford: Blackwell: 439-63.

Santos, M. and Silveira, M. L. (2008) [2001]. O Brasil: Território e sociedade no início do século XXI. 10th ed. Rio de Janeiro, Brazil: Editora Record.

Scheper-Hughes, N. (1992). *Death Without Weeping. The Violence of Everyday Life in Brazil.* Berkeley: University of California Press.

Scott, P. (1996). "Matrifocal Males: Gender, Perception and Experience of the Domestic Domain in Brazil". In: *Gender, Kinship and Power. A Comparative and Interdisciplinary History, pp.* 287-301. New York, London: Routledge.

Sexual Health and Medicine (2006). "Erectile Dysfunction and Diabetes". [cited December 10, 2009]; Available from: sexhealthmatters.com/v2/data/health/sexualhealthmedicine/EDdiabetes_shm8%2006.pdf.

Silberschmidt, M. (2001). "Disempowerment of Men in Rural and Urban East Africa: Implications for Male Identity and Sexual behavior". In: *World Development.* Vol. 29 (4): 657-671.

Silberschmidt, M. (2003). "Male disempowerment, male sexuality and HIV/AIDS in East Africa: Are disempowered men motivated for responsible sexual behaviour and HIV/AIDS prevention?" In: *Proceedings from the seminar. Gender, Sexuality, and HIV/AIDS. Research and Intervention in Africa.* Tersbøl, B. P. (ed.), pp. 126-149. Copenhagen: University of Copenhagen.

Silberschmidt, M. (2005). "Poverty, Male Disempowerment, and Male Sexuality: Rethinking Men and Masculinities in Rural and Urban East Africa" In: *African Masculinities - Men in Africa from the Late Nineteenth Century to the Present, pp.* 189-203. New York: Palgrave-Macmillan.

Silink, M. (2009). "The great awakening". *Diabetes Voice.* Vol. 54: 2.

Schmidt, M., Duncan, B. B., Azevedo, G., Menezes, A. M., Monteiro, C. A., Barreto, S. M., Chor, D. and Menezes, P. R. (2011). Health in Brazil 4. Chronic non-communicable diseases in Brazil: burden and current challenges. *Lancet.* Vol. 377: 1949-1961.

Tamler, R. (2009). "Diabetes, Obesity, and Erectyle dysfunction". *Gender Medicine.* Vol. 6: 4-16.

Último Segundo [Newspaper]. April 26, 2010 [cited June 10, 2011]; Available from: http://ultimosegundo.ig.com.br/brasil/cidades+do+interior+lideram+homicidios+no+pais/n1237596742022.html

Unwin, N. and Marlin, A. (2004). "Diabetes Action Now: WHO and IDF working together to raise awareness worldwide". *Diabetes Voice.* Vol. 49 (2): 27-31.

Vallis, M. (2009). "Barriers to self-management in people affected by chronic disease". *Diabetes Voice.* Vol. 54: 5-8.

Weiss, M. and Funnel, M. (2007). *The Little Diabetes Book You Need to Read.* Philadelphia: Running Press.

Whyte, S. (1997). *Questioning Misfortune: The Pragmatics of Uncertainty in Eastern Uganda.* Cambridge: University Press: 1-33, 224-251.

Wilkinson, R. (1996). *Unhealthy Societies: The Afflictions of Inequality.* London: Routledge, pp. 1-72.

World Health Organization (2004). *Diabetes Action Now Booklet.* Geneva. [cited November 2, 2010]; Available from: www.who.int/diabetes/actionnow/en/DANbooklet.pdf

Reviewed by assistant professor Dr. Bjarke Oxlund, University of Copenhagen.

In: Socioeconomic Status and Health Implications
Editor: Sarah Reibert and Alice Jannings, pp. 29-55
ISBN: 978-1-62100-675-6

Chapter 2

SOCIO-ECONOMIC ASPECTS OF HEALTH SERVICE IN THE SOUTHERN-PERIPHERY OF ISRAEL

Hasia Lubetzky, Shifra Shvarts, Galit Lubetzky and Lora Warshawsky-Livne

ABSTRACT

The southern peripheral area of Israel is characterized by a widely dispersed, culturally-diverse and polarized socio-economic population creating special needs in the healthcare delivery system. This chapter explores quantitatively the main issues influencing the delivery and use of the central health specialty clinics in Beer-Sheva (the main city in the southern-periphery). The findings were complemented by qualitative research that analyzed issues considered important by the population in regard to health-service delivery.

The quantitative study population consisted of patients that visited specialist clinics in a central medical care facility in Beer-Sheva between 2000-2005. The number of patient visits was analyzed (parametric and non-parametric) according to independent variables – population size, age-distribution, gender, family size, cars/household, socio-economic-level and distance from Beer-Sheva.

The findings show that the distance from Beer-Sheva and socio-economical-level have a negative correlation to the number of patient visits to the specialist clinics.

The qualitative study consisted of interviews with public administrators, health-service deliverers, and local residents (Jews and Bedouin). Using Extracting-Field-Theory and Content-Analysis, three main topics that represent "Socio-economic Aspects of Health Service in the Southern-Periphery of Israel", were identified:

(1) Distance, an objective aspect measured in kilometers, includes other elements revealed in the interviews, such as the direct cost of travel to the clinics in Beer-Sheva, car availability, public transportation availability, distance from home to bus stop, time wasted in traveling, and affect on work and domestic routines.

Residents living in different areas of the region relate differently to the travel issue to health clinics: A mother with a developmentally disabled child living in a rural town, thinks that "*it is hard work*" to get to the clinic; a family from kibbutz says that "*Every time we needed follow-up, we made the visit into a fun outing in the big city*".

The Bedouin population living outside the recognized towns surrounding Beer-Sheva encounters the hardest difficulties and barriers in accessing health care in the main city. Public transportation is often not accessible and the low socio-economic level prevents private transportation. One interviewee explained: "*I have to walk 4 kilometers with my child in my arms to the main road and then wait for someone to do me a favor and stop to give me a ride*".

These interviews indicate that distance does have impact on the use of health services, however economic level, accessibility and availability of transportation are just as important.

(2) Level of social identification with the community is based on the individuals' sense of belonging to their local place of residence, the geographical area, and to the state. A virtual scale divides the population according to the variety of culture, and level of foreignness and belonging.

At the high extreme are the Kibbutz-members: "*The kibbutz-community is in many ways the highest level in Israel*".

The middle section contains Jewish and Bedouin communities, a woman from a recognized Bedouin town says: "*If a woman has self-confidence she should have no problem doing anything she wants. I drive a car and can go easily to the market, medical care or anywhere I want*".

The low-extreme is the Bedouin from outside the recognized towns. One man says "*It is a disgrace to ask a neighbor for help. I alone have to take care of my issues. Everything – alone*".

(3) The inequality of health services in the periphery in comparison with the center is an issue the interviewees included even though it was not in the scope of the interview.

One mayor stated the general feeling of frustration of the population: "*If I would sum all the budget promises given to me by the government, they would total the budget of the USA*". On the other hand, many have a good personal feeling: "*When we lived in the center it was good but here, we have a good life here...different attitude, better ...we feel we are in a good place*".

It is clear that a fitting health system in the periphery has to build programs that take into consideration the needs of specific communities, such as distance to health services, the socio-economic level, and culture.

1. Health Policy Development in Connection with Social, Economic and Political Issues in Israel

The State of Israel was established in 1948 with strong socialistic elements. The first years of the young state were characterized as a "melting pot", an attempt to mold a new society from the immigrants coming from around the world. The next Israeli generations were born into the existing nation and felt less of an obligation towards the collective society. Therefore, the state's involvement decreased in the molding of the individual and personal identity. In the 1970's, conservative values started to conquer the main social groups in Israel, and for the first time, a right wing-conservative government was established in 1977.[1]

In the 1980s, the change continued and strengthened. Conservative and capitalistic characteristics took the place of the socialist and nationalistic values. This process influenced different factors in the state in different ways including the health system. In the 1990's, the Israel health system was modified. Besides the social changes that occurred over the years, three additional elements contributed to these health system changes: National Health Insurance Law enacted in 1995, large groups of new immigrants from the former USSR and

Ethiopia, and the use of medical-economic health models (rather than medical-biological) where the personnel is also required to make positive revenues for the health institution.[2]

Israel was not alone in changing in the 1980s and 1990s. In these decades, there were also global changes - relations between the countries of the world strengthened and immigration processes from eastern countries to western countries enhanced. This caused demographic, social and economic change in many fields including the health systems. Young people from diverse cultures and populations living in the periphery moved to the metropolises in the Western World. This created a heterogenic population of differing immigrants and the "original" residents of the cities. One outstanding difference is the amount and pattern of health service consumption, the immigrant being the needier and larger consumer of health services.[3,4]

The adapted health systems of the 21st century also needed to deal with new concepts and trends. The first concept comes from the marketing field. The fundamentals of any system are the interface with consumers. Health systems today treat the population in their care as clients and not as patients. The second comes from the social field. Highly researched and implemented field concerns the periphery and minorities. There is a whole spectrum of social healthcare that is defined by "periphery health" and "minority health". These definitions were together labeled as "Health services provision to culturally diverse populations".[5]

2. Demographics and Geography of the Southern-Periphery of Israel

In this section, different aspects pertaining to the southern-periphery of Israel will be introduced: the connection between the center and periphery in Israel, the metropolis space of the southern-periphery, Beer-Sheva and its surroundings, the demographics of the southern-periphery and the Bedouin living in the region.

Periphery is a geographic and demographic term describing the characteristics of a region such as distance from other cities, population density, transportation level, and other issues.[17] In Israel, like in other countries, a political and geographical process has been taking place over the years resulting in the defining of two areas.: The Core Area – the center of activity were decision-making of the state takes place, and the Periphery – geographically not in the center but influenced by the activities and events of the center. The core and periphery differ by geographical, demographic, economic, cultural and social characteristics. The main factors that differentiate the two is the term "commuting" - daily traveling from place of dwelling to the big city, mostly to work. Areas further from the center, which are not in a daily commute range, lack social and economic investment and therefore, are less attractive.[2,6,7]

Like in other countries, the decisions regarding the periphery are decided in the core. There is usually little consultation with the leaders of the periphery and minor consideration of the unique needs of these periphery areas.[7,8] This process started with the declaration of the State of Israel in 1948. The young state prepared a comprehensive national plan to formulate the concept of population distribution, development of the periphery and immigrant absorption which included the establishment of several towns referred to as "development towns". The national division of planning implemented national and social values that were then at the highest preference: working the land and settling the land (northern and southern areas of the country). These guidelines of the 1950s are the grounds for social, economical, cultural and health diversity that accelerated in later years. Therefore, distance from the core of the country positioned the periphery population as inferior – distant from higher quality sources of income, education and culture.

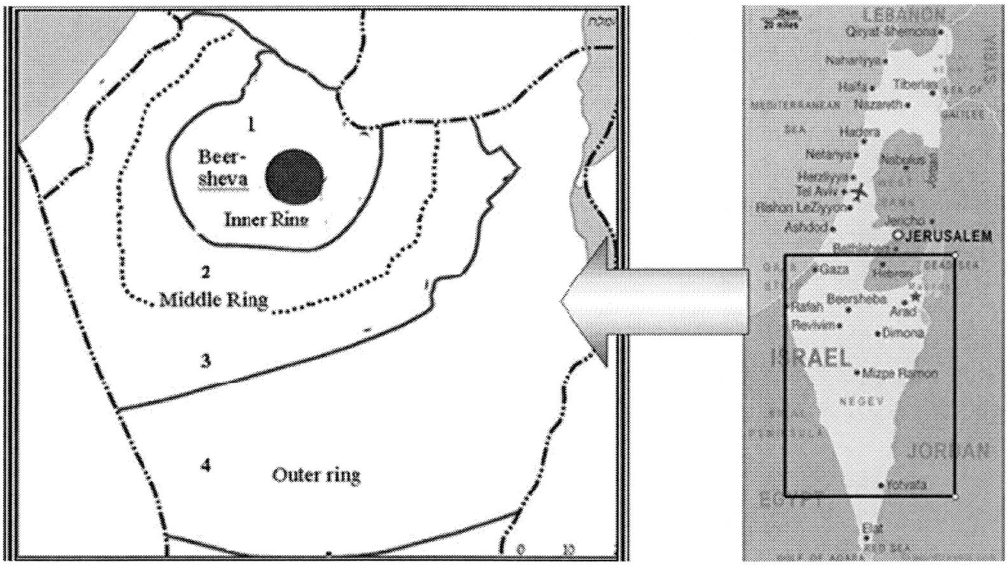

Illustration 1. Map of the southern region of Israel, divided by geographical rings[11,41].

In the 1960s, it was realized that sending the new immigrants to the periphery was a mistake. To correct the injustice, industrial grants were given to factories in the northern and southern periphery. Although these factories were plentiful in job possibilities, they also offered low pay. This course of action caused more damage than benefit. The existing gap only got larger. In the 1980s, there was another attempt to strengthen the southern-periphery. Following the peace treaty with Egypt in 1979, the government needed new settlement solutions for the population evacuated from the areas that were transferred to Egypt. The population was sent to settle in the southern-periphery of Israel without thinking through a plan.[1,2] In the 1990's, the new immigrants from the former USSR were sent to live in the southern-periphery, but not as a part of a national plan to strengthen the periphery. In retrospect, twenty years later, it can be said that the last wave of new residents did reinforce the towns and population of the southern periphery[10]. This population now is 30-50% of the population in most of the cities and large towns in the southern-periphery (while immigrants from the former USSR are only 15% of the general population of Israel).[6]

As in other countries of the world, in the Israeli society, especially in the southern-periphery, different ethnic and cultural groups exist side by side. Some of these groups are a part of the majority group, some integrate in only certain interfaces with the "Israeli society" and some groups differ from the majority in almost any aspect possible[11]. Israel defines itself as a Jewish state with a large diversity of Jewish and non-Jewish ethnic groups. The Israeli society is institutionalized to keep the rules of a democracy by allowing freedom of speech to all cultures and religions.[10,11]

The southern-periphery includes population groups that differ by culture, language, clothing, and tradition, but with many points of interface. This diversity is not only between new immigrants and long time residents or between Jews and Bedouin, but also among the varying types of communities, social-economic clusters, community resilience, level of religion tradition and political views.[10,12]

The southern-periphery region of Israel is geographically bigger than other geographical areas in the country. The distance to the core of the country and the distances within the area are the largest in Israel. The social-economic gaps are the most prevalent, sometimes between settlements that actually physically border each other. The variety of cultural groups in this area is the largest in the country. Any national process existing in the south is an extreme example for national procedures (such as health services provision to culturally diverse populations).[2,13,14,15,16]

According to the Israeli Bureau of Statistics,[15] there are four metropolises in Israel: Tel-Aviv (center/core), Haifa (north), Jerusalem (middle, capital), and Beer-Sheva (south). The metropolis of Beer-Sheva is divided according to its structure. The core encompasses an area of the main city with a radius of 15 km which is the center of population activity. Surrounding the metropolis are three rings defined according to the distance from the core: inner ring (15-30 km), middle ring (30-50 km), and the outer ring (above 50 km). Each ring also has a sub-division of north, east, south and west. The inner ring includes two cities (one mostly Jewish and one Bedouin) and a few local municipalities (Jewish municipalities are ranked in the highest socio-economic level while the Bedouin municipalities are ranked at the lowest socio-economical level). The middle ring contains the largest area and the most municipalities, with almost 80 local and regional municipalities serving Jews and Bedouins, secular and religious, agriculture and urban. The outer ring is the largest area with the lowest density in Israel.[10]

The "Beer-Sheva metropolis" encompasses the southern area of Israel (referred to as the Negev desert) which is 60% of Israel's total area. This area, although the largest in Israel, has the least number of residents (15% of Israel's population), therefore having the lowest population density area in Israel. In 2010, the population of the southern periphery was about a half of million.[16] About 40% live in the city of Beer-Sheva, 25% in the inner ring, 33% in the middle ring, and only a few percent in the outer ring. About 25% of the population is Bedouin. The Bedouin of this area live in Bedouin-permanent towns recognized by the state of Israel (66%) or outside the permanent towns (33%). The forecast for 2020 is that the southern periphery will reach a total population of one million with 33% Bedouin.[17, 18]

The city of Beer-Sheva has a lengthy history. It was first established in the Byzantine period (4th-7th century) and was a large and active village characterized by an active life. With the Arab invasion in the 7th century, the city was abandoned. In the 19th century, the Ottoman Empire conquered the area and rebuilt the city as a small service and commerce center for the Bedouin tribes of the south.

After the establishment of the State of Israel, the city of Beer-Sheva was chosen to be the district city, providing services for the growing population of the southern periphery of Israel. As the metropolis core, the city of Beer-Sheva till this day has all the proper services of a city with this status. Among these services are government offices, wholesale commerce markets, cultural centers, education institutions, police headquarters, legal courts, army recruitment bureau, and health service facilities.

In the 1990s, there was significant growth in the percentage of workers in the public sector because of the industrial works. This pattern is appropriate for a metropolis core serving not only the population of the city but also the entire population of the metropolis.[6,11]

The Bedouins are settled mostly in the inner and middle rings. They are divided into two official types of municipal authorities - one city (population of about 50,000) and 6 local municipalities (also about 50,000 altogether). Another 50,000 live outside the Bedouin permanent towns in surrounding towns or in dispersed areas throughout the Negev. Over the years, the State of Israel has tried to settle the issue of the population that lives outside the recognized towns by offering planned communities in designated areas. The conflict at large has not been resolved because of issues regarding land ownership and traditional lifestyle.[10,11]

Polarization is the unique socio-economic characteristic of the southern periphery of Israel. Most of the population is either in the highest socio-economic level or the lowest. A small percentage of the population does belong to the middle level, living in neighborhoods of a city with a low socio-economic level. Another fact is that these very diverse populations may live in adjunct neighborhoods or villages.[10]

The population of the southern periphery is the poorest in Israel. This is reflected in many social and economical measures.[16] A large percent of the working force are employed in manual labor. Average wages are 90% of the national average. An unproportional percentage (16%) receives government subsidy. Unemployment is higher than the rest of the country. The birth rate is the highest in Israel (25% of the Jewish families have 4 children or more and 60% of the Bedouin have 4 children or more.[7,19])

3. Health Issues in the Southern-Periphery of Israel

In the health field, there are a number of indices defining the socio-economic level of a family and their ability to use health services for treatment and prevention. These measures are used for international and intercultural comparisons. As in other peripheries of the world, all the indices of the southern periphery are inferior to the measures of the center and of the national average. Table 1 presents quantitative evidence of the differences between the national estimations, the southern periphery situation and the Bedouins (part of the southern periphery population) condition. The population of the southern periphery is also younger than the national average and therefore, should have lower morbidity.[7,12] These known findings and facts are not integrated enough in government policy regarding allocation of economic and medical resources.

As in the rest of Israel, medical and health services are given at three different levels in the peripheral southern region: Primary care –local clinics, Secondary care –county clinics and core city clinics; Tertiary care –specialist clinics and hospital – only in the metropolis core city of Beer-Sheva. The geographical spread of the population of the periphery causes extra financial and accessibility issues.[6] The doctors and medical staff demand extra incentives to commute to the primary and secondary clinics. The population living outside of the core city encounters barriers in commuting to the secondary and tertiary centers such as direct travel costs and indirect travel costs (loss of time) as well as lack of transportation.

Table 1. Comparison of health indicators[7,12]

	Israel	Southern periphery	Bedouins of the southern periphery
Life expectancy – Men	75.7	73.3	71.7
Life expectancy –Women	79.6	79.6	75.6
Birth rate (births per 1000 people)	19.3	23.8	55.4
Infant mortality rate (deaths per 1000 people)	3.9	9.8	5.2
Number of hospital beds (beds per 1000 people)	66.680	58.241	--
Number of rehabilitation beds (beds per 1000) people)	0.107	0	--

Most communities of the southern periphery have developed primary healthcare solutions adapted to the necessary social and cultural concerns. But these communities are still very dependent on the medical center in the metropolis core city. This dependence, along with commuting barriers, is the main reason for not receiving or discontinuing healthcare.[20]

The Bedouin population of the Negev received special attention after the National Health Insurance Law was passed in 1994. The law set a financial capitation formula for the allocation of funds among the Health Medical Organizations (HMO). The HMO receives money according to the number of members and the age of the insured. The Bedouin family is young and large – therefore, each HMO wants them as their clients. Many of these attractive new clients at large do not pay health taxes because they are unemployed or receiving government subsidies.[17] These changes gave a big boost to the network of primary care health services for the Bedouin. More primary care clinics were established in the permanent towns and mobile health services are available outside the permanent towns. This only partially solved the health issues of the Bedouin community. Besides the known barriers receiving secondary and tertiary services of peripheral populations, the Bedouin have other obstacles to pass, such as lack of knowledge regarding healthy lifestyles and cultural barriers.[13,20,21,22]

Objectives

The southern peripheral area of Israel, as presented, is widely dispersed, culturally-diverse and has a polarized socio-economic population all of which create special needs in healthcare delivery. This chapter explores quantitatively the main issues influencing the delivery and use of the central health specialty clinics in Beer-Sheva (the core city of the metropolis and of the southern-periphery). Also, this chapter will present qualitative findings which complement the prior research and analyze issues considered important by the population in regard to health-service delivery. The qualitative research, exploring the differences within the peripheral area, is based on the known theory regarding differences between periphery and central (core) areas of a country.(theory testing). The objective of the qualitative research is to define themes for "peripheral health" and "health services provision to culturally diverse populations" by using personal experiences of the population (patients, caregivers, and public officials) and building theory.[23,24] Research shows that socio-economic level, physical distance and perceived distance are three important factors compiling a social, economic and political effect on the health system of the southern periphery of Israel.

4. Quantitative Research - Distance and Socio–Economic Level as a Health Service Predictor within the Southern-Periphery of Israel[20]

This quantitative research was designed to identify the main factors that influence the utilization of health services. The populations of the research were patients that frequented specialist clinics at the main medical center in Beer-Sheva between 2000 and 2005.[25] The research population did not include Beer-Sheva residents (34% of the southern region population) since distance to the clinic is not an issue. Thirteen specialist clinics were observed (excluding specialist clinics that are available at other clinics within the region). The thirteen clinics were divided into five specialty categories: (1) Pediatrics (hematology, metabolic, nephrology, diabetes); (2) Orthopedics (knees, hands, shoulder); (3) Audiology (hearing and speech); (4) Sleep (sleeping disorders); (5) Geriatrics. The dependent variable of the study was the sum total of patients' visits by residents of the southern region at clinics, by specialty category (62,000 visits out of population of 350,000). On average, every patient of these clinics visited the clinics 1.5 times. The independent variables included 2004 demographic parameters for towns in the southern periphery region, as listed in Israeli Central Bureau of Statistics (ICBS) data.[7] Information was obtained regarding 120 settlements: population size, distribution by age, gender, families with over four children, vehicles per household, socio-economic level (by percentiles), and distance from Beer-Sheva gauged by concentric geographical rings.

The distance from each town to Beer-Sheva was recorded, based on data from the Israel Central Bureau of Statistics, the Negev Development Authority and the Negev Center for Regional Development.[7,10,26] This data was correlated for the four geographical rings surrounding Beer-Sheva.[18] Table 2 shows the distribution of 62,000 visits of the study population.[25]

Table 2. Study Population

	Number of visits [25]	Number of residents[7]
Jews	40,500	200,000
Bedouins, permanent towns	20,000	100,000
Bedouins, outside the permanent towns	1,500	50,000
Total	62,000	350,000

The first step of data analysis included descriptive tests: average, standard deviation, median, minimum and maximum (Table 3). The variables include number of residents (town size), age distribution – by percentage, percentage of families with more than 4 children, percentage of women in the population, level of motor vehicle ownership in the town – per 1000 residents. The table also includes the number of visits at each clinic and the total number of visits at all thirteen clinics. Pearson correlation was used to test correlation between various demographic variables and the number of visits at different clinics. The data is presented in Table 4. Significant correlations are marked for $p < 0.05$.

Table 3. Descriptive Statistics

Variable	Valid n	Mean	Std dev	Median	Minimum	Maximum
Number of residents	129	2,328*	5831.04	368*	56	35,800
Age 0-19	23	46.3%	12.8%	41.0%	26.6%	66.5%
Age 20-64	23	48.2%	10.0%	49.6%	32.3%	63.2%
Age 65+	23	5.5%	4.1%	5.2%	1%	14.1%
Families > 4 children	16	35.9%	21.0%	26.5%	7.7%	63%
Women in population	23	49.4%	1.4%	49.7%	46.7%	52%
Motorized per 1000	15	187.3	130.9	147.7	71.1	553
Pediatrics	88	92.19*	207.41	10*	0	1315
Orthopedics	100	403.75*	851.85	64*	1	5145
Audiology	97	252.25*	566.21	43*	1	3272
Sleep	89	24.72*	53.61	5*	0	287
Geriatrics	43	9.61*	15.83	3*	0	82
Number of visits	123	550.33*	1312.19	86*	0	9289

Table 4. Pearson correlation between demographic variables and number of visits

Variable	Pediatrics	Orthopedics	Audiology	Sleep	Geriatrics	Number of visits
Geographical Ring	-0.26 N=80 p=0.021	-0.28 N=92 p=0.006	-0.22 N=889 p=0.036	-0.18 N=81 p=0.104	-0.17 N=35 p=0.321	-0.27 N=115 p≤0.001
Socio-economical Percentile	-0.49 N=88 p≤0.001	-0.18 N=100 p=0.071	-0.28 N=97 p=0.006	-0.13 N=80 p=0.221	0.32 N=43 p=0.038	-0.33 N=123 p≤0.001
Sum residents	0.84 N=88 p≤0.001	0.74 N=100 p≤0.001	0.88 N=97 p≤0.001	0.76 N=89 p≤0.001	0.14 N=43 p=0.357	0.95 N=123 p≤0.001
Age (%) 0-19	0.36 N=23 p=0.088	-0.13 N=23 p=0.542	-0.13 N=23 p=0.554	-0.24 N=23 p=0.276	-0.5 N=23 p=0.016	0.05 N=23 p=0.809
Age (%) 20-64	-0.38 N=23 p=0.542	0.15 N=23 p=0.498	0.12 N=23 p=0.600	0.28 N=23 p=0.210	0.53 N=23 p=0.010	-0.16 N=23 p=0.454
Age (%) 65+	-0.22 N=23 p=0.319	0.05 N=23 p=0.803	0.12 N=23 p=0.574	0.08 N=23 p=0.210	0.26 N=23 p=0.010	0.23 N=23 p=0.280
Families over 4 children (%)	0.4 N=16 p=0.122	-0.07 N=16 p=0.787	-0.15 N=16 p=0.575	-0.25 N=16 p=0.350	-0.58 N=16 p=0.018	-0.05 N=16 p=0.850
Women in population (%)	0.35 N=23 p=0.096	0.42 N=23 p=0.044	0.41 N=23 p=0.049	0.34 N=23 p=0.110	0.13 N=23 p=0.540	0.41 N=23 p=0.050
Motorized per 1000	-0.34 N=15 p=0.220	-0.07 N=15 p=0.792	-0.03 N=15 p=0.792	0.07 N=15 p=0.801	0.6 N=15 p=0.017	-0.02 N=15 p=0.948

Distance

The data demonstrates that distance and travel-time from Beer-Sheva, represented by the four geographical rings, is negatively correlated to the number of visits to specialty clinics. In other words, patients that live further away visit specialist clinics at medical centers in Beer-Sheva less frequently. There is a significant correlation for pediatrics, orthopedics, audiology and the overall total number of visits.

The Spearman Test was used to measure the influence of distance, by concentric rings, on the number of visits to the different clinics. The results are presented in Table 5. Spearman's correlation strengthens the hypothesis that distance – measured in geographical rings - has a considerable negative influence on the number of clinic visits.

Table 5. Spearman correlation between number of visits and distance or percentile

Pair of variables	Valid N	Spearman's r	T(N-2)	P-level
Geographical ring and number of visits	115	-0.33	-3.74	0.01
Percentile and number of visits	123	-0.19	-2.07	0.04

Previous research sited shows that in general, the distance from a person's home to the clinic is one of the most important factors contributing to the level of utilization of healthcare services.[27,28] The purpose of this research was to test the hypothesis that distance in the southern region of Israel – that is, comparing accessibility within the periphery – is also a significant factor influencing the use of healthcare services, measured by patient visits to specialist clinics at medical centers in Beer-Sheva. This research shows an inverse correlation between the distance of a town from Beer-Sheva and the number of visits to the specialist clinics. This result matches findings of other researchers. Ken found in interviews with family practitioners that differences in levels of utilization vary and are a function of geographical factors.[29] A study in the United Kingdom by Hayness found similar results showing that distance was the main barrier to health service accessibility on the periphery; 80 percent of the populations living up to 15 kilometers from the health center are the main clients of the health services, significantly higher than those living over 50 kilometers from the health center.[27] A later American study in Michigan, United States by Billi sought to define the maximum distance for effective accessibility.[30] This study found that the optimal distance between home and clinic for optimal accessibility was no more than 10 miles (16 kilometers), while distances over 50 kilometers constitutes a serious barrier to the accessibility of healthcare. A Canadian study by Seidel that examined the use of a pre-surgery clinic in Alberta, Canada found that 66 percent of the patients living up to 50 kilometers from the clinic opted for this service prior to surgery, compared to 52 percent living over 50 kilometers from the clinic.[28] To date, no similar work had been done in Israel.

Previous research in Israel is devoted to issues of equal health services for the periphery. Peled and Lubetzky showed that the level of service use and quality of services among the population of the southern region are considerably lower than what is available to residents of the central region, the most densely-populated section of the country.[17,31] Most healthcare services research on the southern periphery in Israel compares the south to the center of the country. Gross, Nirel and Warshawsky-Livne studies' found that the southern region suffers from health service barriers due to a lower ratio of healthcare providers per population, lower availability of healthcare providers, longer waiting times, difficulty recruiting and retaining staff, and higher operating expenses due to geographical factors.[14,21,32]

Socio-Economical Level

Socio-economic level (gauged in percentiles) also has an influence on the total number of visits. A significant positive correlation was found for geriatrics while pediatrics, audiology and the total number of visits showed a negative correlation. This indicates that people of better means frequented clinics less than those of lesser means, with the exception of geriatric patients. The Spearman Test was used to measure the influence of the socio-economic level, according to CBS percentiles, on the number of visits to the different clinics. The results are presented in Table 5. Spearman's correlation strengthens the hypothesis that socio-economic level, measured in percentile, has a considerable negative influence on clinic, population of lower socio-economic level use expert clinics more than the population of high socio-economic level.

This finding matches patterns found among different socio-economic levels in Israel[17] and out of Israel.[9,29] These all demonstrate that lower socio-economic sectors of society utilize health services more.

Chernichovsky and Borkan claim that the different patterns of healthcare utilization are the result of a heterogenic population in the southern-periphery; This work, based on Israel Central Bureau of Statistics (ICBS) data, reveals that Jews receive better service then Arabs, populations from higher socio-economic neighborhoods (or towns) receive better service then populations in low socio-economic development towns, and those with economic means have better access to private health service.[7,19,33] Different researchers have sought to explain different levels of health service utilization based on "socio-economical percentiles" of the research population. Becker explains those populations from low economic percentiles visit acute and sub-acute clinics more due to a lower frequency of routine follow-up and preventive medicine, resulting in late detection reflected in elevated utilization of acute and sub-acute clinics.[34] Glasgow and Dunlop link the high utilization of the sub-acute clinics with higher use of public health services by low-income populations, while more affluent populations have private insurance and avail themselves similar health services outside hospitals.[9,35] This phenomenon also exists in countries such as Australia and Canada that offer universal health services, where theoretically, there is no need for non-public health services. From the above three studies, one can conclude that the variances between high and low socio-economic status confirm that higher socio-economic populations utilize services more effectively, not necessarily less frequently.

Only the correlation between the number of patients' visits and geriatrics had a positive correlation–indicating that lower socio-economic sectors use this clinic less. This could be explained by the uniqueness of geriatrics, a health service unit perceived as a quality of life enhancement, not a life saving matter. Borkan and Dunlop found that health-enhancing services are mainly utilized by secular, educated, high-income, high socio-economic level populations.[33,35] A possible explanation for this result is that people living in a town of a higher socio-economical level use health services in a educated matter and manage a life style that promotes health—including diet, physical activity, and use of advanced health services that are not included in the public health system.

Size of Town

It was also found that the size of the town has a strong positive correlation on the frequency with which residents visited specialist clinics, with the exception of geriatrics.

There is a direct correlation between the number of patient visits and the number of residents in towns surrounding Beer-Sheva. This finding was calculated according to proportions and not absolute numbers.

The towns in the southern region of Israel are located in the inner and middle geographical rings. The transportation system in these large towns is accessible and reliable due to high demand and high utilization which can explain the direct correlation between size and utilization of health services at the medical center in Beer-Sheva.

The Mann–Whitney Test was used to examine the influence of the population size of the town of residence on the number of visits. This test was chosen because the sum total of residents did not distribute normally.

Therefore, a new variable was introduced into the research: the ratio between total number of visits and the sum total of residents (sum total visits/sum total of residents). The findings were as follows: valid N= 123, mean= 0.25, median = 0.20, minimum= 0. Maximum= 1.19, standard deviation = 0.23. The data for the visit ratio by geographical distance (concentric rings), was plotted in Graph 1.

Every geographical ring was compared with the previous ring. Two parameters were employed: levels of freedom (F) and average plotted as points and horizontal bars for confidence interval.

Graph 1 further substantiates that the farther a resident lives from Beer-Sheva, the smaller the ratio of clinic visits per total residents in a given location of settlement. Follow-up testing, based on the same data set and using the same methods, showed that there is a significant difference ($p \leq 0.001$) between all pairs of rings (1 and 2, 1 and 3, 1 and 4, 2 and 3, 2 and 4) except for rings 3 and 4 ($p = 0.25$).

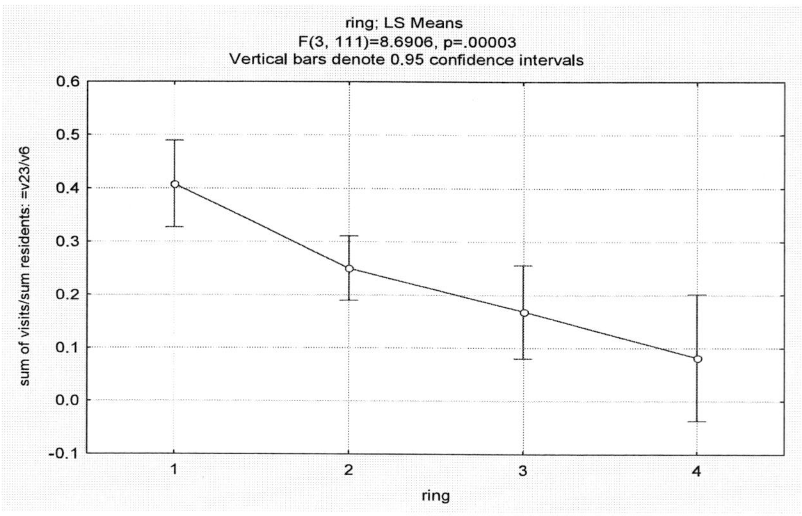

Graph 1. The difference between the means of [visit/size] ratio as a dependent of the geographical ring.

Table 6. Multiple regression for the variables: geographical ring, percentile, sum of residents on the dependent variable of number of visits

R=0.97, R2=0.93, Adjusted R2=0.93 F(3,111)=501.37. p≤0.01, Std error of estimate: 348.46					
N=115	B	Std Error of B	Beta	Std error of Beta	p value
Intercept	-98.08	140.72			0.49
Geographical Ring	-124.84	36.03	-0.09	0.02	≤0.001
Percentile	69.07	20.47	0.095	0.03	≤0.001
Sum of residents	0.21	0.006	0.98	0.03	≤0.001

The variables identified as statistically significant in Table 4 (geographical ring, percentile, sum of residents), were applied as independent variables in a multiple regression model to determine their influence on utilization of specialist clinics, as a dependent variable. The results are presented in Table 6. From Table 6, we learn that distance, socio-economic level and town population have a strong affect on the utilization of healthcare, as found previously in Tables 4 and 5. This demonstrates, again, that the increased distance and high socio-economic statuses are negatively correlated, while town population has a positive correlation.

Other Independent Variables

The percent of women in the population has a positive correlation on the number of visits to orthopedics and audiology clinics; access to a motor vehicle has a positive connection with the number of visits to the geriatrics clinic. No significant correlation was found between age and family size and visits to the clinics. Except for geriatrics that is irrelevant for age cohorts 0–19 and 20–64; therefore the correlation is significant and negative. Likewise, families with over 4 children (e.g. under the age of 18), are irrelevant for the geriatrics category.

It should be noted: Age distribution, family size, percentage of women and level of motorization, do not have any significant influence on the number of patient visits at clinics.

The Bedouin of the Southern Periphery

The Mann-Whitney test was used to test the influence of the population size of the town (Bedouin permanent towns or Jewish) on the number of visits from the town to the specialist clinics. Comparing these two populations shows that there is no difference in the pediatrics, orthopedics, and audiology clinics while there is a significant difference in the sleep and geriatrics clinics (Table 7).

Two proportion tests were used to test the influence of the population size of the town, Bedouin (permanent and outside the permanent) or Jewish on the number of visits to the specialist clinics. The first test compared the number of visits from the permanent Bedouin towns (Group1) to the number of visits from the Jewish towns (Group 2). No significant difference was found between the groups. (Table 8)

The second test compared the number of visits from the permanent Bedouin towns (Group1) to the number of visits of Bedouins from outside the permanent Bedouin towns (Group 2). A significant difference was found between these two groups. (Table 9)

Table 7. Comparison of the number of visits of Bedouin from permanent towns and Jews (Mann-Whitney U-test)

Variable	Rank sum Jews	Valid N group1	Rank sum Bedouin	Valid N group 2	Z	p-values
Pediatrics	64	9	72	7	-1.32	0.18
Orthopedics	85	9	51	7	0.9	0.37
Audiology	90	9	46	7	1.43	0.15
Sleep	96	9	40	7	2.06*	0.04*
Geriatrics	101	9	35	7	2.59*	0.004*
Number of visits	87	9	49	7	1.11	0.27

*Significant $p<0.05$

Table 8. Comparison of the number of visits from Bedouin permanent towns and from Jewish towns (% group1=0.21, N=20000; % group 2=0.20, N=1500 p=0.36, two sided test)

	Number visits	Sum residents	Number visits/sum residents
Bedouin, permanent towns	20,000	100,000	0.2
Jews	40,500	200,000	0.2

Table 9. Comparison of the number of visits of Bedouin permanent towns and Bedouin non-permanent towns (% group1=0.21, N=20000; % group 2=0.03, N=1500, two sided test)

	Number visits	Number residents	Number visits/number residents
Bedouin permanent towns	20,000	100,000	0.2
Bedouin non-permanent towns	1,500	50,000	0.03

No significant difference was found between the proportion of visits from Jewish towns and Bedouin permanent towns. However, a significant difference was found between Bedouin permanent towns and Bedouin from outside the Bedouin permanent towns ($p\leq0.01$).

This indicates that the Bedouin population may not have confidence in these services.[17,22]

In a continuous pursuit to understand the diverse heterogenic nature of Israel's southern region population, Lubetzky found that the proportion of visits of the Bedouin population that live outside permanent towns is significantly lower than the proportion of visits of the Bedouin population that live in permanent towns.[20] The second surprising finding is that the proportion of visits of the Bedouin population that live in permanent towns is the same proportion of visits of the Jewish population.

Previous research and current data show that when making a decision to seek healthcare, the individual checks the level of adaption to one's health needs economic situation and life style.[15,17] In non-acute health situations, the life style and culture aspects are emphasized. This explains the difference between Bedouin and Jews when comparing the use of a sleep clinic and geriatric clinic, clinics that improve health but are not life-saving. Different cultures look at sleep and geriatrics as a disease and others as a part of a normal life cycle. The health services and solutions provided in these clinics are appropriate for western, non-religious populations, from higher economical levels, who believe that these are health issues that can be solved. The Bedouin population does not seek medical attention and health services to improve a situation of compromised quality of life.

Summary

The three main variables identified as statistically significant in Table 4 (geographical ring, percentile, sum of residents), were applied as independent variables in a multiple regression model to determine their influence on utilization of specialist clinics, as a dependent variable. The results are presented in Table 6. From Table 6 we learn that distance, socio-economic level and town size have a strong affect on utilization of health care, as found previously in Tables 4 and 5. This demonstrates, again, that increased distance and high socio-economic statuses are negatively correlated, while town size has a positive correlation.

These findings not only strengthen the findings of previous researchers from around the world regarding distance and socio–economical level as a Health Service Predictor, but also show the social and economical aspects within the southern-periphery of Israel.

5. Qualitative Research – Distance and Socio–Economic Aspects of Health Service in the Southern-Periphery of Israel from the Perspective of the Residents

The qualitative research was conducted as a continuation of the quantitative aspects of the research in order to find possible explanations for the results of the quantitive research and to aid in building new concepts in the health service field and health service delivery to the diverse cultural populations in the southern periphery of Israel. This qualitative research is based on the personal experiences of the interviewees.

The objective of the research is to identify the main issues in the Israel southern periphery health care delivery as perceived by policy makers of the south, key people in different communities and healthcare receivers (Jews and Bedouins of the southern periphery).

The research question: What are the main issues of healthcare delivery in the south, from the interviewees' point of view?

This study extracts field theory (Grounded Theory) in order to identify the main themes that represent a health services provision to residents of the southern-periphery, and distinguish it from other fields of health services in Israel. Extraction methodology from the field theory assumes that people with common life circumstances have similar social patterns that allow the researcher to indentify themes that explain the phenomenon under investigation. Using these themes, social structures, relationships between groups and power struggles between them are examined. This interpretation gives the perspective of the participants.[23,24] Grounded theory relies on data collected from interviews, constantly comparing interviews and examining reasons with a social-cultural context.[23]

The study population consisted of twenty interviewees associated with the southern periphery of Israel: 3 public administrators of the community, 4 health system policy makers and 13 local residents (Jews and Bedouins).

"The Southern Experience" – The Picture That Emerges from the Themes

The selected themes, summarizing a long process of collecting, sorting and interpretation, are those that give a broad and comprehensive picture of the "southern experience" in the health field. Themes were selected with respect to the general research purpose, research findings of the quantitative research and responses to the research question about the main issues that characterize health services provision to the southern-periphery of Israel, all from the perspective of residents. This focus results from the need to build a base of knowledge on "Health of the periphery" and "Health care delivery to culturally diverse populations in Israel".[24]

Each theme was given a title that reflects topics included in the narrative described by the interviewees. Provision of the title, as described by Kacen, is the formation of a 'code' to understand the meaning of the story.[36] Unlike the study conducted by Kacen, where the interviewees determined the title of their story, in this study, the selected titles represent the researcher's "story line" at large and help in understanding the general ideas of the story themes. All categories and sub-categories were given a title that emphasizes the phenomenon and provides and immediate picturesque explanation.[24]

The selected themes were intended to provide a broader outlook on the quantitative research findings, highlight the cases that they exemplify and collect them into a grounded theory.[24] Two main themes were identified: (1) Hierarchy sequence of southern settlements according to "foreignness vs. belonging" and its expression in the use of health services, (2) Components of distance and its expression in the use of health services. Since the purpose of the interviews was to strengthen the quantitative findings, the respondents were asked to address the geographical and physical distance as a factor in their decision to use health services. The topic of "foreignness vs. belonging" was not part of the original scheme of the interviews. Only after processing sections of the interview and organization into thematic categories, was the intensity of the term "foreignness vs. belonging" acknowledged in connection with the use of health services in the south.

The First Theme: Hierarchy Sequence of Southern Settlements According to "Foreignness vs. Belonging" and its Expression in the use of Health Services

> "You take a kibbutz and a town nearby. Two completely different worlds"[a]

Analysis of the interviews found a scale of three levels describing the level of social identification with the community. This is based on the individuals' sense of belonging to their local place, and to the nation. This virtual scale divides the population according to the variety of culture, and level of foreignness and belonging. At the high level are the kibbutz members.

The interviewees describe the kibbutz as a place with a large sense of commitment in terms of health and welfare to its members. The middle level is made up of Jewish and Bedouin communities alike. The low level is made up of the Bedouin communities from outside the recognized towns. These are described by respondents as a place where there is a high sense of commitment to family and tribe, but a low commitment to others living in the town but not of the same tribe.

In the 1980's, as described in the introduction, the Israeli society went through many economic and social changes causing a crisis within the kibbutz movement itself and between the kibbutz movement and the rest of the Israeli society. However, the kibbutz has remained and still is considered the most united community in the south. Leaders of the kibbutz know how to get the best health services that are offered by law and to help the community members who cannot fend for themselves. Kibbutz leaders know to take advantage of political situations. One deputy of a peripheral regional council (and a kibbutz member himself)*:

> "We get a lot because of the security situation ... because there's been a war ... and because we know how to demand".

One respondent indicated that the *"community resilience ... membership and friendship is a top value ... we are strong people here"* The kibbutz holds today, even if not as in the past, potential ability to influence government. This power originates from the strength of a homogeneous group, the historical status of the kibbutz, and also the social concept of the kibbutz as a strong community with high and positive involvement in life of the country. The understanding of the health systems and the relevant laws, allows the leaders of the community to obtain the top medical care and treatments best suited to their way of life. This concept was described by one health policy maker in the south:

> "We created a natural controlled experiment", and he explains the difference between the two communities: "You take a kibbutz and a nearby town and compare the medical services. You get two worlds completely different. Totally different.... kibbutz society is the top of the health percentile scale. It's really an experiment conducted for us by nature."

---

*Kibbutz is an Israeli communal settlement in which all wealth is held in common and profits are reinvested in the settlement. Most originally based their income on agricultural. Adults live in private quarters; children are generally housed and cared for as a group. Meals are prepared and eaten communally. Members have regular meetings to discuss business and to take votes on matters requiring decisions. Jobs may be assigned by rotation, by choice, or by skill. The kibbutz movement declined dramatically in the late 20th century.

The ability to provide adapted health services results, as noted, is not only related to the nearness to the establishments but also the ability to use budgets wisely and suitable for the population. The group's unity level affects the general sense of group commitment to the individual and sense of security for the individual in the group. The more the group is united, the individual commitment is higher, but on the condition that there are resources to be distributed among everyone. Without appropriate financial resources, it is hard for the group over time to provide for its members. Even today, after the crisis of the 1980's and the privatization processes in all of the kibbutz communities in Israel, the kibbutz in the southern-periphery is still perceived as a strong society with a high sense of commitment to its members.[37]

The middle level consists of urban communities where the level of individual commitment to the urban community is not homogeneous and the individual sense of belonging to the community varies from community to community.

The interviewees said that in recent years significant changes occurred in the Jewish "development towns" in the south. Some of these town's leaders learned to exploit the connections with the establishment and improve residents' administration systems, including the health system. But still, a lower commitment level is observed compared to the kibbutz.

According to respondents, the cooperation between central government and local government are better today than in the past. "*The main message is not to give them [the residents who have difficulty] fish but fishing rods*," says one school principal in a Jewish southern city, who married a local resident in the fifties and has been living there with her extended family. She is involved in the life of the city and perceives herself as influencing factor. She describes the change in community attitude – from needy, foreign dependent to independence and sense of belonging:

> "The general vision has changed, it is understood that it is impossible to give [money] to people without end. That people need the will to stop saying: I am unemployed, I am disabled, I am despondent, I cannot. This developed a second generation of poverty ... the main message [of the state and municipality] is not to give them fish but what to fish with, learn to help yourself with us. "

Of course, not all cities are similar. Feeling of remoteness and foreignness grows depending on the distance or size of city. Residents of larger cities are less affected by the distance. Smaller cities feel they have less influence on decision-making in all areas of life including the health field. In an interview with a Jewish couple in their sixties, they describe how they see the situation in their city and its impact on them in the future:

> "We will get up and leave, there is no doubt ... there are not many things in our city ... no professional people ... if you want to develop professionally it is not simple... and if we come in need of better medicine we will have to move to the center".

This couple does not feel connected to the community and feels that the city does not meet their health needs. The couple enjoys the city and did not complain about day-to-day difficulties, but know that it will be difficult to get support from the community when they need it, and because of their low sense of "belonging", it will be easy for them to leave when necessary.

In the permanent Bedouin towns, significant changes have occurred in recent years. This trend was reflected in an interview with one of the Bedouin interviewees:

> "Ten years ago, girls were not let out of the house alone; now many girls go out to study and work".

Leaving the house and meeting other young people has affected the women's sense of the personal capability. One interviewee states:

> "If one has self-confidence then she has no problem doing what she wants".

This interviewee was dressed in Bedouin traditional clothes, covering herself in a veil and considered herself very religious. Alongside the strong traditional elements, the friction with the Jewish secular and traditional population reveals ideas regarding the ability to learn and acquire a profession. This allows women self-fulfillment and helps them realize their personal potential and the advancement their children. In some cases this occurs, despite the Bedouin of the permanent towns existing sense of alienation toward the state and the majority Jewish population. There is an understanding that higher education, even if sponsored by the state, and knowledge of state laws are important to promote their community. This means that not everyone is satisfied with the situation, but there is a sense of capability that allows them a better life.

The low level in the hierarchy sequence are the Bedouins living outside of the permanent towns, these residents describe a high sense of commitment to family and tribe, and a low sense of commitment to others in the area. One interviewee describes his ambivalence:

> "We are one big family…but it is an embarrassment that my neighbor is more advanced and needs to help me".

Bedouin from outside-permanent towns have an ongoing struggle with the definition of their community and their relationship with the Bedouin and Jewish neighbors, so they are not available to deal with problems that are not existential problems, even if these are health issues.

Tribal Bedouin communities are seen by many as homogeneous, but the interviewees suggest a different scenario. The commitment of the individual is only to the extended nuclear family, while the element "community", unlike the family, is not so strong. The level of the community committed to the individual is low and depends on the family or tribe pertinence. It is possible that the lack of commitment originates from the difficult economic situation of some of the residents living in outside-permanent towns which also affects the ability to help each other.

Living for many years in closely neighboring areas, often combined with financial distress, contributes to a sense of shame, a desire to avoid the neediness, a need to preserve a sense of capability, and to strengthen the family.

> "We live outside the town. The whole family is together but each has his own problems. We can help each other once or twice but not more".

Another interviewee describes similar difficulties which characterize small population groups where everyone knows each other and compare their financial situation:

> "We have a tribe; it's a shame that the neighbor would need to help me. It's a shame that the neighbor is advanced and needs to help me. Everyone for himself. ".

Weak traditional communities with a high sense of conformity and with low individual independence have a tendency to hide problems from others in the community. This was described by the one of the interviewees:

> "For us it is a shame if the family has a child with a disability...they hide the child, do not let her/him out....This child will not marry, will not go out to and will stay out of sight, this way the family will not ruin things for the siblings".

Polygamy is extant in the Bedouin society. The Koran allows a man to marry up to four women, but under Israeli law, multiple marriages are prohibited and the offense is punishable by up to five years in prison. During the twentieth century, the multiple marriages phenomenon was limited among the Muslim community in Israel, but this changed after the 1967 war. The Bedouins of Israel have a better economic situation then the residents of the Gaza Strip and Hebron area and it is possible to get young women for a low dowry. It is difficult to estimate the extent of this phenomenon because a large percentage of the polygamy marriages are not officially registered. The main reasons are legally related and unmarried mothers get financial benefits. Even though the Bedouin of the southern-periphery of Israel are experiencing a modernization process, the phenomenon of polygamy is not decreasing and is also common among the young and educated.[38] Interior Ministry data between the years 2000 to 2005 reports nearly four hundred polygamous marriages among the general Muslim population in Israel in contrast to 20% -35% among the of southern periphery Bedouin.[39] The polygamous family structure is seen as non-egalitarian which directly affects the women and the status of women at large. Studies conducted among Bedouin women indicate that this family structure leads to frustration and hostility between the women. The status of each one of them is ….and her self-image is lower than women in "normal" family units.[38] The polygamous family unit brings foreignness and alienation within the family which should be the individual's main source of support and protection. One interviewee was asked about the status struggle within the family (which woman is more "important" and whose children receive better conditions), she said:

> "because I was angry I went to live with my mother. The second wife put her things in my house and she wanted to take everything from my house. So I came back and threw all her things out. Then there were lots of problems and she left.

Life in a polygamous family also affects the use of health systems. Many of the Bedouin women who were not born in Israel do not speak Hebrew and are not familiar with the Jewish-Israeli society. One husband described what happens when his wife needs a medical test:

> "She does not go...She does not know the place. She does not know how to read…No…No... She cannot get along...I always go. She does not know...not know".

The husband's repeated use of the word *'not know* ' shows the perception of the Bedouin woman as a complete outsider. Bedouin women outside-permanent towns are completely dependent on their husband for anything outside the village. The husband is an intermediary between the woman and the world, and is also a buffer (does not allow her to develop and be exposed to the world). They are totally dependent on their husband and his expanded family.

The child of a second wife has the lowest chance of getting medical treatment (in comparison to any other patient in Israel). The woman has to argue with her husband and explain the necessity of treatment:

> "He says the child will be alright and does not need an appointment ... he eats, he sees, he hears, there are lots of children like him... But I'm worried about the child... do not see why you cannot give money. I tell him - you have a lot of children and I have only four".

The constant conflicts and competition within the nuclear family members creates alienation. The nuclear family members are in constant tension, instead of sharing intimacy, causing individuals feelings of isolation.[40]

Bedouin families who live outside permanent towns are in constant struggle for their place in the tribe, for recognition of their lifestyle, for their communication with both Arab and Jewish surrounding societies. This factor could explain the community leaders' difficulties in helping the needy inside the communities. When there is no support and help, individuals in the group prefer to hide their difficulties and not reveal to others and therefore their ability to utilize mandatory and free health services are limited (needless to say they have no ability to receive health services that cost extra money even if subsidized). It is not only the additional insurance costs, but also the ability to reach the appropriate doctors and other medical services. Every individual needs a certain level of personal resilience and basic understanding of state laws and regulations in order to take advantage of medical rights (without them you cannot get health services). This is why Bedouin interviewees from outside the permanent towns say it is difficult to receive appropriate medical care and give up on treatments that they consider not important or not lifesaving.

In summary, the first theme: "Hierarchy sequence of southern settlements according to 'foreignness vs. belonging' and its expression in the use of health services" was defined according to respondents' perception of belonging to the community and the perception of community commitment to its members. The scale was also defined in reference to the utilization of health services provided outside the community. Analysis of the interviews positioned the members of the kibbutz at the highest rank with reference to the sense of belonging to their country and community-commitment to the individual. As a result, on the kibbutz, health services are perceived and rated the highest in the south and possibly for all of Israel. In the middle of the scale are Jewish and Bedouin residents of towns including various forms of community such as regional councils, cities and Bedouin permanent towns. Every community differs from each other and within, by culture and levels of sense of belonging. Health services provided in these communities are not homogeneous - some perceived as good, some are perceived as inadequate, but all are perceived as less good than those provided to kibbutz members. The lowest end of the hierarchy are the Bedouins from outside-permanent towns, which are a tribal groups with a high commitment to the concept of family, and low commitment to others in the community and country. As a result, health services are perceived by them as not suitable to them, their culture and way of life, forcing them to give up treatments they consider less important or not life-saving.

The Second Theme: Components of Distance – "The Distance is Relative and has a lot of Vectors"

> "Every time we needed a doctor, we made the visit into a fun outing in the big city" "It is like a full time job but without a salary"

The second theme presents explanations given by the residents of the southern periphery for the results found in the quantitative study which showed a negative relationship between the distance from Beer-Sheva and the number of clinic visits in Beer-Sheva. There is no doubt that distance is a significant factor in the quantitative research, but geographic distance is not the only factor influencing the use of medical services in the city. Other components described by interviewees are related to the economic situation of the interviewee and his family; amount of help from the community, ability to maintain routine necessary for medical treatments, availability of transportation services, wasted time traveling and availability of services offered to patients living in communities in the periphery – all of these affect the decision-making of the residents of the southern periphery of Israel on how and to what extent to use health services. Without help and support on these issues, there is attrition, lack of will and ability to get to medical treatments that are not perceived as necessary in the eyes of the respondents.[20] These difficulties increased with the last change in Israel's health system that introduced a medical model that was essentially a medical-economical system where there is a need to maximize profits. The current model allows for less personal relationships which had characterized the relationship in the past. Many of the interviewees indicated that they feel the new focus on profitability has created a sense of alienation towards the health system. The economic health model and the necessity of a competitive system is something that cannot be changed but it must be known that this is a significant barrier in using health services for people living in remote communities or with a different cultural background. Many countries around the world have developed models for providing high quality medical care for culturally diverse populations, recognizing the insurers' responsibility to preserve clientele and also stay within budget limits.[9]

There are three components that define the vector of the effect of distance on the decision to use central heath services: (1) The perception of the distance to the Beer-Sheva metropolis, (2) Additional components involved in traveling outside the community (3) The harm to the family income and budget (Everything falls apart).

1) The Perception of the Distance to Beer-Sheva Metropolis

Many respondents noted that the distance measured in kilometers is an important factor in the decision to use health services, but is just one of the components in the decision to travel outside the community for medical care. However, the objective distance (in kilometers), is not similarly perceived by different people, and is not portrayed equally among all interviewees. One health policy maker in the south explains:

> "relative distance has a lot of vectors, vector of education, vector of income, vector of the form of life, and vector of opportunities in seeking medical care."

Interviews showed that there are different costs for people from different communities. For example, a mother of eight children from a religious community in a southern city refers to the long drive for treatments as hard work. She feels:

> "It is work but I do not work. In terms of my time, it is like I am working - trips to the hospital for child care. It is like a full time job but I do not have a salary."

In contrast, a Bedouin who came with her son to a clinic describes the added value that Bedouin women get from coming to the city:

> "It is better for me to come to the city because I leave home. It's good for me to get out. It feels free. Even if the treatment is not so helpful and worthwhile, it is a chance to leave the cooking, cleaning and noise at home".

This shows that one can interpret the trip as hard work without pay, waste of time, and will contemplate future treatments, while the other considers the added value of the trip as an encounter with a different culture. The medical personnel are strangers and enable an intimate conversation that sometimes exists between people who are close. The direct encounter with a staff member from a different culture is often a negative incentive to seek medical care, but sometimes it actually is an incentive to get medical care which goes beyond the actual treatment.

2) Additional Components Involved In Traveling To Special Clinics Outside The Community

There are a few categories that described distance, as perceived by the interviewees, as components in utilizing health services provided outside their communities such as public transportation and service accessibility. Distance is one of the most important components in the decision to use health services, especially for those who are reliant on public transportation, whether it is bus, taxi or another type of fee vehicle. As previously presented, many of the residents of the southern periphery have a low socio-economic level, forcing them to use public transport which lowers accessibility to health services outside the community. The difficulty is not only the actual dependence on public transport but also its availability and home-station distance. This was explained by a female Bedouin from outside the permanent towns:

> "This is the difference – If I live in Beer-Sheva, I pick up the phone, the taxi will come, here the taxi will not come ....If someone wants to take a bus in Beer-Sheva there is a station a hundred meters away, and here I walk three kilometers to the road. It is hard to walk with a small child in your arms for such a distance".

> "There's a shuttle from the village" explains a Bedouin woman from a permanent town. She has a nicely arranged and organized life: All we have to do is ask the village driver if he will agree to take me to Beer- Sheva. He always says 'Yes'… I feel comfortable because it is only people from the village ... I go and pay like the bus fare".

The ability of Bedouin women to converse with men who are not members of the family and the ability to hitchhike out of the village without fear of the husband's anger, facilitates and makes the health services outside the community user-friendly and are perceived as breaking routine events. From the interviews it was found that part of the decision to use health services is based on access and availability of health services. Residents of the recognized villages versus residents from outside-permanent towns strengthen and explain the significant quantitative research outcome in use of health services. Despite the similarity of the Bedouin cultures, there are accessibility and availability differences between them that influence the health services use.

3) The harm to the family income and budget (Everything falls apart)

Prolonged medical treatments outside the community disrupt the family life routine and create tension over the necessity of these treatments, the travel costs and the fear of losing one's job (or loss of income if the caregiver is independent or an agricultural worker). Many people in the southern periphery work in agriculture that requires daily work with livestock and crops. Traveling outside the community and leaving routine work requires outside assistance, whether for a fee or requesting a favor from a relative. A farmer from a remote village describes what happens when a child is diagnosed with a chronic disease:

> "The family actually breaks down into pieces. The father continues to take care of the farm but also has to take care of the other children. The wife took off a year from work to accompany the child. ... The whole family and financial structure falls apart into pieces".

The head of a Bedouin tribe from outside the permanent towns describes the significance of cultural prohibitions that apply to the woman and prevent her from leaving her home and the effect on the family income:

> "A woman in need of medical care at a clinic must bring her husband … This is because many women cannot leave their home alone and are restricted in meeting men from outside the family … They need their husband or another man from the family to bring her to the hospital … this absence from work can cause his dismissal from work that it is not plentiful in the Bedouin community". Another Bedouin described a specific incident: "the husband approached the manager frequently requesting to take his wife to the doctor or a clinic … the manager will say 'isn't there someone else who can take her instead of you, if not, I will find someone else with more stability to work here instead of you".

In summary, the second theme: "Components of distance –distance is relative and has a lot of vectors" deals with the fact that many of the residents living in the southern periphery of Israel earn minimum wage or are paid social security, therefore it is difficult to pay the sum required for the travel and expense of getting treatment.

This discourages the use of health services which are perceived as unnecessary to them. Interpreting health issues as monetary values causes tension in the modern society. The competitive and medical economical health model causes health utilization barriers for the low socio-economic communities.

SUMMARY

This research is one of the first to analyze the public health service utilization in the southern region of Israel, comparing accessibility within the periphery. This research shows that greater distance and higher socio-economic status have a clear cut negative influence on health service utilization which results in inequality in access to health service by peripheral populations. This information can help build programs for health delivery, health promotion and preventive medicine, based on the needs of peripheral populations and the resources available to the health providers. In order to be effective (equality of availability and accessibility), it is recommended that a public health system in the periphery be built with programs that take into consideration the needs of the population, the specific localities, distance to health services, the socio-economic level, the culture of the residents and the size of the community. All of this has to be considered in relation to the resources allocated by the treasury to the health system.

This study's main limitation is that it only investigates possible linkages between the utilization of expert clinics and independent variables related to distance and socio-economic status. Another limitation is that a cross-correlation among the independent variables was not carried out, thus, for example, it is still unclear whether differences will be found between the populations of two cities at the same distance from specialist clinics, but typified by a population with different socio-economic characteristics.

On another level, it is important to notice that there is no culture difference when comparing Jews and Bedouin (from permanent towns). This information can help build programs for health delivery, health promotion and preventive medicine, based on the needs of peripheral populations and the resources available to the health providers.

REFERENCES

[1] Mautner M, Sagi A, Shamir R. *Multi-culturalism in a Democratic and Jewish State*, Ramot- T.A. University1998

[2] Kimmerling B. *Immigrants, Settlers, Natives: Israel Between Plurality of Cultures and Cultural Wars*. Tel Aviv:Am oved , 2004 (Hebrew,).

[3] Tawara D. Goode TD. Dunne M. Bronheim M. *The evidence base for cultural and linguistic competency in health care,* National Center for Cultural Competence, Georgetown University, October 2006

[4] Betancourt J, Green A, and Carrillo, E. *Cultural Competence And Health Care Disparities: Key Perspectives And Trends*. Health Affairs, no. 24, 2, 2005.

[5] Hunt, D. *Building Organizational Cultural Competence*. Conference on Quality Health Care for Culturally Diverse Populations. 24.9.2008-21 Minneapolis-St. Paul

[6] Grados Y. *From city hierarchy to a metropolis approach, changes in the Development of Beer-Sheva and the surrounding cities*. Ecology and surroundings, 1996 (*Hebrew*)
[7] The Israel Central Bureau of Statistics (Nov 2009). http://www1.cbs.gov.il/reader/?MIval=cw_usr_view_SHTMLandID=389
[8] Batty K. McTaggart K. *Development of a model for sustainable delivery of outreach allied health services to remote north-west Queensland, Australia.*. The international Electronic journal of rural and remote health research, education, practice and policy. 12.2003
[9] Glasgow N, Morton L. *Critical Issues in Rural Health*, Blackwell; 2004.
[10] The Negev Development Authority (Nov 2009) *http://www.negev.co.il/statis/ch6.asp*
[11] Asif, S. *Master plan, zoning and development of Beer-Sheva Metropolis,*. 1996. (*Hebrew*)
[12] Levinson, http://www.negev.co.il/ven/ven/xara/profile.htm .2004
[13] Shvarts S., Borkan, J.M., and Morad M. *Satisfaction, perception and use of the health System in the Bedouin sector after the enactment of the National Health Law .Research Report*, Ben-Gurion University, Beer-Sheva 1997
[14] Nirel N, Pilpel D, Rosen B, Zmora I, Greenstein M, Zalcberg, S. *The Accessibility and Availability of Health Services in the South of Israel: Has the Gap between the South and Other Regions in Israel Been Reduced in the Wake of the National Health Insurance Law*. The Myers-JDC-Brookdale Institute, Israel, 2000 (*Hebrew*).
[15] Lubetzky H, Shvarts S, Merrick J, Vardi G, Galil A. *The use of developmental rehabilitation services. Comparison between Bedouins and Jews in the South of Israel.*Scientific World Journal(4) 2004
[16] Warshawsky-Livne L, Cwikel J, Pliskin JS, *A Perception of health care delivery in Israel: women's voices*, Health Care Women International. 2005; 26(5):448-55.
[17] Lubetzky H, Shvarts S, Galil A, Tesler H, Vardi G, Merrick J. *Impact of Co-payment Requirements on Therapy Utilization for Children with Developmental Disabilities in Israeli Jewish and Arab Bedouin Populations*, Journal of Policy and Practice in Intellectual Disabilities. 2004; 4:164–168.
[18] The Robert H. Arnow Center for Bedouin Studies, *annual static report of the Negev Bedouin*, 2004 (*Hebrew*)
[19] Chernichovsky D. *Equality and the Israeli Health System: Relative Poverty as a Risk Factor for Health Inquiry Center for Social Policy in Israel*; 2003 (*Hebrew*)
[20] Lubetzky H, Friger M, Warshawsky-Livne L, Shvarts S *Distance and socioeconomic status as a health service predictor on the periphery in the southern region of Israel*. Health Policy. 2011 May;100(2-3):310-6.
[21] Warshawsky-Livne L. *Women's health services delivery in Israel: organizational and managerial analysis*, Public Health Review. 2009; 29(2-4):119-26; discussion 127-8.
[22] Galil, A. Carmel, S. Lubetzky, H., Vered, S. Haiman, N. *Compliance with home rehabilitation therapy by parents of children with disabilities Among Israeli Jews And Bedouin In Negev Region.* Developmental Medicine and Child Neurology, 2001
[23] Shkedy, *A Words Of Meaning, Qualitative Research – Theory and Practice*, Ramot T.A. University, 2004
[24] Shlasky S, Alpert B , *Ways to write qualitative research: dismantling the reality into text*. Mekhon Mofet (Tel Aviv, Israel) 2007 (*Hebrew*)
[25] Soroka Medical University Center database, 2006

[26] Negev Center for Regional Development, 2009 (*Hebrew*)
[27] Hayness R, Bentham *Community Hospitals and Rural Accessibility.* Teakfield Ltd. Westmead, Farnborough; 1979.
[28] Seidel JE, Beck CA, Pocobelli G, Lemaire JB, Bugar JM, Quan H, Ghali WA. *Location of residence associated with the likelihood of patient visit to the pre-operative assessment clinic.* BMC Health Services Research.2006;6,13
[29] Ken S, David J, Briggs B. *Socio-economic and locational determinants of accessibility and utilization of primary health-care, Health and Social Care in the Community.* 2001; 9.
[30] Billi C, Pahlinger D. *The effect of distance to primary care physician on health care utilization and disease burden*, Health Care Manage Review. 2007; 32(1).
[31] Peled R. Daroma. Ben-Gurion University; 2005 (*Hebrew*).
[32] Gross R, Shirom A. *Reforming the Israeli health system: Findings of a 3-year evaluation*, Health Policy. 2001; 56 (4).
[33] Borkan J. Morad, M. Shvarts, S. *Universal health care? The views of Negev Bedouin Arabs on Health Services.* Health Policy and Planning. 15 (2) 2000Pp. 207-217
[34] Becker G, Newsom E. *Socio-economic Status and Dissatisfaction with Health Care among Chronically Ill African-Americans*, American Journal of Public Health. 2003; 5.
[35] Dunlop S, Coyte P, McIsaac W. *Socio-economic status and the utilization of physicians' services: results from the Canadian National Population Health survey, Social Science and Medicine*, 2000; 51.
[36] Kacen, L. *Supercodes reflected in titles battered women accord to their life stories.* International Journal of Qualitative Methods, (1) 2002.
[37] Nir H. *Only paths my feet conquered, the history of the Kibbutz*, Ben-Gurion University of the Negev, 2008. (*Hebrew*)
[38] Isareli court decision 185/82, *Ben-Attia vs. the state of Israel* 37(1) 85,87, 1982. (*Hebrew*)
[39] Israel Knesset, October 2006)
[40] Zimmel G, Park R, Virath L. *Urbanism, The sociology of a modern city*, Resling Publication, 2007 (*Hebrew*)
[41] World Travel internet site (March; 2010). *www.wordtravels.com/...../Countries/Israel/Map.*

In: Socioeconomic Status and Health Implications
Editor: Sarah Reibert and Alice Jannings, pp. 57-83
ISBN: 978-1-62100-675-6

Chapter 3

The Impact of Low Socioeconomic Status on Child Mental Health and Strategies for Reducing Disparities across Sectors of Care

Catherine DeCarlo Santiago**, *Sheryl H. Kataoka*, *Jeanne Miranda and Bonnie T. Zima
University of California, Los Angeles, Department of Psychiatry and Biobehavioral Sciences, Center for Health Services and Society, 10920 Wilshire Blvd, Suite 300, Los Angeles, CA 90024, U.S.A.

Abstract

The link between low socioeconomic status (SES) and child mental health problems is well established. Nevertheless, the mechanisms underlying this relationship are multi-faceted and complex, involving factors at the child, parent, community, and system levels. For children living in low-income families, disparities in mental health are further accentuated by limited access to care, fragmented care, and poor quality of care. Thus, in this chapter we review the influential role of social determinants of mental health for children living in poverty. Next, we review disparities in mental health services access and utilization. Finally, we discuss strategies for reducing disparities among low SES children through interventions targeted to prevent, detect, and treat mental health problems within and across community-based care sectors serving low-income children.

Introduction

Poverty has consistently been found to be associated with an increased risk for child mental health problems and functional impairment across multiple domains, such as school achievement and relationships with family and peers (Conger et al., 2002; Farrington and Loeber, 2000; Lipman and Boyle, 2008). Among U.S. children, more than one in five

* Corresponding author, Email: csantiago@mednet.ucla.edu.

children live in poverty and an astounding 42% are living in low-income families (Chau, Thampi, and Wight, 2010). Ethnic minority children are also overrepresented in low-income families. Compared to 11% of White children, an estimated 35% of African American children, 31% of Latino children, 31% of Native American children, and 15% of Asian children live below the federal poverty line (Fass and Cauthen, 2008). In this chapter, we review the major mental health disparities for children from low socioeconomic status (SES), with a focus on their social determinants of mental health, such as exposure to violence, family conflict, and neighborhood disadvantage. Next, we review disparities in mental health services access and utilization. Children of low SES are not only at higher risk for mental health problems, but they are also much less likely to receive needed mental health services. Lack of insurance and limited access to mental health services contribute to further mental health disparities across SES. Further, families with low SES often experience barriers to obtaining mental health services, including inflexible work schedules and lack of child-care and transportation. Finally, we discuss prevention and intervention strategies for reducing these disparities among low SES children who are being served across various sectors of care, including primary care and school-based programs, as well as for those children in the child welfare and juvenile justice systems. We discuss the need for preventive interventions that can help reduce the risk for developing mental health problems given the burden of stress faced by low-income families. Primary care may be a crucial screening and access point for many low SES families, while school-based programs can reduce barriers and increase access to mental healthcare for all children by providing services in the school. Examples of interventions targeted to incorporate evidence-based practices and improved coordination of care for high-risk child populations in the child welfare and juvenile justice systems are also presented.

SES Disparities in Child Mental Health

The link between low SES and child mental health problems is well established. Poverty contributes to a multitude of negative outcomes for children, including symptoms of both internalizing and externalizing disorders (Conger et al., 2002; Grant et al., 2003). Internalizing problems include symptoms of anxiety, depression, and post-traumatic stress disorder (PTSD), while externalizing problems include behavioral problems, aggression, and delinquency. For children of low SES, the incidence of child mental health disorders increases substantially—21% of low-income children have at least one mental health problem (Howell, 2004), with children from low-income families having three times the odds for a mental health problem as compared to their counterparts from higher income families (Lipman and Boyle, 2008). Among preschool children, the incidence of behavioral problems is estimated at 30% for low-income children (Feil, Walker, Severson, and Ball, 2000; Gross, Sambrook, and Fogg, 1999), compared to between 3% and 6% in the general population (Achenbach and Edelbrock, 1981; Qi and Kaiser, 2003). Likewise, a large study examining DSM-IV diagnoses among elementary school children found that children exposed to early poverty, living in concurrent poverty, and who had been exposed to violence in the previous year, were more likely to have internalizing disorders (Carter et al., 2010). The relationship between poverty and the child's risk for mental health problems is robust, as it has been found to be stable and consistent across countries, measures of poverty, and methods of determining diagnosis (Lipman and Boyle, 2008). Given that poverty is consistently implicated in risk for mental health disorders among children, explanatory factors associated with this link have been explored. We review these major risk factors across children and adolescents.

Poverty-Related Risk Factors

Researchers have identified numerous psychosocial factors associated with low SES that often contribute to an increased risk for mental health problems. Within the child's immediate physical living and family environment, such factors as food insecurity, poor quality housing, and family or parent problems have been associated with worse child mental health (Evans, 2004; Perkins, 1997). Further, children living in poverty are exposed to broader community and environmental factors that increase their risk for mental health problems, including neighborhood disadvantage, exposure to violence, and discrimination (Evans, 2004; Wadsworth et al., 2008). The accumulation of these stressors compromises both physiological and psychological functioning for children (Evans, Kim, Ting, Tesher, and Shannis, 2007; Wadsworth et al., 2008) and predicts teen pregnancy, school dropout, and substance use, which have long-term adverse effects (Farrington and Loeber, 2000).

Physical Living and Family Environment

Low-income children have limited resources for necessities such as food and often live in poor quality housing. Research on food insecurity, or limited or uncertain availability of food because of inadequate resources, has been linked to increased likelihood of internalizing problems (Slopen, Fitzmaurice, Williams, and Gilman, 2010). Living with less money than one needs for food and other resources can contribute to feelings of depression and anxiety for parents and children alike. For children, this insecurity in their environment contributes to the development of internalizing disorders even among early elementary school children (Carter et al., 2010). In a study conducted by Wadsworth and Compas (2002), adolescents endorsed a variety of stressors related to a lack of money with which to purchase basic needs, such as food, school supplies, and clothing. This type of economic strain is grueling and demoralizing for children and adolescents, undermining a sense of self-efficacy or control. Low sense of control is common among children and adolescents coping with economic strain, which has been associated with both depression and anxiety (Conger et al., 2002).

In addition to food insecurity and economic strain, poor families often live in poor quality, small, multi-unit dwellings that are in need of repair and have less access to positive environmental spaces (Evans, Wells, and Moch, 2003). Low-income housing has less green open space and fewer parks nearby (McLoyd, 1998). This lack of access restricts opportunities for outdoor play and recreation and increases children's risk for behavioral problems and delinquency (Evans et al., 2003). Living in poor quality housing is a constant reminder of one's economic situation, which can ultimately undermine a sense of hope for the future and can increase a youth's risk for depression (Gibb and Alloy, 2006).

Parents with low SES have greater risk for depression, interparental conflict, poor parenting, and alcohol use, which can have both direct and indirect effects on their children's psychological functioning. There is considerable evidence for a direct link between parental depression and child depression, though both genetic and non-genetic factors contribute to this relationship (Foster et al., 2008; Hammen, Brennan, and Keenan-Miller, 2008). Direct connections have also been found between parental depression and children's externalizing symptoms, such as aggression and delinquency (Gross, Shaw, and Moilanen, 2008). Not only does parental depression directly affect children's emotional and behavioral functioning, but it also contributes to interparental conflict and poor parenting, which have detrimental effects on child functioning as well.

Parental depression can lead to feelings of insecurity about the marital relationship and more negative couple interactions, which contributes to increased conflict (Shelton and Harold, 2008). Higher levels and more intense conflicts in the family then contribute to child internalizing symptoms and externalizing problems (Caples and Barrera, 2006; Cui, Donnellan, and Conger, 2007; Garbarino, Sebes, and Schellenbach, 1984; Gerard, Krishnakumar, and Buehler, 2006). Stress associated with low-income can further exacerbate family conflict and its effects on child mental health (Santiago and Wadsworth, 2009).

Both parental depression and interparental conflict are also associated with parenting behavior that is intrusive, harsh, withdrawn, and less warm and responsive. This disrupted parenting is a primary mechanism for how interparental conflict affects children's externalizing symptoms (Benson, Buehler, and Gerard, 2008; Cui and Conger, 2008; Salafia, Gondoli, and Grundy, 2008). This type of parenting also mediates the relationship between maternal depression and child depression and anxiety (Foster, Garber, and Durlak, 2008). Poverty-related stressors also increase the likelihood of harsh and inconsistent discipline (Qi and Kaiser, 2003), which in turn leads to child behavioral problems (Brody et al., 2003; Conger et al., 2002; Mistry, Vandewater, Huston, and McLoyd, 2002). Similarly, parental alcohol abuse lessens a parent's warmth and sensitivity towards his or her children, and this compromised parenting links alcohol abuse to child externalizing and antisocial behavior (Eiden, Edwards, and Leonard, 2007). Whether stemming from parental depression, conflict, stress, or alcohol abuse, parenting that is inconsistent or harsh is consistently identified as a risk factor for both child internalizing and externalizing symptoms.

Community and Broader Social Environment

Neighborhood disadvantage is another type of chronic stress that poor children and adolescents face, that extends community-level factors to include neighborhood cohesion and safety. Neighborhood disadvantage contributes to crime and delinquency through factors such as residential mobility and high poverty rates. These problems tend to reduce interconnectedness within and commitment to the community, weaken ties to the community and reduce adult monitoring of children (Brooks-Gunn, Duncan, Klebanov, and Sealand, 1993; Farrington and Loeber, 2000; Sampson and Groves, 1989). Communities that cannot afford to support formal organizations such as community centers, libraries, gyms, or churches provide fewer opportunities for positive interactions among community members, while zoning laws in poor neighborhoods often allow for more bars, liquor stores, and multi-family dwellings (Jargowsky, Desmond, and Crutchfield, 2005). Additionally, people in neighborhoods with high residential turnover find it difficult to create or maintain neighborly bonds. This creates a socially discouraging and stressful environment where crime and delinquency among poor adolescents may be more appealing and more possible due to less collective socialization (Farrington and Loeber, 2000; Sampson, Raudenbush, and Earls, 1997). Research has shown that neighborhood disadvantage intensifies the negative effects of daily stressors on psychological problems (Attar, Guerra, and Tolan, 1994), placing adolescents in communities with fewer resources at greater risk for juvenile delinquency (Brooks-Gunn, Duncan, and Aber, 1997). Along with broad neighborhood disadvantage, low SES children are more likely to be exposed to violence in their homes, schools, and neighborhoods. Violence exposure, in particular, increases risk for PTSD, anxiety, and depression. In fact, 20-50% of American children have been exposed to violence in their homes, schools, and communities (Finkelhor and Dziuba-Leatherman, 1994), and poor and ethnic minority youth are at highest risk for exposure to violence (Perkins, 1997). Children experience violence directly via victimization, and also witness violence by seeing it or hearing about it. Both victimization and witnessing violence are related to increased intrusive thoughts, depression, and anxiety for poor middle-school children (Jaycox et al., 2002; Kliewer, Lepore, Oskin, and Johnson, 1998). High rates of community violence are common for low-income urban families, and for many poor children who witness or are victims of violence, this exposure undermines a sense of control and contributes to anxiety, depression, and hopelessness (Ceballo, Ramirez, Hearn, and Maltese, 2003). Some studies estimate that one third of children exposed to community violence develop posttraumatic stress disorder (PTSD) (Berman, Kurtines, Silverman, and Serafini, 1996; Fitzpatrick and Boldizar, 1993; Jaycox et al., 2002). In addition to increasing risk for internalizing problems (i.e., PTSD, anxiety and depression), exposure to violence also contributes to aggression and delinquency (Farrell and Sullivan, 2004; Gorman-Smith and Tolan, 1998; Li, Nussbaum, and Richards, 2007; Plybon and Kliewer, 2001), alcohol use, tobacco use, and drug problems (Kliewer et al., 2006; Taylor and Kliewer, 2006). In addition to other risk factors (e.g., genetic, peer influence), use of drugs and alcohol may be an ineffective attempt to cope with violence exposure and victimization. Adolescents inclined to use alcohol to cope with stress can quickly develop more serious alcohol problems (Rafnsson, Jonsson, and Windle, 2006). Domestic violence among family members or directed at children also increases risk for substance and alcohol use, as does peer victimization (Sullivan, Farrell, and Kliewer, 2006). Use of alcohol and drugs in these contexts is, in turn, linked to aggressive behavior and delinquency (Mejia, Kliewer, and Williams, 2006; Sullivan et al., 2006). Exposure to violence has long-term negative health consequences for children including PTSD, but also anxiety, depression, aggression, poor school performance and attendance, decreased cognitive functioning, and decreased rates of high school graduation (Jaycox et al., 2002; Saigh, Mroueh, and Bremner, 1997; Singer, Anglin, Song, and Lunghofer, 1995). In addition, poor youth are at greater risk for discrimination given that ethnic minority children are overrepresented. Unfortunately, discrimination is a frequent experience for ethnic minority children within their schools, neighborhoods, and broader social environment and has negative mental health consequences (Cooper, McLoyd, Wood, and Hardaway, 2008). Discrimination negatively impacts self-esteem and is associated with more depression among Latino adolescents (Umaña-Taylor and Updegraff, 2007). Similarly, experiences of racial discrimination are linked to more depressive symptoms among African American children (Simons et al., 2002). These experiences likely invoke feelings of sadness or anger, but chronic discrimination can ultimately lead to feelings of despair, hopelessness, resignation, and depression. Discrimination also has been linked to behavior problems including aggression and delinquency (DuBois, Burk-Braxton, Swenson, Tevendale, and Hardesty, 2002; Simons et al., 2002). In addition to undermining a sense of control and creating hopelessness, discrimination also results in anger and continual frustration. When young adolescents believe that discrimination negatively affects their chance to move up the ladder of social mobility, lives of crime may become a more attractive alternative.

Protective Factors

Though ethnic and racial minority children are more likely to face economic disadvantage compared to White children (Fass and Cauthen, 2008), research has found that culture can sometimes serve as a protective factor that may reduce a child's risk for mental health problems despite poverty. For example, Latino adults who are immigrants have a lower prevalence rate of mental health disorders than those who are born in the United States despite extreme poverty (U.S. Department of Health and Human Services, 2001). Although less is understood about the effects of immigrant status on Latino children and adolescents, Suárez-Orozco and Suárez-Orozco (1995) suggest that Latino middle-school children who are immigrants also do well due to a dual frame of reference. Immigrant children use their families back home as reference points, whose social and economic conditions are often worse, while U.S. born Latino children are more likely to compare themselves to their peers in the U.S. (Suárez-Orozco and Suárez-Orozco, 1995). Latinos are also more likely to use family and spirituality as forms of coping, which can also have protective effects (Santiago and Wadsworth, 2011; U.S. Department of Health and Human Services, 2001).

Another noteworthy finding is that African American youth consistently have lower prevalence rates of both alcohol and substance use as compared to White youth, despite higher likelihood of economic disadvantage (Botvin, Schinke, and Orlandi, 1995; Wallace et al., 1999). Further, among youths aged 12 to 17 in 2003, African American and Asian youth were least likely to report past month alcohol use, with 8.7% of Asian youth and 10.1% of African American youth endorsing that they are current drinkers, while rates were above 15 percent for other racial/ethnic groups (Substance Abuse and Mental Health Services Administration, 2004). Although there are likely a number of factors that contribute to these differences, the importance of religion and spirituality among African American families has been linked to lower rates of alcohol and substance use (Wallace, Myers, and Osai, 2004).

Disparities in Mental Health Services for Children

Children of low SES are not only at higher risk for poor mental health outcomes, but they are also much less likely to receive needed care. Access to health insurance, mental healthcare, and preventive services contribute to health disparities (McGinnis, Williams-Russo, and Knickman, 2002).

Further, families with low SES often experience barriers to obtaining mental health services, including lack of or limited access to mental health care, child-care, and transportation (McGrath, Keita, Strickland, and Russo, 1990).

Access to Mental Health Services

Among children in need of mental healthcare, 75-80% do not get that care (Kataoka, Zhang, and Wells, 2002). Factors associated with lower SES often exacerbate these statistics. For example, uninsured children have even more unmet mental healthcare needs, with an estimated 87% of uninsured children not receiving needed care (Kataoka et al., 2002). Other factors, such as single-parent status, neighborhood disadvantage, and social isolation are linked to less service utilization (Snell-Johns, Mendez, and Smith, 2004). Children of single parents are more likely to drop out of treatment prematurely and have worse treatment outcomes (Kazdin and Mazurick, 1994; Taylor and Biglan, 1998). Families residing in low-income neighborhoods are less likely to receive services and are also more likely to drop out (Bischoff and Sprenkle, 1993; Kazdin, 1996; McKay, Quintana, Kim, Gonzales, and Adil, 1999). In a study of children in need of mental health care who also have special health needs, children of low SES were the least likely to receive needed care (Fulda, Lykens, Bae, and Singh, 2009).

Ethnic minority children are also identified as having lower rates of use of mental health services and are disproportionately poor (Fass and Cauthen, 2008). Studies have identified both Latino and/or African American children as less likely to receive needed care compared to White children (Padgett, Patrick, Burns, Schlesinger, and Cohen, 1993; Zahner and Daskalakis, 1997). In a national study, Latino children had the most unmet need, with 88% of these children having unmet mental healthcare needs (Kataoka et al., 2002). These troubling disparities may be due, in part, to logistical and engagement barriers.

Logistical Barriers

In addition to limited access to services, barriers associated with the stress of low-income often prevent utilization of services and are predictive of poor engagement and retention in mental health services (Snell-Johns et al., 2004). Low-income families often have less access to mental health services, have to travel longer distances for care, and face additional transportation and childcare barriers (McGrath et al., 1990). However, some research suggests that offering transportation, childcare, and low-cost services will reduce barriers to access and increase service providers' ability to reach underserved families (Miller and Prinz, 1990; Sayger and Heid, 1990; Taylor and Biglan, 1998). Thus, addressing logistical barriers is key for successful intervention and prevention efforts for low-income families.

Engagement Barriers

In addition to logistical barriers such as time and transportation, researchers have identified other barriers to engaging low SES families in services. For example, engaging low-income Latino parents in mental health services has proven challenging due to factors such as language, perceived barriers to treatment, cultural beliefs, client-therapist match, and education level (McCabe, 2002). Clinicians working with immigrant families need to have awareness and competence to assess for and intervene around issues of immigration trauma or stress and acculturation stressors families may be faced with (Pumariega, Rothe, and

Pumariega, 2005). Immigrant families also appear to benefit from relational engagement, thus working towards a collaborative relationship with parents may increase retention in services (Suárez-Orozco, Rhodes, and Milburn, 2009). Further, interventions in which clinicians and all program support staff are trained on engagement barriers and strategies, or interventions that address program barriers improve family engagement (Korfmacher et al., 2008; McKay et al., 2004; Staudt, 2003). Significant reductions in the no-show rate for first appointments have been found when clinicians employ strategies such as telephone engagement that aims to restructure logistical barriers, explore parental concerns and beliefs about coming to treatment, and highlight parental strengths (McKay, McCadam, and Gonzales, 1996). Engagement strategies need to be incorporated into prevention and intervention programs to ensure attendance and acceptability of services.

Strategies for Reducing Disparities

Given disparities in both mental health and service use, implementing strategies to reduce them among low-income children is of high public health significance. A major priority area for the U.S. National Prevention Strategy (2011) is the reduction of mental health disparities, with prevention and intervention with children, early identification of needs and access to quality services, and integration of care across sectors and settings identified as key strategies for reaching this goal. Preventive and early interventions delivered in universal settings such as schools and primary care may reduce the risk of mental health problems and improve early access to services when treatment may be most beneficial. Further, evidence-based intervention strategies targeted to the needs of children at-risk and within each sector of care that serves low-income families are needed. Children of low SES backgrounds are over-represented in the child welfare and juvenile justice sectors of care and 50% and 67-70% of children in these respective systems have a diagnosable mental health disorder (Burns et al., 2004; Skowyra and Cocozza, 2006). In combination with their higher absolute need for services, these high risk child populations are also more likely to rely on restrictive and costly services, such as juvenile detention, residential treatment, and emergency room treatment (Smithgall, Gladden, Yang, and Goerge, 2005; U.S. House of Representatives, 2004). Given this spectrum of clinical need for care, we provide a number of examples of prevention and intervention programs that are promising in reducing mental health problems among poor children.

Prevention Programs

Given the burden of stress that many low SES children face, preventive interventions can help reduce risk for developing mental health problems. Many effective prevention programs incorporate skill building to manage chronic and transitional stressors. Coping strategies that include problem solving, emotion regulation, cognitive reframing, and positive distraction are effective for managing poverty-related stressors (Wadsworth and Santiago, 2008). Thus, programs that teach these types of strategies are likely to be effective for reducing risk for mental health problems. For example, the Improving Social Awareness – Social Problem-

Solving (ISA-SPS) Program led to improvements in coping with stressors related to middle school transition along with significant reductions in problem behavior over six years (Bruene-Butler, Hampson, Elias, Clabby, and Schuyler, 1997). The Promoting Alternative THinking Strategies (PATHS) Program is another program that has demonstrated improvement in emotion regulation and problem-solving skills and reductions of internalizing and externalizing problems (Greenberg and Kusché, 1998; Conduct Problems Prevention Research Group, 1999). PATHS is an elementary school-based program that focuses on teaching students to identify, understand, and regulate their emotions, and includes components for parents and school contexts beyond the classroom to increase generalizability of the students' newly-acquired skills. Other effective prevention programs that target skill building include the Anger Coping Program, which consists of 18 sessions that teach affect identification, self-control, and problem-solving skills (Lochman, 1985). The Anger Coping Program has grown into the Coping Power Program, which has demonstrated positive effects on delinquent and aggressive behavior as well as substance use (Lochman and Wells, 2003). Further, some programs designed as treatment have now been applied in a prevention framework. For example, prevention programs targeting parents have been adapted from the Parent and Children Training Series (Webster-Stratton, 1992a; Webster-Stratton, 1992b), now referred to as The Incredible Years: Parents, Teachers, and Children Series, and the Helping the Noncompliant Child curriculum (Forehand and McMahon, 1981).

In addition, preventive interventions for older children and youth may reduce the risk of serious adverse consequences of mental health problems, such as suicide and substance abuse. For example, Signs of Suicide (SOS) significantly reduced rates of suicide attempts and increased knowledge and adaptive attitudes about depression and suicide among high school students (Aseltine and DeMartino, 2004). SOS is a 2-day secondary school-based prevention program that combines education to raise awareness and screening for depression and other suicide risk factors. Substance abuse is another adverse consequence of mental health problems among older children. Numerous prevention programs are promising, including Project STAR, a multicomponent drug abuse prevention program that includes a coordinated effort that encompasses schools, parents and community organizations (Chou et al., 1998; U.S. Department of Education, 2001). Strategies range from individual- and family-level change, such as teaching youth drug resistance skills and positive family communication, to school and community-change, including limiting youth access to alcohol or drugs. Long-term follow-up studies showed significant reductions in drug use among youth who receive the program.

In a summary of successful prevention programs, the majority of which were aimed at low-income children and families, Greenberg, Domitrovich, and Bumbarger (2000) outlined a number of key points. First, short-term preventive interventions produce very time-limited benefits, while multi-year programs are more likely to foster long-term benefits for at-risk children. Further, preventive interventions are best directed at risk and protective factors rather than at categorical problem behaviors, and should target multiple domains, changing institutions and environments as well as individuals. For example, programs that target children and school and home environments are most successful. Likewise, prevention programs should be coordinated and collaborative in nature. Prevention programs should coordinate multiple strategies for preventing psychological disorders (e.g. skill-building, family and school supports), but also partner with community systems of care for sustainability. For example, combining school-wide primary prevention together with secondary prevention and treatment will likely create a more comprehensive and sustainable system.

Further, prevention programs must consider the obstacles to obtaining these services that are common among low-income families. Programs delivered in schools or other community settings reduce the burden on parents and families in terms of time, transportation, and cost. Other strategies, such as videotaped interventions, may reduce barriers for parents and make prevention and educational materials more accessible. For example, Webster-Stratton's videotape series (Webster-Stratton, 1998) was effective for improving parenting practices.

Primary Care Strategies

In addition to prevention programs, early identification and intervention through primary care settings can also reduce disparities among low-income children. The estimated prevalence of mental health problems among children receiving care in primary care settings ranges from 17% to 25% (Briggs-Gowan, Horwitz, Schwab-Stone, Leventhal, and Leaf, 2000; Briggs-Gowan et al., 2003; Costello et al., 1988), and may be higher among children who are poor (Briggs-Gowan et al., 2000; Starfield et al., 1980). Yet despite the relatively high prevalence of mental health problems among children seen in pediatric primary care outpatient settings, rates of detection of mental health problems are relatively low (Crone, Bekkema, Wiefferink, and Reijneveld, 2010; Katon, Richardson, Russo, Lozano, and McCauley, 2006), especially among children from racial/ethnic minority backgrounds (Tarshis, Jutte, and Huffman, 2006). In a study involving 53 primary care providers and 767 patients age 5-16 years, providers failed to identify a mental health problem among 78% of the children who were Latino and 55% who were African-American compared to 27% of White children (Brown and Wissow, 2010). Better identification of mental health problems within primary care is needed to assist ethnic minority and low-income families in accessing care.

One mechanism potentially underlying low detection rates is poor communication between parents and providers. In a large, representative sample of children in pediatric practices, more than one-half of parents who were aware of their child's symptoms did not discuss their concerns about an emotional or behavioral problem with their pediatrician, and when they did discuss their concerns, less than one-half of these children successfully accessed specialty mental health care (Briggs-Gowan et al., 2000). Communicating concerns about child mental health problems may be particularly problematic for low-income parents who are at greater risk for poor education and health literacy. For example, among a large sample of high-risk youth, mothers with lower education were less likely to endorse ADHD inattentive symptoms (Leslie, Aarons, Haine, and Hough, 2007).

One strategy that may facilitate parent-provider communication and improve early detection of child mental health problems is the use of standardized screening measures in primary care. The Pediatric Symptom Checklist and Children with Special Health Care Needs Screener are examples of options that are feasible for use in primary care settings with low-income and ethnic minority children (The Child and Health Measurement Initiative; Jellinek et al., 1999; Murphy et al., 1996; Murphy, Reede, Jellinek, and Bishop, 1992). Use of global screening may assist primary care clinicians in identifying children in need of mental healthcare and facilitate communication between families and providers regarding children's mental health needs. In addition to global screening measures for child mental health, brief screening tools are available to detect specific disorders, such as depression or PTSD, for which low-income children are at increased risk. For example, two measures of child depression that have demonstrated good sensitivity and specificity in adolescents in primary care settings are the Beck Depression Inventory-Primary Care Version (BDI-PC) and the Patient Health Questionnaire for Adolescents (PHQ-A) (Force, 2009; Richardson et al., 2011). Screening for violence exposure (e.g., "Since the last time I saw you, has anything really scary or upsetting happened to you or your family?") and following up with a screener, such as the UCLA PTSD Reaction Index also improves detection of PTSD in pediatric primary care settings (Cohen, Kelleher, and Mannarino, 2008; Steinberg, Brymer, Decker, and Pynoos, 2004). More consistent use of screening tools within primary care can improve detection of mental health problems and connect low-income children to needed care.

Though screening may improve access to care (Horwitz, Leaf, Leventhal, Forsyth, and Speechley, 1992), quality of care remains variable. For those children that receive mental health care in primary care settings, the quality of care may fall short of recommended treatment guidelines (Hoagwood, Kelleher, Feil, and Comer, 2000; Leslie, Weckerly, Plemmons, Landsverk, and Eastman, 2004). Among children receiving care for Attention Deficit/Hyperactivity Disorder (ADHD) in a large managed care Medicaid program, few if any children who received care in primary care settings accessed specialty mental health services (Zima et al., 2010). Among children who received care in primary care outpatient clinics, 80-85% of children had at least one stimulant prescription filled that is consistent with guideline concordant care, but almost one-half of these children did not have a follow-up visit within 6 months and only 36% had an adequate supply of stimulant medication (Zima et al., 2010). Further, symptoms, functioning, academic achievement, caregiver distress, and family functioning did not improve over time and were similar to children who received no care (Zima et al., 2010). These sobering findings support the call for strategies to improve not only identification of mental health needs in primary care, but also access to quality mental healthcare.

In addition to ADHD, depression is frequently encountered in primary care settings and may be a crucial access point for medication and/or psychosocial intervention, especially for low-income families. However, many primary care providers are uncomfortable medicating adolescents due to controversies over efficacy and concerns about side effects (Bridge et al., 2007), yet access to CBT or other evidence-based approaches outside of primary care may be limited. One quality improvement study for adolescent depression in primary care, Youth Partners in Care (YPIC), found improvement in treatment uptake, depressive symptoms, and functioning relative to usual care (Asarnow et al., 2005). The study included screening, supervised treatments, and education and support for primary care clinicians, raising concerns about long-term feasibility and sustainability in practice. Still, the study highlights that adolescents can not only access screening and treatment through primary care, but that access can improve mental health outcomes when primary care clinicians are supported and trained (Asarnow et al., 2005).

Strategies for better identification and treatment in primary care include the integration of mental health into pediatric primary care (National Institute for Health Care Management Foundation, 2009), use of the Pediatric Medical Home Model (Homer et al., 2008), and changes in reimbursement of mental health services in primary care settings to sustain change in health care delivery over time (Kautz, Mauch, and Smith, 2008). In addition, collaborative care models for improving care for ADHD (Epstein et al., 2007) and use of health information and communication technologies (i.e., web-based or computer assisted screening, telepsychiatry) are promising (Julian, Kelleher, Julian, and Chisolm, 2007; Myers, Valentine, and Melzer, 2007). A more integrated primary care and mental healthcare system would likely improve detection and access to mental health services for many low-income children translating to reduced disparities over time, yet the validity of this model is not well established.

School-Based Programs

For poor children, the school system can be another key access point for the detection and treatment of mental health problems, with fewer financial and structural barriers preventing access to care than often exists in specialty mental health care settings (Garrison, Roy, and Azar, 1999). For example, a randomized study comparing two efficacious treatments for youth with posttraumatic stress symptoms in post-Katrina New Orleans found that 91% of the youth completed the school-based intervention compared to only 15% who completed the clinic-based intervention (Jaycox et al., 2010). Especially when delivering programs that are valued and needed by schools, mental health interventions can not only be a way to improve access, but at least in some cases, may also contribute to the educational mission of schools by also improving the ability of students to learn (Hoagwood et al., 2007). This is a key issue especially for low income ethnic minority students who are not only at risk for mental health problems but at risk for poor academic achievement and high school dropout (McKinsey and Company, 2009; Leventhal and Brooks-Gunn, 2004).

School-based mental health services for children living in poverty can capitalize on schools' inherent capacity to support development and mental health (Cappella, Frazier, Atkins, Schoenwald, and Glisson, 2008). Schools often provide a broad range of prevention and early intervention mental health services. Nationally, it is estimated that 63% of public schools have mental health prevention services such as suicide and drug abuse prevention and 59% of U.S. schools have services that address behavioral problems (Foster et al., 2005). There are also a various models of delivering these services to students, with some schools using only school or district personnel to provide services, while others depend on community providers to co-locate onto campuses to deliver mental health services (Foster et al., 2005).

Schools have many different roles in providing mental health services to low-income students, including mental health screening and referral (Weist, Rubin, Moore, Adelsheim, and Wrobel, 2007). School mental health screening can be an important means of identification of previously undetected mental health problems that can impact students' emotional well-being and learning. However, close coordination of community outreach and mobilization of school-based and community resources is paramount when screening for mental health problems to ensure that there is adequate capacity to provide appropriate services to all students identified as needing care (Weist et al., 2007).

Implementing evidence-based mental health practices in schools is one way to increase access to quality services for children who otherwise would likely not receive care. Schools commonly provide universal prevention programs as discussed earlier, which can help address some of heightened psychosocial stressors that children living in poverty experience, through the development of better social skills, problem-solving strategies, and suicide prevention strategies (Greenberg, Domitrovich, and Bumbarger, 2000). In addition, school-based interventions have been developed that provide treatment for a number of mental health problems. Some have provided support for students with ADHD, such as the Challenging Horizons Program, which targets the educational needs, social skills deficits, and family conflict issues of these students to improve functioning at school and home (Evans, Schultz, DeMars, and Davis, 2011). Other programs have focused on symptoms of depression, providing interpersonal psychotherapy in school-based health centers to reduce depressive symptoms (Mufson et al., 2004).

As discussed earlier, low-income youth report high rates of exposure to traumatic and violent experiences, which puts them at risk for posttraumatic stress symptoms and grief and can ultimately impact their social emotional and academic functioning. Cognitive behavioral therapy (CBT) approaches have been found to be effective in addressing trauma-related mental health symptoms (Amaya-Jackson et al., 2003; Cohen, Deblinger, Mannarino, and Steer, 2004). The Cognitive Behavioral Intervention for Trauma in Schools (CBITS) program, a brief, ten-session group school-based program, has improved posttraumatic stress disorder (PTSD) and depressive symptoms among poor Latino elementary and middle school students exposed to community violence (Kataoka et al., 2003; Stein et al., 2003). Preliminary findings also suggest that this program may have effects on school performance (Kataoka et al., in press). Given the shortage of mental health care providers, especially in neighborhoods of poverty, Support for Students Exposed to Trauma (SSET), was developed as an adaptation of CBITS. SSET, which can be delivered by non-mental health trained school staff (teachers, school counselors) has been found to improve trauma symptoms and is a promising intervention that can be feasibly delivered in schools (Jaycox et al., 2009).

Other trauma interventions have also been developed and studied in the context of schools. The Multimodality Trauma Treatment (MMTT) or Trauma-Focused Coping is a 14-session group intervention program that adapts basic cognitive behavioral techniques for students who have experienced a single incident trauma (March, Amaya-Jackson, Murray, and Schulte, 1998). The University of California Trauma Grief Component Treatment (TGCT) program is designed for adolescents exposed to multiple types of violence and traumatic loss and has improved PTSD, depression, and complicated grief symptoms (Saltzman, Pynoos, Layne, Steinberg, and Aisenberg, 2001). By providing these types of treatments in the school setting, the barriers to mental health services are significantly decreased for low-income students and mental health functioning can be improved.

Child Welfare System

Low-income children are largely represented in the child welfare system, though utilization of mental health services remains low despite need of care—85% of youth in need of mental health services in the child welfare system do not get that care (Burns et al., 2004). Further, children in foster care are at extremely high risk for mental health disorders and long-term functional impairment across multiple domains that do not dissipate in adulthood (Racusin, Maerlender, Sengupta, Isquith, and Straus, 2005). Incorporating or coordinating mental health services within child welfare system is crucial avenue for reaching a particularly high-risk group of low-income children.

A promising approach within the child welfare system is Multidimensional Treatment Foster Care (Chamberlain, 1998a). Treatment Foster Care programs were first designed to target delinquency and aimed to integrate service delivery systems to include foster parents as members of the treatment team, who also receive specialized training and support (Steib, 2002). MTFC is a three-tiered approach that includes system level supports, family and individual treatment, and school interventions (Chamberlain and Reid, 1998b). Foster parents receive substantial training in behavior management, along with individual therapy for the child, family therapy with foster and/or biological families, and coordination with school interventions. When compared with outcomes for adolescents living in group-homes, those who received MTFC engaged in less criminal activity and were more likely to return to live with biological relatives (Chamberlain and Reid, 1998b).

Treatment Foster Care has also been investigated with preschool children experiencing their first out-of-home placement—Early Intervention Foster Care (EIFC). In a small pilot study, EIFC foster parents utilized more positive parenting strategies and EIFC children showed better behavioral adjustment, while non-EIFC children showed declines in functioning (Fisher, Gunnar, Chamberlain, and Reid, 2000). In a later and larger study, Fisher and Kim (2007) applied the Multidimensional Treatment Foster Care approach again with preschoolers. Preschool children who received MTFC showed significant increases in secure attachment behavior and decreases in avoidant behavior compared to children assigned to regular foster care (Fisher and Kim, 2007).

A less intensive version of Treatment Foster Care has also been applied as a universal intervention with the goal of reducing child problem behaviors and strengthening foster parents' skills (Chamberlain et al., 2008). KEEP was examined within a sample of 700 foster care families with children ages 5-12. Families assigned to KEEP, received 16 weeks of training and support in behavioral management methods in groups. Emphasis was placed on reinforcement relative to discipline. Child behavior problems significantly improved and parenting practices mediated these reductions for families receiving KEEP (Chamberlain et al., 2008). These multi-level interventions are promising in their ability to improve functioning and mental health outcomes in a particularly high-risk group of low-income children.

Juvenile Justice System

Poor and ethnic minority youth are also significantly over-represented in juvenile justice settings. Although juvenile detention and residential facilities for youth have been designed to be rehabilitative, evidence suggests that these programs have instead increased criminal activity (Henggeler and Schoenwald, 2011). Within these systems for juvenile offenders, there is a great need to address the high level of psychological problems that these youth experience. One promising screening tool that has been used in detention centers is the Massachusetts Youth Screening Instrument, Version 2 (MAYSI-2), which is a self-report questionnaire that identifies which youth need further psychological assessment (Grisso and Barnum, 2006). It has six clinical scales including: alcohol and drug use, anger and irritability, depressed and anxious, somatic symptoms, suicidality, and thought disturbance (i.e. hallucinations) and traumatic experiences. Juvenile justice systems frequently are faced with youth with multiple problems, including psychiatric disorders, substance abuse, medical problems, and psychosocial challenges. It is recommended that those youth who have significant mental health problems should be diverted from the justice system when possible (Henggeler and Schoenwald, 2011).

To prevent juvenile justice involvement, several interventions have been found to be effective in decreasing antisocial behavior. Multisystemic therapy (MST) has been found to be effective in reducing re-arrest rates, time incarcerated, and self-reported offenses (Borduin et al., 1995; Henggeler, Clingempeel, Brondino, and Pickrel, 2002; Henggeler, Melton, Brondino, Scherer, and Hanley, 1997; Henggeler, Melton, and Smith, 1992). Intervening with multiple systems, MST individualizes the treatment with the family, peers, and school by taking into account the sociocultural context of each youth and family (Henggeler et al., 1992). Studies of MST have demonstrated its positive impact on family correlates of antisocial behavior as well as adjustment in family members.

Functional Family Therapy (FFT) is another effective program that has been found to decrease antisocial behavior in youth by addressing dysfunctional family relationships. FFT targets changing behaviors at the family-level and anger management and communication training on the individual level (Sexton and Alexander, 2000). Multifaceted approaches such as MST and FFT can create change on multiple levels and prevent placement in juvenile justice for many low-income children and adolescents.

Summary of Strategies

Despite effective prevention and intervention programs, many low-income children do not receive needed care. Prevention and intervention programs must address logistical and engagement barriers in order to improve attendance and treatment retention of low-income families. Further, improving access to and quality of services across sectors of care in important to reduce disparities long-term. Primary care settings can improve screening and coordination of care to identify mental health problems early and connect families to services, while schools can serve as another access point that minimizes barriers to services for children and families. Finally, multicomponent and coordinated treatments are needed within the child welfare and juvenile justice systems to improve mental health functioning and long-term outcomes of the high-risk youth served in these sectors.

Conclusion

Low SES children are at increased risk for mental health problems. Though low-income, food insecurity, neighborhood disadvantage, exposure to violence, disrupted parent and family functioning, and discrimination have all been implicated in this risk, it is likely the accumulation of stress that is particularly damaging. It is imperative that children of low SES have access to high quality mental health services in order to reduce mental health disparities across SES. In addition to working to decrease logistical and engagement barriers in mental health services, there is a growing need to increase early identification and access to care.

Preventive interventions can reduce disparities by preventing the incidence of new mental health problems, while standardized screening in primary care can increase identification of mental health problems and link services. An integrated primary care and mental healthcare system may also increase both identification of mental healthcare need and access to services for low-income children. Research findings further suggest a pressing need for wide dissemination of prevention and intervention efforts for low-income children whose poverty status places them at increased risk for mental health problems. Intervention targets include providing supportive home and school environments, increasing children's language and social skills, increasing adaptive coping skills, increasing positive parent-child interactions, and reducing patterns of harsh discipline. Disseminating such evidence-based practices in schools increases access to and quality of care for many underserved children. Other systems of care that serve low SES families like the child welfare system and juvenile justice system may best reduce mental health problems through multifaceted approaches that intervene on multiple levels (e.g., MTFC and MST).

Prevention and intervention services can be improved and disseminated across sectors of care to reduce SES mental health disparities. Further implications for policy aimed at reducing disparities might include programs for decreasing community violence or increasing neighborhood cohesion, green spaces, and afterschool programs. Projects like the Harlem Children's Zone that weave together family, social service, and health programs with community building programs, and services that follow children from birth to college are promising in their ability to take on mental health disparities and the risk factors that are associated with them.

Acknowledgements

This research was supported by Award Numbers P30MH082760 and T32MH073517 from the National Institute of Mental Health. The content is solely the responsibility of the authors and does not necessarily represent the official views of the National Institute of Mental Health or the National Institutes of Health.

References

Achenbach, T. M., and Edelbrock, C. S. (1981). Behavioral problems and competencies reported by parents of normal and disturbed children aged four through sixteen. *Monographs of the Society for Research in Child Development, 46*, 1-82.

Amaya-Jackson, L., Reynolds, V., Murray, M. C., McCarthy, G., Nelson, A., Cherney, M. S., et al. (2003). Cognitive-behavioral treatment for pediatric posttraumatic stress disorder: Protocol and application in school and community settings. *Cognitive and Behavioral Practice, 10*, 204-213.

Asarnow, J. R., Jaycox, L. H., Duan, N., LaBorde, A. P., Rea, M. M., Murray, P., et al. (2005). Effectiveness of a quality improvement intervention for adolescent depression in primary care clinics. *The Journal of the American Medical Association, 293*, 311-319.

Aseltine, R. H., Jr., and DeMartino, R. (2004). An outcome evaluation of the SOS suicide prevention program. *American Journal of Public Health, 94*, 446-451.

Attar, B. D., Guerra, N. G., and Tolan, P. H. (1994). Neighborhood disadvantage, stressful life events, and adjustment in urban elementary-school children. *Journal of Clinical Child Psychology, 23*, 391-400

Benson, M. J., Buehler, C., and Gerard, J. M. (2008). Interparental hostility and early adolescent problem behavior. *The Journal of Early Adolescence, 28*, 428-454.

Berman, S. L., Kurtines, W. M., Silverman, W. K., and Serafini, L. T. (1996). The impact of exposure to crime and violence on urban youth. *American Journal of Orthopsychiatry, 66*, 329-336.

Bischoff, R. J., and Sprenkle, D. H. (1993). Dropping out of marriage and family therapy: A critical review of research. *Family Process, 32*, 353-375.

Borduin, C. M., Mann, B. J., Cone, L. T., Henggeler, S. W., Fucci, B. R., Blaske, D. M., et al. (1995). Multisystemic treatment of serious juvenile offenders: Long-term prevention of criminality and violence. *Journal of Consulting and Clinical Psychology 63*, 569-578.

Botvin, G. J., Schinke, S., and Orlandi, M. A. (1995). School-based health promotion: Substance abuse and sexual behavior. *Applied and Preventive Psychology, 4*, 167-184.

Bridge, J. A., Iyengar, S., Salary, C. B., Barbe, R. P., Birmaher, B., Pincus, H. A., et al. (2007). Clinical response and risk for reported suicidal ideation and suicide attempts in pediatric antidepressant treatment. *The Journal of the American Medical Association, 297*, 1683-1696.

Briggs-Gowan, M. J., Horwitz, S. M., Schwab-Stone, M. E., Leventhal, J. M., and Leaf, P. J. (2000). Mental health in pediatric settings: Distribution of disorders and factors related to service use. *Journal of the American Academy of Child and Adolescent Psychiatry, 39*, 841-849.

Briggs-Gowan, M. J., Owens, P. L., Schwab-Stone, M. E., Leventhal, J. M., Leaf, P. J., and Horwitz, S. M. (2003). Persistence of psychiatric disorders in pediatric settings. *Journal of the American Academy of Child and Adolescent Psychiatry, 42*, 1360-1369.

Brody, G. H., Murry, V. M., Ge, X., Kim, S. Y., Simons, R. L., Gibbons, F. X., et al. (2003). Neighborhood disadvantage moderates associations of parenting and older sibling problem attitudes and behavior with conduct disorders in African American children. *Journal of Consulting and Clinical Psychology, 71*, 211-222.

Brooks-Gunn, J., Duncan, G. J., and Aber, L. (1997). *Neighborhood poverty, Volume 1: Context and consequences for children.* New York: Russell Sage Foundation.

Brooks-Gunn, J., Duncan, G. J., Klebanov, P. K., and Sealand, N. (1993). Do neighborhoods influence child and adolescent development? . *American Journal of Sociology, 99*, 353-395.

Brown, J., and Wissow, L. (2010). Screening to identify mental health problems in pediatricprimary care: Considerations for practice. *International Journal of Psychiatry in Medicine, 40*, 1-19.

Bruene-Butler, L., Hampson, J., Elias, M., Clabby, J., and Schuyler, T. (1997). The improving social awareness-social problem solving project. In G. W. Albee and T. P. Gullotta (Eds.), *Primary prevention works* (pp. 239-267). Thousand Oaks, CA: Sage.

Burns, B., Phillips, S., Wagner, H., Barth, R., Kolko, D., Campbell, Y., et al. (2004). Mental health need and access to mental health services by youths involved with child welfare: A national survey. *Journal of the American Academy of Child and Adolescent Psychiatry, 43*, 960-970.

Caples, H., and Barrera, M. (2006). Conflict, support and coping as mediators of the relation between degrading parenting and adolescent adjustment. *Journal of Youth and Adolescence, 35*, 599-611.

Cappella, E., Frazier, S., Atkins, M., Schoenwald, S., and Glisson, C. (2008). Enhancing schools' capacity to support children in poverty: An ecological model of school-based mental health services. *Administration and Policy in Mental Health and Mental Health Services Research, 35*, 395-409.

Carter, A. S., Wagmiller, R. J., Gray, S. A. O., McCarthy, K. J., Horwitz, S. M., and Briggs-Gowan, M. J. (2010). Prevalence of DSM-IV disorder in a representative, healthy birth cohort at school entry: Sociodemographic risks and social adaptation. *Journal of the American Academy of Child and Adolescent Psychiatry, 49*, 686-698.

Ceballo, R., Ramirez, C., Hearn, K. D., and Maltese, K. L. (2003). Community violence and children's psychological well-being: Does parental monitoring matter? . *Journal of Clinical Child and Adolescent Psychology, 32*, 586-592.

Chamberlain, P. (1998a). *Treatment foster care*: OJJDP Juvenile Justice Bulletin.

Chamberlain, P., Price, J., Leve, L., Laurent, H., Landsverk, J., and Reid, J. (2008). Prevention of behavior problems for children in foster care: Outcomes and mediation effects. *Prevention Science, 9*, 17-27.

Chamberlain, P., and Reid, J. (1998b). Comparison of two community alternatives to incarceration for chronic juvenile offenders. *Journal of Consulting and Clinical Psychology, 6*, 624-633.

Chau, M., Thampi, K., and Wight, V. R. (2010). *Basic facts about low-income children, 2009*. New York: National Center for Children in Poverty.

Chou, C. P., Montgomery, S., Pentz, M. A., Rohrbach, L. A., Johnson, C. A., Flay, B. R., et al. (1998). Effects of a community-based prevention program on decreasing drug use in high-risk adolescents. *American Journal of Public Health, 88*, 944-948.

Cohen, J. A., Deblinger, E., Mannarino, A. P., and Steer, R. A. (2004). A multisite, randomized controlled trial for children with sexual abuse-related PTSD symptoms. *Journal of the American Academy of Child and Adolescent Psychiatry, 43*, 393-402.

Cohen, J. A., Kelleher, K. J., and Mannarino, A. P. (2008). Identifying, treating, and referring traumatized children: The role of pediatric providers. *Archives of Pediatrics and Adolescent Medicine, 162*, 447-452.

Conduct Problems Prevention Research Group (1999). Initial impact of the Fast Track prevention trial for conduct problems: I. The high-risk sample. *Journal of Consulting and Clinical Psychology, 67*, 631-647.

Conger, R. D., Wallace, L. D., Sun, Y., Simons, R. L., McLoyd, V. C., and Brody, G. H. (2002). Economic pressure in African American families: A replication and extension of the family stress model. *Developmental Psychology, 38*, 179-193.

Cooper, S. M., McLoyd, V. C., Wood, D., and Hardaway, C. R. (2008). The mental health consequences of racial discrimination for African American adolescents. In S. Quintana and C. McKown (Eds.), *Handbook of race, racism and the developing child* (pp. 278-312). Hoboken, NJ: Wiley.

Costello, E. J., Costello, A. J., Edelbrock, C., Burns, B. J., Dulcan, M. K., Brent, D., et al. (1988). Psychiatric disorders in pediatric primary care: Prevalence and risk factors. *Archives of General Psychiatry, 45*, 1107-1116.

Crone, M. R., Bekkema, N., Wiefferink, C. H., and Reijneveld, S. A. (2010). Professional identification of psychosocial problems among children from ethnic minority groups: Room for improvement. *The Journal of Pediatrics, 156*, 277-284.e271.

Cui, M., and Conger, R. D. (2008). Parenting behavior as mediator and moderator of the association between marital problems and adolescent maladjustment. *Journal of Research on Adolescence, 18*, 261-284.

Cui, M., Donnellan, M. B., and Conger, R. D. (2007). Reciprocal influences between parents' marital problems and adolescent internalizing and externalizing behavior. *Developmental Psychology, 43*, 1544-1552.

DuBois, D. L., Burk-Braxton, C., Swenson, L. P., Tevendale, H. D., and Hardesty, J. L. (2002). Race and gender influences on adjustment in early adolescence: Investigation of an integrative model. *Child Development, 73*, 1573-1592.

Eiden, R. D., Edwards, E. P., and Leonard, K. E. (2007). A conceptual model for the development of externalizing behavior problems among kindergarten children of alcoholic families: Role of parenting and children's self-regulation. *Developmental Psychology, 43*, 1187-1201.

Epstein, J. N., Rabiner, D., Johnson, D. E., FitzGerald, D. P., Chrisman, A., Erkanli, A., et al. (2007). Improving Attention-Deficit/Hyperactivity Disorder treatment outcomes through use of a collaborative consultation treatment service by community-based pediatricians: A cluster randomized trial. *Archives of Pediatrics and Adolescent Medicine, 161*, 835-840.

Evans, G. W. (2004). The environment of childhood poverty. *American Psychologist, 59*, 77-92.

Evans, G. W., Kim, P., Ting, A. H., Tesher, H. B., and Shannis, D. (2007). Cumulative risk, maternal responsiveness, and allostatic load among young adolescents. *Developmental Psychology, 43*, 341-351.

Evans, G. W., Wells, N. M., and Moch, A. (2003). Housing and mental health: A review of the evidence and a methodological and conceptual critique. *Journal of Social Issues, 59*, 475-500.

Evans, S. W., Schultz, B. K., DeMars, C. E., and Davis, H. (2011). Effectiveness of the challenging horizons after-school program for young adolescents with ADHD. *Behavior Therapy, 42*, 462-474.

Farrell, A. D., and Sullivan, T. N. (2004). Impact of witnessing violence on growth curves for problem behaviors among early adolescents in urban and rural settings. *Journal of Community Psychology, 32*, 505-525.

Farrington, D. P., and Loeber, R. (2000). Epidemiology of juvenile violence. *Child and Adolescent Psychiatric Clinics of North America, 9*, 733-748.

Fass, S., and Cauthen, N. K. (2008). *Measuring poverty in the United States*. New York: Columbia University.

Feil, E. G., Walker, H. M., Severson, H. H., and Ball, A. (2000). Proactive screening for emotional/behavioral concerns in Head Start preschools: Promising practices and challenges in applied research. *Behavioral Disorders, 26*, 13-25.

Finkelhor, D., and Dziuba-Leatherman, J. (1994). Children as victims of violence: A national survey. *Pediatrics, 94*, 413-420.

Fisher, P., and Kim, H. (2007). Intervention effects on foster preschoolers' attachment-related behaviors from a randomized trial. *Prevention Science, 8*, 161-170.

Fisher, P. A., Gunnar, M. R., Chamberlain, P., and Reid, J. B. (2000). Preventive intervention for maltreated preschool children: Impact on children's behavior, neuroendocrine activity, and foster parent functioning. *Journal of the American Academy of Child and Adolescent Psychiatry, 39*, 1356-1364.

Fitzpatrick, K. M., and Boldizar, J. P. (1993). The prevalence and consequences of exposure to violence among African-American youth. *Journal of the American Academy of Child and Adolescent Psychiatry, 32*, 424-430.

Forehand, R., and McMahon, R. J. (1981). *Helping the noncompliant child: A clinician's guide to effective parent training*. New York: Guilford Publications.

Foster, C., Webster, M., Weissman, M., Pilowsky, D., Wickramaratne, P., Rush, A., et al. (2008). Course and severity of maternal depression: Associations with family functioning and child adjustment. *Journal of Youth and Adolescence, 37*, 906-916.

Foster, C. E., Garber, J., and Durlak, J. A. (2008). Current and past maternal depression, maternal interaction behaviors, and children's externalizing and internalizing symptoms. *Journal of Abnormal Child Psychology, 36*, 527-537.

Foster, S., Rollefson, M., Doksum, T., Noonan, D., Robinson, G., and Teich, J. (2005). *School mental health services in the United States, 2002-2003*. Rockville, MD: Department of Health and Human Services.

Fulda, K., Lykens, K., Bae, S., and Singh, K. (2009). Factors for accessing a medical home vary among CSHCN from different levels of socioeconomic status. *Maternal and Child Health Journal, 13*, 445-456.

Garbarino, J., Sebes, J., and Schellenbach, C. (1984). Families at risk for destructive parent-child relations in adolescence. *Child Development, 55*, 174-183.

Garrison, E. G., Roy, I. S., and Azar, V. (1999). Responding to the mental health needs of Latino children and families through school-based services. *Clinical Psychology Review, 19*, 199-219.

Gerard, J. M., Krishnakumar, A., and Buehler, C. (2006). Marital conflict, parent-child relations, and youth maladjustment. *Journal of Family Issues, 27*, 951-975.

Gibb, B. E., and Alloy, L. B. (2006). A prospective test of the hopelessness theory of depression in children. *Journal of Clinical Child and Adolescent Psychology, 35*, 264-274.

Gorman-Smith, D., and Tolan, P. (1998). The role of exposure to community violence and developmental problems among inner-city youth. *Development and Psychopathology, 10*, 101-116.

Grant, K. E., Compas, B. E., Stuhlmacher, A. F., Thurm, A. E., McMahon, S. D., and Halpert, J. A. (2003). Stressors and child and adolescent psychopathology: Moving from markers to mechanisms of risk. *Psychological Bulletin, 129*, 447-466.

Greenberg, M. T., Domitrovich, C., and Bumbarger, B. (2000). *Effectiveness of prevention programs for mental disorders in school-age children.* Paper presented at the A System of Care for Children's Mental Health: Expanding the Research Base. Proceedings of the Annual Research Conference, Tampa, FL.

Greenberg, M. T., and Kusché, C. A. (1998). Preventive intervention for school-aged deaf children: The PATHS curriculum. *Journal of Deaf Studies and Deaf Education, 3*, 49-63.

Grisso, T., and Barnum, R. (2006). *Massachusetts youth screening instrument, version 2 (MAYSI-2): User's manual and technical report.* Sarasota, FL Professional Resource Press.

Gross, D., Sambrook, A., and Fogg, L. (1999). Behavior problems among young children in low-income urban day care centers. *Research in Nursing and Health, 22*, 15-25.

Gross, H., Shaw, D., and Moilanen, K. (2008). Reciprocal associations between boys' externalizing problems and mothers' depressive symptoms. *Journal of Abnormal Child Psychology, 36*, 693-709.

Hammen, C., Brennan, P., and Keenan-Miller, D. (2008). Patterns of adolescent depression to age 20: The role of maternal depression and youth interpersonal dysfunction. *Journal of Abnormal Child Psychology, 36*, 1189-1198.

Henggeler, S. W., Clingempeel, W. G., Brondino, M. J., and Pickrel, S. G. (2002). Four-year follow-up of multisystemic therapy with substance-abusing and substance-dependent juvenile offenders. *Journal of the American Academy of Child and Adolescent Psychiatry, 41*, 868-874.

Henggeler, S. W., Melton, G. B., Brondino, M. J., Scherer, D. G., and Hanley, J. H. (1997). Multisystemic Therapy with violent and chronic juvenile offenders and their families: The role of treatment fidelity in successful dissemination. *Journal of Consulting and Clinical Psychology, 65*, 821-833.

Henggeler, S. W., Melton, G. B., and Smith, L. A. (1992). Family preservation using Multisystemic Therapy: An effective alternative to incarcerating serious juvenile offenders. *Journal of Consulting and Clinical Psychology, 60*, 953-961.

Henggeler, S. W., and Schoenwald, S. K. (2011). Evidence-based interventions for juvenile offenders and juvenile justice policies that support them. *Social Policy Report, 25*.

Hoagwood, K., Kelleher, K. J., Feil, M., and Comer, D. M. (2000). Treatment services for children with ADHD: A national perspective. *Journal of the American Academy of Child and Adolescent Psychiatry, 39*, 198-206.

Hoagwood, K. E., Serene Olin, S., Kerker, B. D., Kratochwill, T. R., Crowe, M., and Saka, N. (2007). Empirically based school interventions targeted at academic and mental health functioning. *Journal of Emotional and Behavioral Disorders, 15*, 66-92.

Homer, C. J., Klatka, K., Romm, D., Kuhlthau, K., Bloom, S., Newacheck, P., et al. (2008). A review of the evidence for the medical home for children with special health care needs. *Pediatrics, 122*, e922-e937.

Horwitz, S. M., Leaf, P. J., Leventhal, J. M., Forsyth, B., and Speechley, K. N. (1992). Identification and management of psychosocial and developmental problems in community-based, primary care pediatric practices. *Pediatrics, 89*, 480-485.

Howell, E. (2004). *Access to children's mental health services under Medicaid and SCHIP*. Washington, D.C.: Urban Institute.

Jargowsky, P. A., Desmond, S. A., and Crutchfield, R. D. (2005). Suburban sprawl, race, and juvenile justice. In D. F. Hawkins and K. Kempf-Leonard (Eds.), *Our children, their children: Confronting racial and ethnic differences in American juvenile justice* (pp. 167-201). Chicago: University of Chicago Press.

Jaycox, L.H, Langley, A., Stein, B., Wong, M., Sharma, P., Scott, M., et al. (2009). Support for students exposed to trauma: A pilot study. *School Mental Health, 1*, 49-60.

Jaycox, L. H., Cohen, J. A., Mannarino, A. P., Walker, D. W., Langley, A. K., Gegenheimer, K. L., et al. (2010). Children's mental health care following Hurricane Katrina: A field trial of trauma-focused psychotherapies. *Journal of Traumatic Stress, 23*, 223-231.

Jaycox, L. H., Stein, B. D., Kataoka, S. H., Wong, M., Fink, A., Escudero, P. I. A., et al. (2002). Violence exposure, posttraumatic stress disorder, and depressive symptoms among recent immigrant schoolchildren. *Journal of the American Academy of Child and Adolescent Psychiatry, 41*, 1104-1110.

Jellinek, M. S., Murphy, J. M., Little, M., Pagano, M. E., Comer, D. M., and Kelleher, K. J. (1999). Use of the pediatric symptom checklist to screen for psychosocial problems in pediatric primary care: A national feasibility study. *Archives of Pediatrics and Adolescent Medicine, 153*, 254-260.

Julian, T., Kelleher, K., Julian, D., and Chisolm, D. (2007). Using technology to enhance prevention services for children in primary care. *The Journal of Primary Prevention, 28*, 155-165.

Kataoka, S., Jaycox, L. H., Wong, M., Nadeem, E., Langley, A., Tang, L., et al. (in press). Effects on school outcomes in low-income minority youth: Preliminary findings from a community-partnered study of a school trauma intervention. *Ethnicity and Disease*.

Kataoka, S., Zhang, L., and Wells, K. (2002). Unmet need for mental health care among U.S. children: Variation by ethnicity and insurance status. *American Journal of Psychiatry, 159*, 1548-1555.

Kataoka, S. H., Stein, B. D., Jaycox, L. H., Wong, M., Escudero, P. I. A., Tu, W., et al. (2003). A school-based mental health program for traumatized latino immigrant children. *Journal of the American Academy of Child and Adolescent Psychiatry, 42*, 311-318.

Katon, W. J., Richardson, L., Russo, J., Lozano, P., and McCauley, E. (2006). Quality of mental health care for youth with asthma and comorbid anxiety and depression. *Medical Care, 44*, 1064-1072

Kautz, C., Mauch, D., and Smith, S. (2008). *Reimbursement of mental health services in primary care settings* (No. HHS PUB SMA-08-4324). Rockville, MD.

Kazdin, A. E. (1996). Dropping out of child psychotherapy: Issues for research and implications for practice. *Clinical Child Psychology and Psychiatry, 1*, 133-156.

Kazdin, A. E., and Mazurick, J. L. (1994). Dropping out of child psychotherapy: Distinguishing early and late dropouts over the course of treatment. *Journal of Consulting and Clinical Psychology, 62*, 1069-1074.

Kliewer, W., Lepore, S. J., Oskin, D., and Johnson, P. D. (1998). The role of social and cognitive processes in children's adjustment to community violence. *Journal of Consulting and Clinical Psychology, 66*, 199-209.

Kliewer, W., Murrelle, L., Prom, E., Ramirez, M., Obando, P., Sandi, L., et al. (2006). Violence exposure and drug use in Central American youth: Family cohesion and parental monitoring as protective factors. *Journal of Research on Adolescence, 16*, 455-478.

Korfmacher, J., Green, B., Staerkel, F., Peterson, C., Cook, G., Roggman, L., et al. (2008). Parent involvement in early childhood home visiting. *Child and Youth Care Forum, 37*, 171-196.

Leslie, L. K., Aarons, G. A., Haine, R. A., and Hough, R. L. (2007). Caregiver depression and medication use by youths with ADHD who receive services in the public sector. *Psychiatric Services, 58*, 131-134.

Leslie, L. K., Weckerly, J., Plemmons, D., Landsverk, J., and Eastman, S. (2004). Implementing the American Academy of Pediatrics Attention-Deficit/Hyperactivity Disorder diagnostic guidelines in primary care settings. *Pediatrics, 114*, 129-140.

Leventhal, T., and Brooks-Gunn, J. (2004). A Randomized study of neighborhood effects on low-income children's educational outcomes. *Developmental Psychology, 40*, 488-507.

Li, S. T., Nussbaum, K. M., and Richards, M. H. (2007). Risk and protective factors for urban African American youth. *American Journal of Community Psychology, 39*, 21-35.

Lipman, E. L., and Boyle, M. H. (2008). *Linking poverty and mental health: A lifespan view*. Ontario, Canada: The Provincial Centre of Excellence for Child and Youth Mental Health at CHEO.

Lochman, J. E. (1985). Effects of different treatment lengths in cognitive behavioral interventions with aggressive boys. *Child Psychiatry and Human Development 16* 45-56.

Lochman, J. E., and Wells, K. C. (2003). Effectiveness of the coping power program and of classroom intervention with aggressive children: Outcomes at a 1-year follow-up. *Behavior Therapy, 34*, 493-515.

March, J. S., Amaya-Jackson, L., Murray, M. C., and Schulte, A. N. N. (1998). Cognitive-behavioral psychotherapy for children and adolescents With posttraumatic stress disorder after a single-incident stressor. *Journal of the American Academy of Child and Adolescent Psychiatry, 37*, 585-593.

McCabe, K. M. (2002). Factors that predict premature termination among Mexican-American children in outpatient psychotherapy. *Journal of Child and Family Studies, 11*, 347-359.

McGinnis, J. M., Williams-Russo, P., and Knickman, J. R. (2002). The case for more active policy attention to health promotion. *Health Affairs, 21*, 78-93.

McGrath, E., Keita, G. P., Strickland, B. R., and Russo, N. F. (Eds.). (1990). *Women and depression: Risk factors and treatment issues*. Washington, DC.

McKay, M., McCadam, K., and Gonzales, J. (1996). Addressing the barriers to mental health services for inner city children and their caretakers. *Community Mental Health Journal, 32*, 353-361.

McKay, M., Paikoff, R., Baptiste, D., Bell, C., Coleman, D., Madison, S., et al. (2004). Family-level impact of the CHAMP Family Program: A community collaborative effort to support urban families and reduce youth HIV risk exposure. *Family Process, 43*, 79-93.

McKay, M., Quintana, E., Kim, L., Gonzales, J., and Adil, J. (1999). Multiple family groups: An alternative for reducing disruptive behavioral difficulties of urban children. *Research on Social Work Practice, 9*, 414-428.

McKinsey and Company. (2009). The Economic Impact of the Achievement Gap in America's Schools [Electronic Version] from http://www.mckinsey.com/clientservice/socialsector/achievement_gap.

McLoyd, V. C. (1998). Socioeconomic disadvantage and child development. *American Psychologist, 53*, 185-204.

Mejia, R., Kliewer, W., and Williams, L. (2006). Domestic violence exposure in Colombian adolescents: Pathways to violent and prosocial behavior. *Journal of Traumatic Stress, 19*, 257-267.

Miller, G. E., and Prinz, R. J. (1990). The enhancement of social learning family interventions for childhood conduct disorder. *Psychological Bulletin, 108*, 291-307.

Mistry, R. S., Vandewater, E. A., Huston, A. C., and McLoyd, V. C. (2002). Economic well-being and children's social adjustment: The role of family process in an ethnically diverse low-income sample. *Child Development, 73*, 935-951.

Mufson, L., Dorta, K. P., Wickramaratne, P., Nomura, Y., Olfson, M., and Weissman, M. M. (2004). A randomized effectiveness trial of interpersonal psychotherapy for depressed adolescents. *Archives of General Psychiatry, 61*, 577-584.

Murphy, J. M., Ichinose, C., Hicks, R. C., Kingdon, D., Crist-Whitzel, J., Jordan, P., et al. (1996). Utility of the pediatric symptom checklist as a psychosocial screen to meet the federal Early and Periodic Screening, Diagnosis, and Treatment (EPSDT) standards: A pilot study. *The Journal of Pediatrics, 129*, 864-869.

Murphy, J. M., Reede, J., Jellinek, M. S., and Bishop, S. J. (1992). Screening for psychosocial dysfunction in inner-city children: Further validation of the pediatric symptom checklist. *Journal of the American Academy of Child and Adolescent Psychiatry, 31*, 1105-1111.

Myers, K. M., Valentine, J. M., and Melzer, S. M. (2007). Feasibility, acceptability, and sustainability of telepsychiatry for children and adolescents. *Psychiatric Services, 58*, 1493-1496.

National Institute for Health Care Management Foundation (2009). Strategries to support the integration of mental health into pediatric primary care. from http://www.nihcm.org/pdf/PediatricMH-FINAL.pdf

National Prevention Council (2011). *U.S. National Prevention Strategy*. Washington, DC: U.S. Department of Health and Human Services, Office of the Surgeon General.

Padgett, D. K., Patrick, C., Burns, B. J., Schlesinger, H. J., and Cohen, J. (1993). The effect of insurance benefit changes on use of child and adolescent outpatient mental health services. *Medical Care, 31*, 96-110.

Perkins, C. A. (1997). *Age patterns of victims of serious violent crime*. Washington, DC: US Dept of Justice.

Plybon, L. E., and Kliewer, W. (2001). Neighborhood types and externalizing behavior in urban school-age children: Tests of direct, mediated, and moderated effects. *Journal of Child and Family Studies, 10*, 419-437.

Pumariega, A. J., Rothe, E., and Pumariega, J. B. (2005). Mental health of immigrants and refugees. *Community Mental Health Journal, 41*, 581-597.

Qi, C., and Kaiser, A. P. (2003). Behavior problems of preschool children from low-income families: Review of the literature. *Topics in Early Childhood Special Education, 23*, 188-216.

Racusin, R., Maerlender, A. C., Sengupta, A., Isquith, P. K., and Straus, M. B. (2005). Psychosocial treatment of children in foster care: A review. *Community Mental Health Journal, 41*, 199-221.

Rafnsson, F. D., Jonsson, F. H., and Windle, M. (2006). Coping strategies, stressful life events, problem behaviors, and depressed affect. *Anxiety, Stress and Coping: An International Journal, 19*, 241-257.

Richardson, L. P., McCauley, E., Grossman, D. C., McCarty, C. A., Richards, J., Russo, J. E., et al. (2011). Evaluation of the patient health questionnaire-9 Item for detecting major depression among adolescents. *Pediatrics, 126*, 1117-1123.

Saigh, P. A., Mroueh, M., and Bremner, J. D. (1997). Scholastic impairments among traumatized adolescents. *Behaviour Research and Therapy, 35*, 429-436.

Salafia , E. B., Gondoli, D., and Grundy, A. (2008). Marital conflict as a mediator of the longitudinal connections between maternal emotional distress and early adolescent maladjustment. *Journal of Child and Family Studies, 17*, 928-950.

Saltzman, W. R., Pynoos, R. S., Layne, C. M., Steinberg, A. M., and Aisenberg, E. (2001). Trauma- and grief-focused intervention for adolescents exposed to community violence: Results of a school-based screening and group treatment protocol. *Group Dynamics: Theory, Research, and Practice, 5*, 291-303.

Sampson, R. J., and Groves, B. W. (1989). Community structure and crime: Testing social-disorganization theory. *American Journal of Sociology, 94*, 774-802.

Sampson, R. J., Raudenbush, S. W., and Earls, F. (1997). Neighborhoods and violent crime: A multilevel study of collective efficacy. *Science, 277*, 918-924.

Santiago, C. D., and Wadsworth, M. (2009). Coping with family conflict: What's helpful and what's not for low-income adolescents. *Journal of Child and Family Studies, 18*, 192-202.

Santiago, C. D., and Wadsworth, M. E. (2011). Family and cultural influences on low-income Latino children's adjustment. *Journal of Clinical Child and Adolescent Psychology, 40*, 332-337.

Sayger, T. V., and Heid, K. O. (1990). Counseling the impoverished rural client: Issues for family therapists. *Psychotherapy Patient, 7*, 161-168.

Sexton, T. L., and Alexander, J. F. (2000). Functional Family Therapy (FFT). *Juvenile Justice Bulletin*, 1-8.

Shelton, K. H., and Harold, G. T. (2008). Interparental conflict, negative parenting, and children's adjustment: Bridging links between parents' depression and children's psychological distress. *Journal of Family Psychology, 22*, 712-724.

Simons, R. L., Murry, V., McLoyd, V., Lin, K., Cutrona, C., and Conger, R. D. (2002). Discrimination, crime, ethnic identity, and parenting as correlates of depressive symptoms among African American children: A multilevel analysis. *Development and Psychopathology, 14*, 371-393.

Singer, M. I., Anglin, T. M., Song, L. y., and Lunghofer, L. (1995). Adolescents' exposure to violence and associated symptoms of psychological trauma. *The Journal of the American Medical Association, 273*, 477-482.

Skowyra, K. R., and Cocozza, J. J. (2006). *Blueprint for change: A comprehensive model for the identification and treatment of youth with mental health needs in contact with juvenile justice system.* Delmar, NY: Policy Research Associates, Inc.

Slopen, N., Fitzmaurice, G., Williams, D. R., and Gilman, S. E. (2010). Poverty, food insecurity, and the behavior for childhood internalizing and externalizing disorders. *Journal of the American Academy of Child and Adolescent Psychiatry, 49*, 444-452.

Smithgall, C., Gladden, R., Yang, D., and Goerge, R. (2005). *Behavioral problems and educational disruptions among children in out-of-home care in Chicago.* Chicago, IL: Chapin Hall Center for Children at the University of Chicago

Snell-Johns, J., Mendez, J. L., and Smith, B. H. (2004). Evidence-based solutions for overcoming access barriers, decreasing attrition, and promoting change with underserved families. *Journal of Family Psychology 18*, 19-35.

Starfield, B., Gross, E., Wood, M., Pantell, R., Allen, C., Gordon, I. B., et al. (1980). Psychosocial and psychosomatic diagnoses in primary care of children. *Pediatrics, 66*, 159-167.

Staudt, M. M. (2003). Mental health services utilization by maltreated children: Research findings and recommendations. *Child Maltreatment, 8*, 195-203.

Steib, S. (2002). *What's so special about specialized foster care: Lessons from the research.* Paper presented at the 16th Annual Conference on Treatment Foster Care, Chicago, IL.

Stein, B. D., Jaycox, L. H., Kataoka, S. H., Wong, M., Tu, W., Elliott, M. N., et al. (2003). A mental health intervention for schoolchildren exposed to violence. *The Journal of the American Medical Association, 290*, 603-611.

Steinberg, A., Brymer, M., Decker, K., and Pynoos, R. (2004). The University of California at Los Angeles post-traumatic stress disorder reaction index. *Current Psychiatry Reports, 6*, 96-100.

Suárez-Orozco, C., Rhodes, J., and Milburn, M. (2009). Unraveling the Immigrant Paradox. *Youth and Society, 41*, 151-185.

Suárez-Orozco, C., and Suárez-Orozco, M. (1995). *Transformations: Immigration, family life, and achievement motivation among Latino adolescents*. Stanford, CA: Stanford University Press.

Substance Abuse and Mental Health Services Administration (2004). *Results from the 2003 national survey on drug use and health: National findings* (No. DHHS Publication SMA 04-3964). Rockville, MD.

Sullivan, T. N., Farrell, A. D., and Kliewer, W. (2006). Peer victimization in early adolescence: Association between physical and relational victimization and drug use, aggression, and delinquent behaviors among urban middle school students. *Development and Psychopathology, 18*, 119-137.

Tarshis, T. P., Jutte, D. P., and Huffman, L. C. (2006). Provider recognition of psychosocial problems in low-income Latino children. *Journal of Health Care for the Poor and Underserved, 17*, 342-357.

Taylor, K. W., and Kliewer, W. (2006). Violence exposure and early adolescent alcohol use: An exploratory study of family risk and protective factors. *Journal of Child and Family Studies, 15*, 207-221.

Taylor, T. K., and Biglan, A. (1998). Behavioral family interventions for improving child-rearing: A review of the literature for clinicians and policy makers. *Clinical Child and Family Psychology Review, 1*, 41-60.

The Child and Health Measurement Initiative Children with special health care needs (CSHCN) screener [Electronic Version]. Retrieved 6-24-11 from http://cahmi.org/ViewDocument.aspx?DocumentID=115.

U.S. Department of Education (2001). *Safe, disciplined, and drug-free schools programs*. Washington, DC: Office of Special Education Research and Improvement, Office of Reform Assistance and Dissemination.

U.S. Department of Health and Human Services (2001). *Mental health culture, race, and ethnicity- A supplement to mental health: A report of the surgeon general*. Rockville, MD: U.S. Department of Health and Human Services, Substance Abuse and Mental Health Services Administration, Center for Mental Health Services.

U.S. House of Representatives, Committee on Government Reform, Minority Staff Special Investigations Division. (2004). *Incarceration of youth who are waiting for community mental health services in the United States* Retrieved. from www.democrats.reform.house.gov/Documents/ 20040817121901-25170.pdf.

U. S. Preventive Services Task Force (2009). Screening and treatment for major depressive disorder in children and adolescents: US Preventive Services Task Force recommendation statement. *Pediatrics, 123*, 1223-1228.

Umaña-Taylor, A. J., and Updegraff, K. A. (2007). Latino adolescents' mental health: Exploring the interrelations among discrimination, ethnic identity, cultural orientation, self-esteem, and depressive symptoms. *Journal of Adolescence, 30*, 549-567.

Wadsworth, M. E., and Compas, B. E. (2002). Coping with family conflict and economic strain: The adolescent perspective. *Journal of Research on Adolescence, 12*, 243-274.

Wadsworth, M. E., Raviv, T., Reinhard, C., Wolff, B., Santiago, C. D., and Einhorn, L. (2008). An indirect effects model of the association between poverty and child functioning: The role of children's poverty-related stress. *Journal of Loss and Trauma, 13*, 156-185.

Wadsworth, M. E., and Santiago, C. D. (2008). Risk and resiliency processes in ethnically diverse families in poverty. *Journal of Family Psychology, 22*, 399-410.

Wallace, J. M., Forman, T. A., Guthrie, B. J., Bachman, J. G., O'Malley, P. M., and Johnston, L. D. (1999). The epidemiology of alcohol, tobacco and other drug use among black youth. *Journal of Studies on Alcohol, 60*, 800-809.

Wallace, J. M., Myers, V. L., and Osai, E. (2004). *Faith matters: Race/ ethnicity, religion, and substance abuse*. Baltimore, MD: Annie E. Casey Foundation Publications

Webster-Stratton, C. (1992a). Individually administered videotape parent training: "who benefits?" *Cognitive Therapy and Research, 16*, 31-52.

Webster-Stratton, C. (1992b). *The incredible years: A trouble-shooting guide for parents of children aged 3-8*. Toronto, Canada: Umbrella Press.

Webster-Stratton, C. (1998). Preventing conduct problems in Head Start children: Strengthening parenting competencies. *Journal of Consulting and Clinical Psychology, 66*, 715-730.

Weist, M. D., Rubin, M., Moore, E., Adelsheim, S., and Wrobel, G. (2007). Mental health screening in schools. *Journal of School Health, 77*, 53-58.

Zahner, G. E., and Daskalakis, C. (1997). Factors associated with mental health, general health, and school-based service use for child psychopathology. *American Journal of Public Health, 87*, 1440-1448.

Zima, B. T., Bussing, R., Tang, L., Zhang, L., Ettner, S., Belin, T. R., et al. (2010). Quality of care for childhood Attention-Deficit/Hyperactivity Disorder in a managed care Medicaid program. *Journal of the American Academy of Child and Adolescent Psychiatry, 49*, 1225-1237.

In: Socioeconomic Status and Health Implications
Editor: Sarah Reibert and Alice Jannings, pp. 85-109
ISBN: 978-1-62100-675-6

Chapter 4

THE QUEST FOR HIGHER SOCIOECONOMIC STATUS AND ADOLESCENT HEALTH RISK BEHAVIOR: CASE STUDY FROM A MIGRANT POPULATION IN THE UNITED ARAB EMIRATES

Caroline Barakat-Haddad[1] and Rania Dghaim[2]
[1] University of Toronto Scarborough, Toronto, Canada.
[2] Zayed University, Dubai, United Arab Emirates.

ABSTRACT

This chapter will explore the relationship between socioeconomic status and health in fast developing nations. Using new data from the United Arab Emirates (UAE), the health status of the expatriate population that resides in the UAE is examined. The UAE is a federation of seven emirates that has experienced unprecedented growth in the past forty years. The federation is situated in the southeast of the Arabian Peninsula in Southwest Asia on the Persian Gulf. The largest emirate, Abu Dhabi is the nation's capital. The remaining six emirates (Dubai, Sharjah, Ajman, Umm al-Quwain (UAQ), Ras al-Khaimah (RAK), Fujairah) form the Northern Emirates. Using oil revenue, the UAE continues to reduce reliance on oil and to diversify its economy from a conventional, labour-intensive economy to one based on knowledge, technology and tourism. In doing so, the UAE relies on a large expatriate population to transfer their skills and to build these sectors. These expatriates seeking financial gains are usually allowed into the country on a work permit. Although their socioeconomic status varies, many face challenges related to access to healthcare, proper housing, and various environmental changes. This chapter will report on data collected under the *National Study of Population Health in the UAE (NSPHUAE)* (2007 – 2009). A comprehensive large-scale cross-sectional survey was administered on expatriate families with children that attend public and private schools in the seven emirates. The survey collected data related to the general health status of this sub-population, exposures to a range of health determinants, demographics, as well as medical diagnoses.

1. Introduction

The relation between socioeconomic status and population health is evident in epidemiological studies (Marmot and Wilkinson, 1999). Socioeconomic status is typically measured using income and financial resources, occupation type, and educational attainment. In some cases, socioeconomic comparability may be problematic given that standard socioeconomic status measurement approaches may not account for marked racial or ethnic differences (Braveman et al., 2005). Measures of population health are diverse and include morbidity, standardized mortality, health expectancy, health capital, and quality of life (Murray, Salomon, Mathers, and Lopez, 2002). Often, in addition to measures of population health, health risk factors are assessed in order to estimate their contribution to population health or to estimate future healthcare needs.

In general, higher socioeconomic status leads to better health status, whereas socioeconomically disadvantaged individuals are more likely to experience negative health outcomes, such as increased mortality and morbidity (Bender and Ioannis, 2009). Exposures to environmental factors are important mediators of this relationship (Evans and Kantrowitz, 2002). Nonetheless, the relationship between socioeconomic status and health is multi-faceted and influenced by a number of factors, many of which are related to national development. For example, in developed nations, income inequalities are significant determinants of health and may have a bigger impact on health than socioeconomic status (Wilkinson, 2003). Negative correlations between life expectancy and increased income inequality have been reported for different countries (Babones, 2008). In developed countries, advances in health care has the potential to improve the health status of people with higher income and socioeconomic status, whereas people of relatively lower socioeconomic status and those from the lower income gradient are more likely to be exposed to health risk factors and behaviors that lead to detriments in health status (Diez-Roux, Link, and Northbridge, 2000). In addition to higher likeliness to engage in high risk behaviors, socioeconomically disadvantaged people are more likely to have less access to health care, be exposed to environmental factors, and more prone to experience psychosocial problems than their counterparts.

In arguing the multi-faceted nature of the link between socio-economic status and health, one can point to research findings of the negative relationship between socioeconomic status and health. For example, a US study that focused on the health profiles among Hispanic and Latino immigrants found that while this group of immigrants has relatively lower socioeconomic status and less access to health care, they exhibit better health behavior and risk profiles than the general population, leading to lower morbidity and mortality outcomes (Abraido-Lanza, Chao, and Florez, 2007). The authors attribute the positive risk behaviours and health outcomes among this group of immigrants to the preservation of cultural habits including strong social networks. This is no surprise given that social capital has long been recognized as an important determinant of health and a helpful construct for identifying conditions that contribute to quality of life and for understanding the relationship between poverty and health and well being (Wilkinson, 1996)(Cattell, 2001). Thus, belonging and ethnicity can also be important predictors of health outcomes.

The link between socioeconomic status, ethnicity, and health has been extensively examined particularly in countries where immigration is an important contributor to ethnic diversity. In most host countries with high immigration rates, ethnic categories are connected to the socioeconomic gradient (Lorant and Bhopal, 2010). Studies have shown that ethnicity can be linked to particular disease patterns, such as cancer, cardiovascular, and respiratory diseases (Nair, Nargundkar, Johansen, and Stachan, 1990; Razum, Zeeb, and Akgün, 1998; Hemminki and Li, 2002). For example, a study that compares risk factors for cardiovascular diseases (such as systolic blood pressure, overall obesity, and smoking) among Australian immigrants found that immigrants had lower prevalence of risk factors for heart disease than their counterparts (Bennett, 1993). However, among immigrants from Asian origins, duration of stay in Australia was positively related to body mass index and participation in physical activity during leisure time, an indication that the prevalence of risk factors changes in time. Likewise, lower mortality due to cardiovascular diseases were found among immigrants from Latin America, China and South Asia to Canada (Nair, Nargundkar, Johansen, and Stachan, 1990), Scandinavian-born immigrants to Canada (Valkonen, Brancker, and Reijo, 1992), and Turkish immigrants to West Germany (Razum, Zeeb, and Akgün, 1998). In relation to cancer, research found that first generation immigrants to Sweden had an overall lower risk of cancer compared with Swedish born individuals (Hemminki and Li, 2002). Factors such as country of birth, age at immigration, and residence duration were major determinants for the incidence of cervical, breast, prostate, and testes cancers. However, large differences in cancer prevalence observed for the first generation of immigrants to Sweden almost completely disappeared in their Sweden-born second generation, pointing to the importance of early life exposures and disease development (Hemminki and Li, 2002).

While ethnicity norms and early childhood exposures are important predictors of immigrant health, other explanations are linked to the 'healthy migrant effect', which suggests that immigrants are in general healthier than the host population. Arguments for this phenomenon include health screening by recipient countries, healthy behavior prior to migration, and immigrant self-selection where healthier and wealthier individuals from relatively higher socioeconomic status tend to search for better opportunities in new host countries (Kennedy, McDonald, and Biddle, 2006). Nonetheless, as Hemminki and Li (2002) found for second generation immigrants to Sweden, the mortality and morbidity pattern of immigrants in the long-term is influenced by determinants of health in the host country. For example, a meta-analysis that investigated the association between acculturation and blood pressure found positive effect sizes from acculturation on systolic blood pressure and diastolic blood pressure (Steffen, Smith, Larson, and Butler, 2006). Acculturation has also been linked to mental health particularly among young adolescent population (Garcia and Saewyc, 2007; Neto, 2009; Galler and Sher, 2010). Indeed, transitioning into a new country can be extremely stressful for immigrants, particularly for adolescents who simultaneouly face additional challenges while their identity and perceptions about life and health are developing. Adapting to a new culture and environment may contribute to deteriorations in mental health and the adoption of new risk behaviours such as substance abuse, unhealthy eating habits, and sedentary lifestyles. In addition, transitioning to a new country may be subject to a period of instability where immigrants, while experiencing their new environments - their surroundings, residential experiences and options, and the availability of resources – may be subject to additional health risk factors such as residential crowding, decreased social capital, and exposures to diverse air and water quality. Thus, along with migration and the search for better life opportunities, individuals particularly adolescents are likely to be exposed to societal norms that influence their diet, physical activity levels, smoking behavior, substance use, identity development, and overall health status.

1.1. Migration and Adolescent Health: Case Study from the United Arab Emirates

The literature on migration often compares the health patterns of a migrant group to that of the host population and / or to their non-immigrant counterpart. In adolescence, migration has been found to have a complex effect on health. For instance, regardless of socioeconomic status, migrant adolescents are more likely to suffer from overweight and obesity (Popkin and Udry, 1998). Research from the US found higher prevalence rates of obesity and overweight in Maya-American children compared to their Guatemalan natives and compared to a reference standard sub-population from the United States (Smith, Bogin, Varela-Silva, Orden, and Loucky, 2002). The same trend is seen among migrant children into Tonga, New Zealand (Stillman, Gibson, and McKenzie, 2010). Research suggests that contributing factors to higher body mass index include living in environments that promote excessive food intake and that discourage physical activities. Indeed, higher levels of physical inactivity were observed among immigrants to the United States, particularly among children from Hispanic origins (Singh, Yu, Siahpush, and Kogan, 2008). Similarly, ethnicity and migration in childhood have been linked to exposure to environmental tobacco smoke. For example, a US study found that exposure to tobacco smoke was high among African American children, moderately high for South East Asian and Native American, moderately low for Hispanic children, and lowest for Somali children attending primary schools in two economically disadvantaged neighborhoods in Minnesota (Sexton et al., 2004).

While migration brings along promises of an improved lifestyle and higher standards of living, often new environments may in fact expose individuals to risk factors that can lead to detriments in health status. This is particularly the case for new adolescent migrants into countries that are experiencing dramatic transitions in relation to demographics and economic growth. Often this is related to the fast emergence of corporate economies, such as fast-food markets, large entertainment chains (movie theatres, internet cafes), and losely planned developments. The United Arab Emirates (UAE) is a country that has experienced unprecedented growth in the past few decades. The country is a federation of seven emirates located on the Arabian Gulf: Abu Dhabi, Dubai, Sharjah, Ajman, Ras al-Khaimah (RAK), Umm al-Quwain (UAQ), and Fujairah. The UAE currently ranks 12th among world economies in relation to gross national income per capita (World Development Indicators Database, 2011). While the UAE has embraced a resource-based industry heavily dependent on oil, more recent economic diversification led to new areas of investment and growth such as in the hospitality industry, real estate, and financial services. Dubai, for example, one of the most populated emirates, has become a center for several ambitious real-estate projects and has established itself as a major financial and tourist hub that attracts expatriate workers and investors from different parts of the world. A recent survey of professionals revealed that the UAE is the sixth most desired destination for migrant professionals (Khondker, 2008). This fast pace economic development has caused a large influx of migrant workers to the UAE, making the UAE one of the most ethnically diverse countries in the world. However, ethnicity is strongly correlated to socioeconomic status in the UAE, with certain ethnic categories disproportionately represented at the lower end of the economic scale. For example, migrants from North America and Europe represent a large proportion of highly skilled professionals, whereas migrants from South East Asia tend to be manual laborers and service workers. According to census data 2005, only 20.1% of the population estimated at 4,104,695 is of Emirati national origin, while the remainder consists of other Arabs and Iranians (23%), South Asians (50%), and others including expatriates from Europe, North America, and East Asia (8%)(Central Intelligence Agency CIA – The World Factbook, 2011). This dramatic transition from a traditional Bedouin society with little resources related to modern living, to one that is accessible to all forms of modern comfort living and culture mix, inadvertently led to changes in the socioeconomic status of the general population and patterns of health and health risk behaviors.

While economic development has brought so many benefits to the area - including improved living conditions, access to high quality healthcare, sanitation, and overall higher standards of living - , in parallel, the migration and demographic transitions have introduced new social values, habits, and patterns of life that changed the traditional societal structure of the UAE. For migrant workers and their families, acculturation to the emerging transitional lifestyle, and exposures to new social and physical environments is likely to have an impact on their behaviors, lifestyles, and health. However, ethnicity and improved socioeconomic status (among many other factors) that results from migration may be linked to specific health risk behaviors. This leads to the following question: which socioeconomic and demographic factors are significant predictors of adolescent health risk behaviors among the UAE adolescent population? To address this research question, data from a sample of over 6000 young expatriate and national adolescents that reside in the UAE was collected in 2006. The aims are to compare patterns of health risk behaviors among the adolescent UAE population and to identify socioeconomic and demographic predictors of specific health risk behaviors; mainly smoking, substance abuse, sedentary habits and physical inactivity, and traffic-related behaviors.

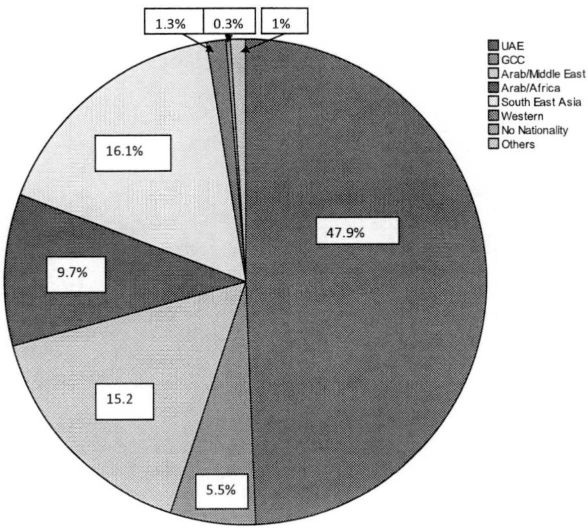

Figure 1. Distribution of the UAE Expatriate Adolescent Population by Ethnic Category.

Table 1. Distribution of the sample in relation to gender and ethnic category by Emirate

Ethnic Categories (n)		Emirate							
		Abu Dhabi	Ajman	Dubai	Fujairah	RAK	Sharjah	UAQ	Total
UAE	M	456	54	168	129	190	250	1	1248
	F	912	47	112	218	216	285	87	1877
	T (%)	1368 (43.8)	101 (3.2)	280 (9)	347 (11.1)	406 (13)	535 (17.1)	88 (2.8)	3125
GCC	M	120	20	60	7	7	20	0	234
	F	61	13	7	9	8	21	9	128
	T (%)	181 (50)	33 (9.1)	67 (18.5)	16 (4.4)	15 (4.1)	41 (11.3)	9 (2.5)	362
Arab / Middle East	M	368	15	26	23	22	80	0	534
	F	240	51	2	29	30	99	10	461
	T (%)	608 (61.1)	66 (6.6)	28 (2.8)	52 (5.2)	52 (5.2)	179 (18)	10 (1)	995
Arab / Africa	M	189	11	46	12	22	52	0	332
	F	156	23	6	36	21	55	6	303
	T (%)	345 (54.3)	34 (5.4)	52 (8.2)	48 (7.6)	43 (6.8)	107 (16.9)	6 (0.9)	635
South East Asia	M	235	0	26	22	51	38	13	385
	F	241	14	124	22	72	170	20	663
	T (%)	476 (45.4)	14 (1.3)	150 (14.3)	44 (4.2)	123 (11.7)	208 (19.8)	33 (3.1)	1048
Western	M	12	0	0	1	0	18	0	31
	F	21	3	0	2	2	23	0	51
	T (%)	33 (40.2)	3 (3.7)	0 (0)	3 (3.7)	2 (2.4)	41 (50)	0 (0)	82
No Nationality	M	1	0	0	0	1	4	0	6
	F	1	5	0	1	0	6	0	13
	T (%)	2 (10.5)	5 (26.3)	0 (0)	1 (5.3)	1 (5.3)	10 (52.6)	0 (0)	19
Others	M	14	1	2	0	4	12	0	33
	F	14	2	3	1	3	7	0	30
	T (%)	28 (44.4)	3 (4.8)	5 (7.9)	1 (1.6)	7 (11.1)	19 (30.2)	0 (0)	63

M – male participants; F – female participants.

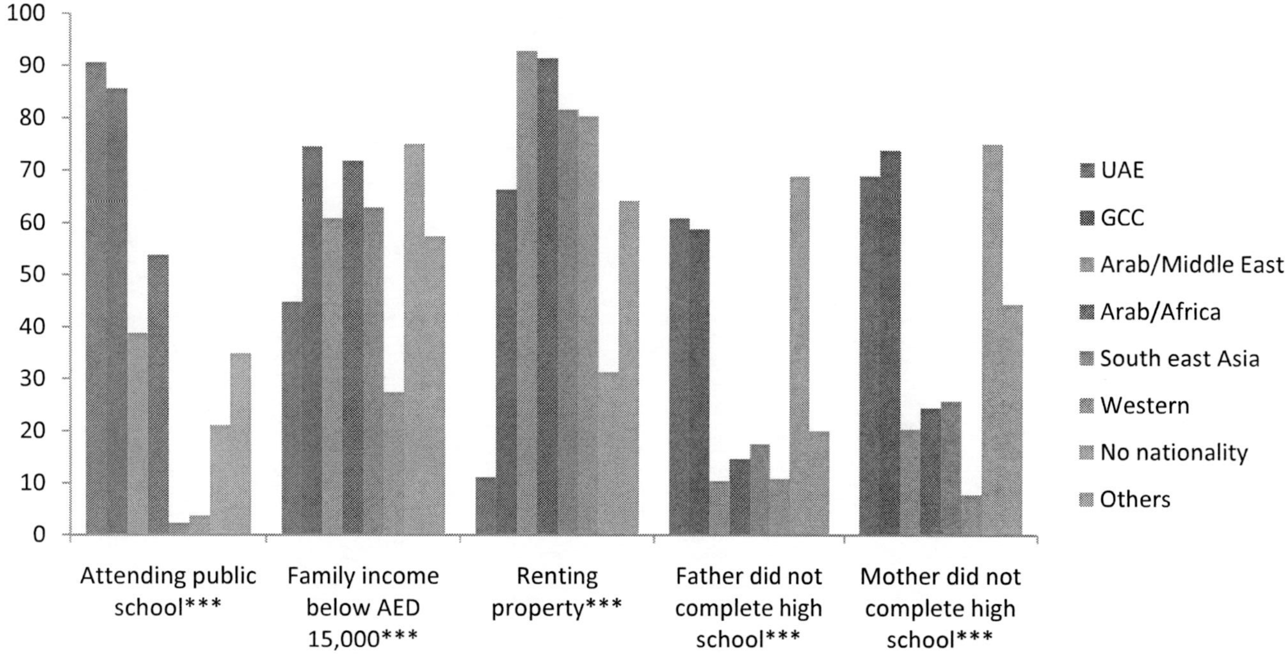

Figure 2. Socio-economic profile of the adolescent UAE population by ethnic category. *** $p < 0.001$.

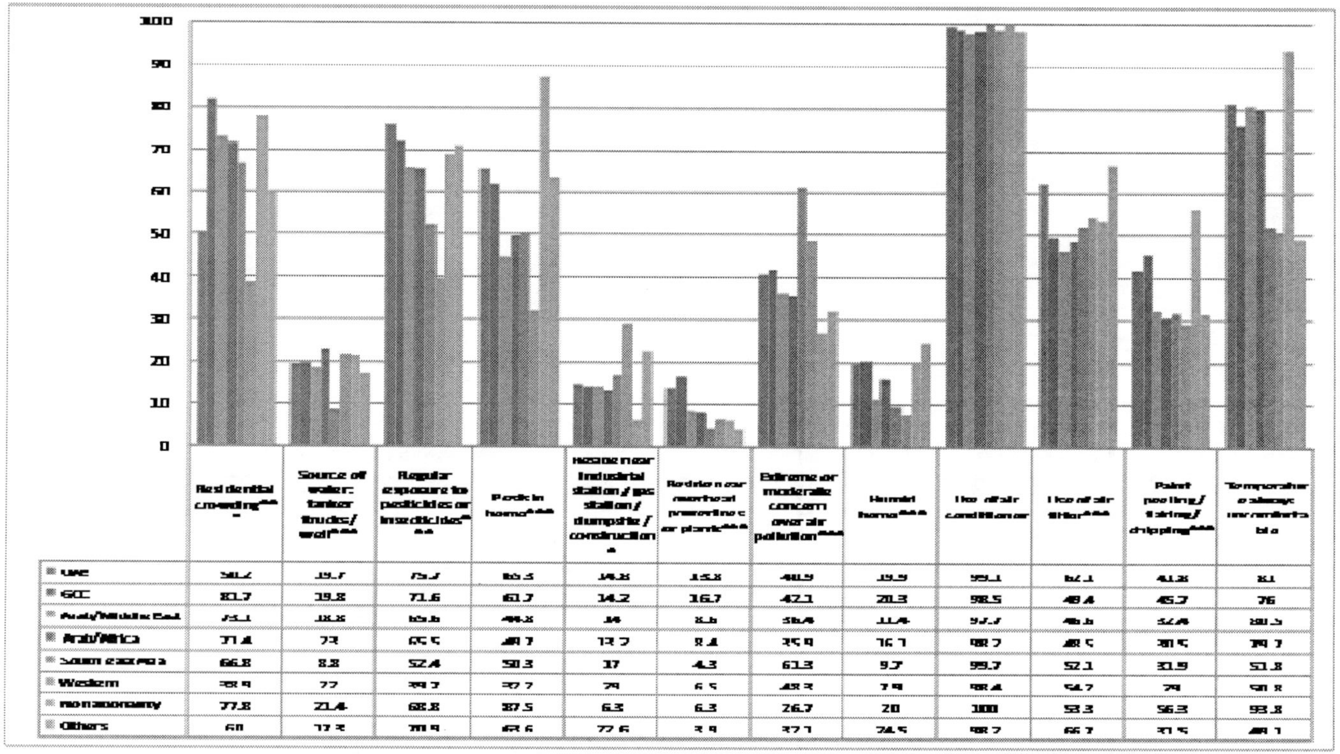

Figure 3. The residential profile of UAE adolescents in relation to ethnic categories (n = 6471). * $p < 0.05$; ** $p < 0.01$; *** $p < 0.001$.

Table 2. Odds Ratios for socioeconomic and demographic predictors of health risk behaviors among adolescents that reside in the United Arab Emirates (OR, 95%CI)

Variable	Classification	Active smoking (n=2970)	Passive smoking (n=3035)	Illegal drugs (n=3340)	Non-conventional drugs (n=3318)	Sedentary habits (n=3381)	Physical Inactivity (n=3464)	Speeding behavior (n=3290)	Not always use of seatbelts (n=3278)
Gender (Female)	Male	5.33 (4.07, 6.98)*** ***	1.75 (1.50,2.04)*** ***	7.13(3.18,16.01)***	0.44 (0.37, 0.52)***	0.92 (0.80, 1.07) ***	0.50 (0.32, 0.79)**	1.49 (1.29,1.73)*** *	0.86 (0.71, 1.04) ***
Ethnic category (UAE)									
	GCC	1.44 (0.89, 2.35)	1.02 (0.73, 1.44)	0.95 (0.27, 3.28)	0.95 (0.65, 1.41)	1.26 (0.91, 1.74)	1.07 (0.40, 2.90)	0.98 (0.71, 1.36)	0.97 (0.61, 1.55)
	Arab/Middle East	2.86 (1.83, 4.47)***	2.12 (1.56,2.90)***	0.26 (0.06, 1.14)	1.03 (0.74, 1.43)	0.74 (0.55, 0.99)*	1.03 (0.41, 2.56)	0.68 (0.51, 0.92)*	0.86 (0.57, 1.27)
	Arab/Africa	1.78 (1.10, 2.89)*	1.36 (0.98, 1.88)	1.54 (0.48, 4.97)	1.11 (0.78, 1.57)	1.05 (0.77, 1.43)	1.00 (0.37, 2.71)	0.76 (0.56, 1.04)	0.87 (0.57, 1.32)
	South East Asia	0.69 (0.40, 1.19)	0.49 (0.34,0.70)***	0.55 (0.15, 1.98)	1.33 (0.94, 1.89)	0.46 (0.33, 0.65)***	1.53 (0.60, 3.91)	0.83 (0.61, 1.15)	0.38 (0.25,0.57)***
	Western	5.10 (2.18, 11.93)***	1.29 (0.63, 2.67)	1.21 (0.13,11.43)	0.72 (0.33, 1.59)	0.69 (0.33, 1.44)	1.37 (0.16, 11.64)	1.64 (0.75, 3.55)	0.57 (0.24, 1.35)
	No nationality	0.01 (0.01, 1.05)	1.46 (0.40, 5.32)	0.01 (0.01, 9.32)	1.70 (0.46, 7.24)	0.90 (0.28, 2.91)	2.14 (0.25, 18.64)	0.42 (0.12, 1.47)	0.01 (0.01, 1.00)
	Others	1.24 (0.40, 3.86)	1.40 (0.68, 2.89) **	0.01 (0.01, 9.78) *	1.71 (0.81, 3.61)	0.66 (0.31, 1.39)	2.87 (0.62, 13.42) *	0.47 (0.23, 0.98)*	0.57 (0.25, 1.32)
Emirate (UAQ)									
	Abu Dhabi	0.86 (0.33, 2.24)	1.87 (1.05, 3.36)*	0.30 (0.03, 2.61)	0.70 (0.43, 1.15)	1.35 (0.81, 2.23)	0.33 (0.15, 0.69)**	0.81 (0.49, 1.33)	0.84 (0.43, 1.63)
	Ajman	1.02 (0.35, 2.94)	1.01 (0.51, 2.03)	2.33 (0.23,23.45)	0.69 (0.37, 1.28)	1.38 (0.76, 2.52)	0.48 (0.16, 1.44)	0.59 (0.32, 1.07)	0.83 (0.37, 1.84)

Table 2. (Continued).

Dubai	0.78 (0.29, 2.12)	1.56 (0.84, 2.89)	0.97 (0.11,8.80)	0.86 (0.50, 1.47)	1.33 (0.77, 2.28)	0.20 (0.07, 0.56)**	0.71 (0.42, 1.21)	0.74 (0.37, 1.49)
Fujairah	0.82 (0.29, 2.30)	1.43 (0.76, 2.69)	0.87 (0.09, 8.84)	0.91 (0.52, 1.58)	0.89 (0.51, 1.56)	0.29 (0.11, 0.75)**	0.86 (0.50, 1.50)	0.81 (0.39, 1.70)
RAK	0.43 (0.15, 1.21)	1.21 (0.65, 2.24)	0.61 (0.06, 5.76)	0.62 (0.36, 1.06)*	1.24 (0.72, 2.12)	0.25 (0.1, 0.61)**	0.81 (0.47, 1.37)	1.01 (0.49, 2.07)
Sharjah	0.84 (0.31, 2.24)	1.61 (0.88, 2.95)	0.63 (0.07, 5.72)	0.86 (0.52, 1.45)	1.19 (0.70, 2.01)	0.26 (0.11, 0.63)**	0.91 (0.54, 1.53)	0.98 (0.49, 1.96)
Income(≥AED 15,000)								
< AED15,000	0.80 (0.61, 1.05)	0.87 (0.73, 1.05)	0.63 (0.31, 1.29)	0.86 (0.72, 1.04)	0.95 (0.80, 1.12)	0.97 (0.60, 1.55)	0.67(0.57, 0.80)***	0.76 (0.60, 0.96)*
School Type (Public)								
Private	1.22 (0.89, 1.68)	1.12 (0.91, 1.37)	1.36 (0.58, 3.20)	0.96 (0.77, 1.20)	1.15 (0.95, 1.40)	1.45 (0.85, 2.49)	1.32 (1.09, 1.60)*	1.04 (0.79, 1.36)
Maternal education (Completed high school)								
Did not complete	1.02 (0.76, 1.38)	1.04 (0.85, 1.27)	0.98 (0.43, 2.26)	1.19 (0.97, 1.46)	0.86 (0.71, 1.04)	0.74 (0.44, 1.23)	0.95 (0.79, 1.14)	1.16 (0.91, 1.49)
Paternal education (Completed high school)								
Did not complete	0.96 (0.67, 1.36)	0.97 (0.76, 1.23)	1.03 (0.42, 2.55)	0.97 (0.76, 1.24)	1.13 (0.90, 1.41)	2.28 (1.23, 4.23)**	1.49(1.20, 1.85)***	0.91 (0.69, 1.22)
Property tenure (Rent)								
Own	1.23 (0.90, 1.70)	0.98 (0.77, 1.23)	3.64(1.41,9.37)**	1.60 (1.24,2.05)***	1.23 (0.98, 1.54)	0.89 (0.43, 1.82)	1.27 (1.01, 1.59)*	0.69 (0.52, 0.93)*

* $p < 0.05$; ** $p < 0.01$; *** $p < 0.001$.

2. Health in the United Arab Emirates

The following section gives an overview of health-related findings from research undertaken during the economic and demographic transition that occurred in the UAE. In general, social and economic advances in the UAE have been accompanied by reductions in the prevalence of communicable diseases, increased life expectancy, and the increased prevalence of non-communicable diseases. Although over 51% of the UAE population is younger than 20 years of age and 38% are less than 14 years of age, chronic non-communicable diseases and their risk factors are relatively prevalent in the UAE. Non-communicable diseases are the main causes of mortality and morbidity in the UAE, with chronic diseases causing 31% of deaths in 2005, and malignant neoplasm and leukemia accounting for 12% of deaths (Belal, 2009). Cardiovascular diseases are known to be the leading causes of morbidity and mortality in the UAE among both the nationals and the expatriates. Risk factors related to cardiovascular diseases include hypertension, cholesterol levels, smoking, body mass index, and physical activity. Hypertension is prevalent in the adult Emirati population aged 30 to 50 years, with higher prevalence rates among females than males (53% versus 47% respectively) (El-Shahat, et al., 1999). The prevalence rates of hypercholesterolemia and mean cholesterol level were found to be significantly higher among Arabs than among non-Arabs that reside in the United Arab Emirates (Agarwal, Hughes, Haliga, Newman, Sheekh-Hussen, and Shalabi, 1995). In addition, smoking is fairly prevalent in the UAE. Results of the Global Youth Tobacco Survey suggest that 30% of male youths and 13% of females use tobacco at least once or more in the past 30 days (Mandil, Hussein, Omer, Turki, and Gaber, 2005).

Of particular concern is the prevalence of overweight or obesity, which reaches 34% among young adolescents (ages 10 to 19) and 39% among female adults (Malik, Bakir, Saab, and King, 2007) (Al-Matroushi, 2005). Obesity and overweight are significantly higher among females than males, with non-Emirati females more likely to be obese than their Emirati counterparts (Malik and Bakir, 2007). However, in a study on adolescent females in the UAE, although only 23% scored above the cut-off in the Eating Attitudes Test (EAT-40), socioeconomic status and nationality did not emerge as significant factors (Eapen, Mabrouk, and Bin-Othman, 2006). Among UAE youth, 22% of children ages 5 to 17 years are overweight and 14% are obese (Malik and Bakir, 2007). Moreover, Type II diabetes has emerged as a major health concern among UAE children and adolescents. In comparing the prevalence of diabetes between UAE migrants and their native non-migrant counterparts, research documents that the prevalence rates of diabetes in Oman (16.8%) and Yemen (6-10%) are significantly lower than the rates reported for Omanis and Yemenis that reside in the UAE (23%) (Baynouna et al. 2009). Indeed, research has highlighted low levels of physical activity among the UAE adolescent population (Barakat-Haddad, 2011). Low rates of physical activity result from a combination of cultural and social norms, a hot climate, preference for car use, and a lifestyle of luxury dependent on the availability of domestic workers who represent a significant proportion of the country's population. Physical inactivity prevalence rates in 2003 were as high as 38% for males and 57% for females (Belal, 2009). Sedentary habits are prevalent among the youth with 38% of males and 43% of females aged 13 to 15 years old spending 3 or more hours per day sitting (Al-Matroushi, 2005).

Following mortality due to cardiovascular diseases, road traffic injuries are the second major cause of death and morbidity in the UAE (Ministry of Health Annual Statistics Report (2007; WHO, 2009; Bener, Berger, and Al-Falasi, 1994). Road traffic injuries have increased steadily by 38% in the Emirate of Dubai between the years 2002 and 2008, with 54% increase in mortality during the same period (Al-Marzooqi, Badi, and El-Jack, 2010). Road traffic injuries are the most frequent cause of hospital admissions in children aged 10 to 14 years, with young adults being most frequent victims of road accidents. Given the large size of the expatriate population that resides in the UAE, gaining knowledge on the health risk factors of migrant adolescents can translate into relevant public health decisions and intervention measures that protect this young vulnerable sub-population.

3. Research Background and Sample Profile

A randomly-selected stratified sample of 147 public and private schools were selected for inclusion in this research. Over 6000 students that attend Grades 10, 11 and 12 were then randomly selected and a cross-sectional survey was administered on the sample. The survey collected a range of data including demographic and socioeconomic data, residential characteristics and exposures, water sources, and residential proximity to industries and overhead power lines. In addition, the survey collected data related to health risk behaviors including smoking, substance abuse, sedentary habits, physical activity, and traffic-related behaviors. In relation to ethnicity, participants were categorized into the following categories based on their nationality: Emirati, GCC (includes participants from GCC - Gulf Cooperation Council - countries or GAFTA - Greater Arab Free Trade Area - including Kuwait, Kingdom of Saudi Arabia, Oman, Qatar, Bahrain, and Yemen), Arab/Middle East (participants from Lebanon, Syria, Jordan, Palestine, and Iraq), Arab/Africa (includes Egypt, Tunisia, Morocco, Algeria, Libya, Sudan, Somalia), South East Asia (includes India, Pakistan, Bangladesh, Sri Lanka, Philippines, and Indonesia), Western (Europe, USA, Australia, Canada), No nationality, and Others (all other nationalities). These ethnic categories were based on similar cultures, traditions, ancestral linkages, or geographical origins. Family income was categorized into annual family income below or above AED 15,000. This cut-off was selected based on recent data from the U.A.E Ministry of Economy indicating that the average monthly income for Emirati households is AED 36,438.10 and that for expatriate households is AED 15,074.30 (Bundhun, 2009).

Respondents consisted of 3,401 migrant and 3,125 Emirati adolescents. In relation to ethnicity, the demographic composition of the sample varies by Emirate. Table 1 displays the distribution of the sample in relation to gender and ethnic category by Emirate. Consistent with the demographic profile of the UAE, a large proportion of the expatriate adolescent population is from South East Asia (31%), and other Arab / Middle East origins (30%) (Figure 1).The gender distribution of the sample is relatively equally represented with 48% males (ranging between 37 and 64% for each ethnic category). Over 90% of the sample is between the ages of 15 and 18 years. Overall, all Emirates were represented with the sample reflecting the demographics in each emirate, with the exception of Dubai and Umm al-Quwain (UAQ), where the sampling method did not capture respondents from Western origins. While the number of migrants from Western origins is limited in UAQ, the unavailability of data from migrant adolescents of Western origins that reside in Dubai is recognized as a study limitation. In addition, the sampling method did not capture a representative male sample in UAQ. Socioeconomic status of the adolescents is measured using public school attendance, monthly family income below AED 15,000, property ownership, and parental education; overall, results indicate that 40% of the respondents' fathers and 30% of mothers did not complete high school (Figure 2).

In relation to the residential profile, overall 60% of the adolescent population report residential crowding (measured using a ratio greater than two for the number of individuals over the number of bedrooms). Residential crowding ranges between 39% and 82% for the different ethnicities, with a significantly lower prevalence among Westerners (Figure 3). Tanker-trucks or well water is the main source of tap water for 23% of Arab/African migrants, 22% of migrants from Western countries, 20% for GCC migrants, 19% for Arabs / Middle East, 9% for South East Asians, and 17% for other migrants. High rates of pesticide or insecticide use in the house, garden, or on pets is reported by migrants from GCC (72%), Other (71%), No nationality (69%), Arab / African (66%), Arab / Middle Eastern (66%), and South East Asians (52%); significantly lower rates are reported by Westerners (40%). In relation to house pests, 32 to 88% of migrants report pests in their houses, with migrants from 'No nationality' most exposed and those from Western countries least exposed to pests. The proportion of adolescents that report residing near industrial plants or gas stations or dumpsite ranges between 13 and 29% for the various ethnic categories (Figure 3). In relation to residing near overhead power lines or plants, the highest proportion is among migrants from GCC (17%), followed by migrants from Arab / Middle East (9%), Arab / Africa (8.5%), Western (7%), those from 'No nationality' (6%), and South East Asia (4%). Overall, 43% of expatriate adolescents are extremely or moderately concerned over air pollution in their neighborhood. Figure 3 compares various residential variables across ethnicities and in comparison to the UAE Emirati population.

4. Comparative Analysis of Immigrant Health Risk Behavioral Factors in the UAE Adolescent Population

The fast rate of economic development that occurred in the UAE made the country an attractive destination for professionals and workers in search for better opportunities and relatively high standards of living. For their adolescent children, exposure to a new culture and environment is coupled with a period of adjustment that slowly introduces new norms and behaviors. The following section will compare the experiences of the ethnic adolescent population categories that reside in the UAE, in relation to the following risk behavioral factors: smoking, substance abuse, sedentary habits and physical inactivity, and road traffic behaviors. Smoking behavior is assessed using active smoking (smoking any form of tobacco) and passive smoking (exposure to environmental tobacco smoke). A distinction is made between substance abuse in the form of illegal drugs and that in the form of other substance abuse. Sedentary lifestyle considers the amount of time that participants watch television or use computers on a regular day. Road traffic behavior is assessed using speeding behavior and regular use of seatbelts during road travels.

4.1. Smoking

The associations between smoking and health outcomes (such as lung cancer, chronic respiratory problems and coronary heart diseases) in both smoking and non-smoking adults are evident in the literature (Shafey O, 2003; Corra M, 2000; Doll, 1998). The age onset of tobacco use and exposure to environmental tobacco smoke (ETS) are common during childhood and adolescence. In this study, 8 items collected data related to smoking. Adolescents are categorized as active smokers if they report occasional or daily use of any form of tobacco (including cigarette, shisha, and midwakh) in the past 30 days. Passive smoking is measured by occasional or daily exposure at home and /or with friends in the past 30 days. The overall prevalence of active smoking among UAE expatriate adolescents is 16%, with significantly higher prevalence among males (25%) compared to females (6%). In examining the link between ethnicity and smoking behavior, high prevalence rates exist among adolescent migrants from Arab / Middle Eastern counties (27.7%) and western origins (27.5%), whereas low rates exist among those from South East Asia (7%) and those from no nationality (5.9%). In relation to gender, the highest prevalence rates for smoking for males was among migrants from Arab / Middle East origins (37%) and those for females were among Western origins (28%). In relation to exposure to ETS, the overall prevalence of passive smoking among the UAE adolescent migrant population is 36%. Overall, a larger proportion of males is exposed to passive smoke (50%) compared to females (31%), with these gender differences seen across all ethnic categories. Similar to the pattern observed for active smoking, migrants from Arab / Middle Eastern origins have the highest prevalence rates (61% for males and 54% for females) while migrants from South East Asian origins have the lowest rates (27% for males and 18% for females). Figure 4 compares gender-related prevalence rates for smoking across the different ethnic categories.

Multivariate analysis reveals that gender and ethnicity are significantly related to active smoking (Table 2). Male adolescents are 5.33 times more likely to be active smokers than females. Compared to the UAE Emirati adolescents, those from Arab / Middle East, Arab / Africa, and Western categories are 2.86, 1.78, and 5.10 times respectively more likely to be active smokers. In relation to passive smoking, significant predictors include gender, ethnicity, and Emirate. Residing in Abu Dhabi, being male, and belonging to the Arab / Middle East category increase the likelihood of exposure to tobacco smoke, whereas participants from South East Asia are less likely to be exposed to tobacco smoke.

In general, apart from migrants from South East Asia, smoking was more prevalent in the migrant adolescent population than that of the host Emirati population. Consistently, in comparing these results to results obtained from the Global Youth Tobacco Survey (GYTS), the prevalence rates of active smoking among the different ethnic categories of UAE expatriate adolescents that is observed in this study are higher than rates reported for all regions except for the Americas and European regions, where the prevalence rates are 22% and 20% respectively (CDC,2006). Specifically, the prevalence rates among Arab/Middle Eastern expatriates residing in the UAE is much higher (28%) than rates reported by the GYTS report for the Eastern Mediterranean region (15%). It is also higher than the averageprevalence rates reported for four Arab / Middle Eastern countries (Lebanon, Syria, Jordan, and Iraq) (26%). Consistent with our results, the GYTS study found the lowest prevalence rates of active smoking among the South East Asian (13%) and Western Pacific regions (11%).

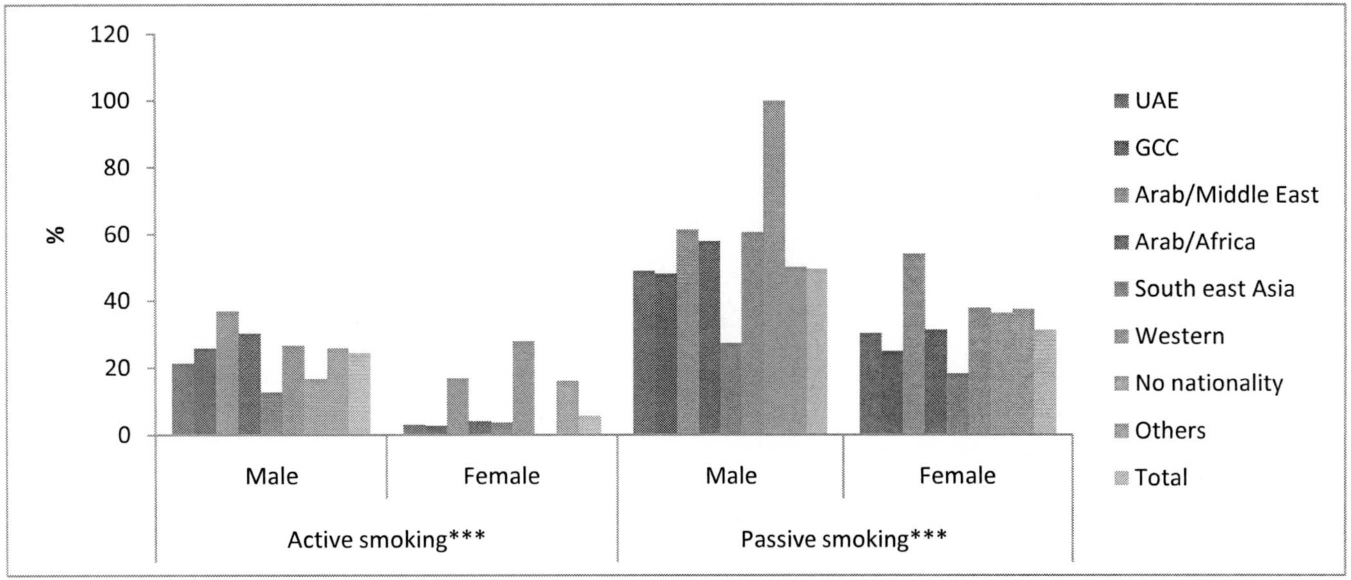

Figure 4. Gender-related prevalence rates for smoking across the different ethnic categories (n=6471).

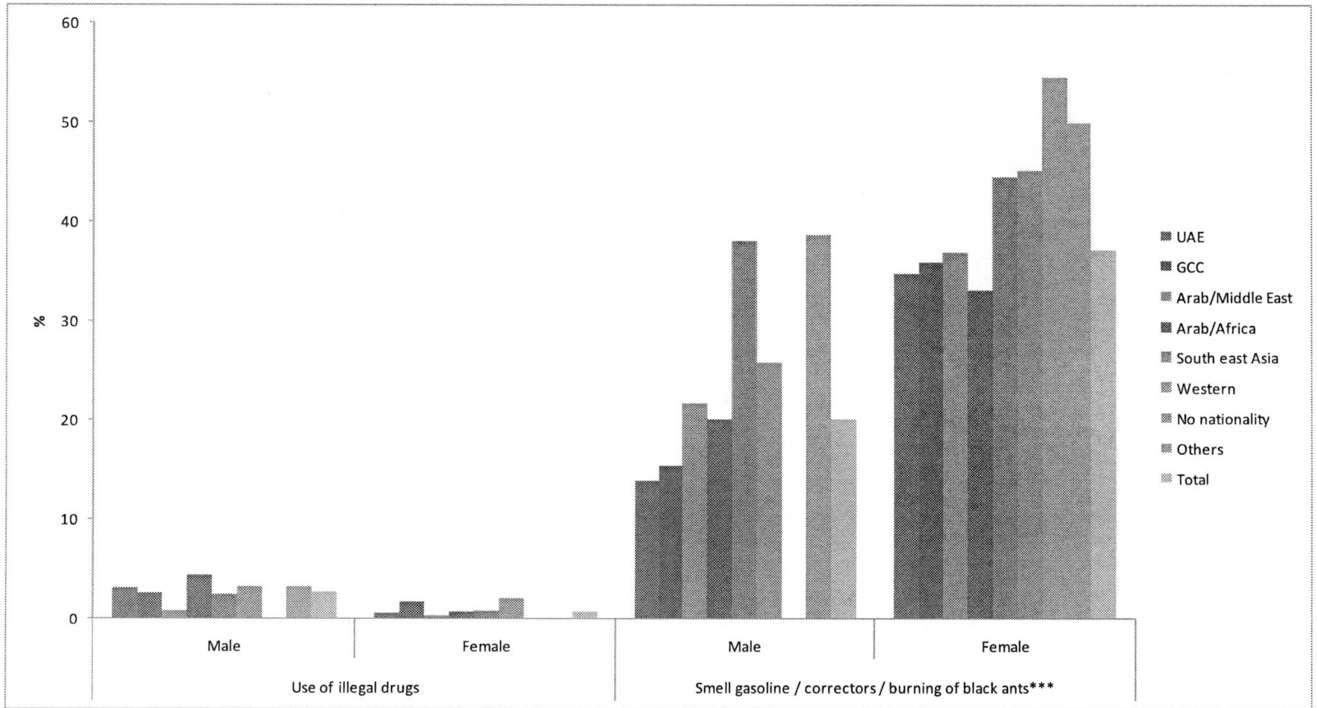

Figure 5. Gender-related prevalence rates for illegal and non-conventional drug-use across the different ethnic categories (n=6471).

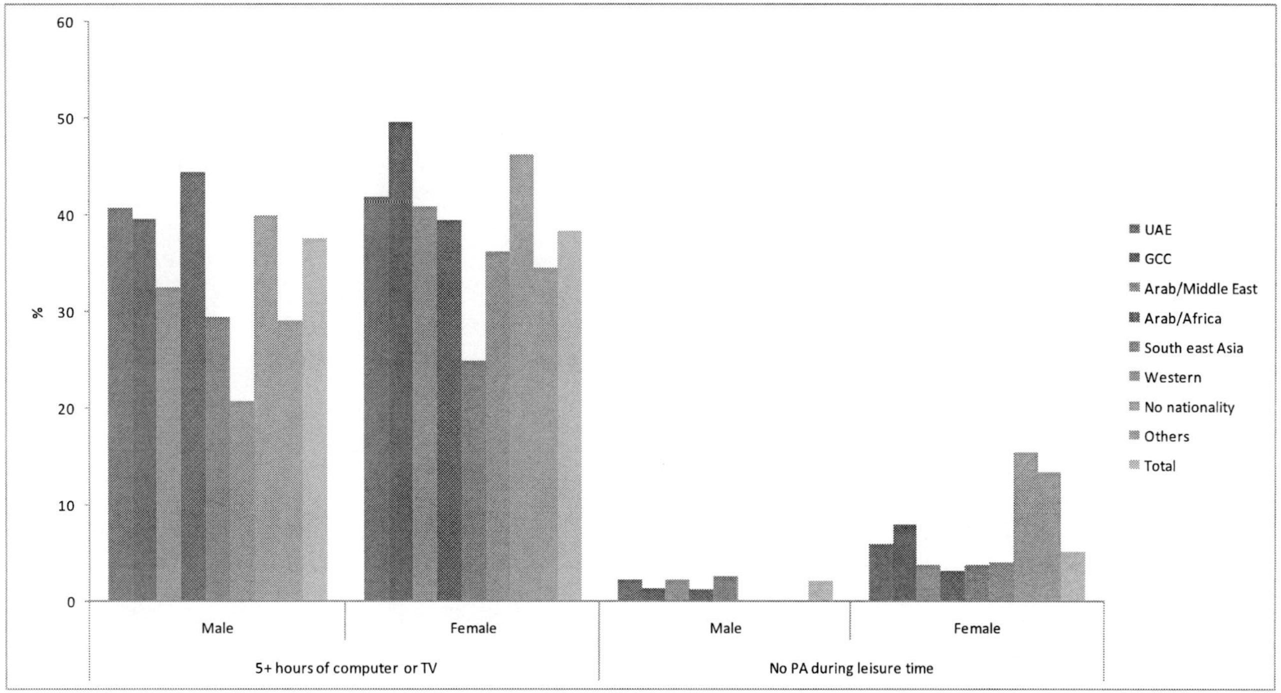

Figure 6. Gender-related prevalence rates for illegal sedentary habits and physical inactivity across the different ethnic categories (n=6471).

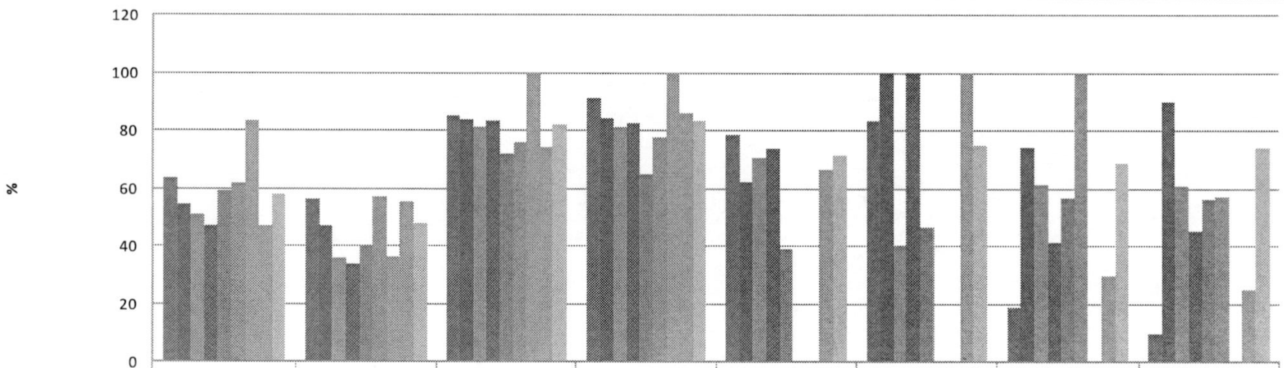

	Always / most of the time exceeds speed limit***		Not always wearing seatbelt		Driver in car accident while not wearing seatbelt		Passenger in car accident while not wearing seatbelt	
	Male	Female	Male	Female	Male	Female	Male	Female
UAE	63.5	56.3	85.2	91.2	78.4	83.3	18.9	9.4
GCC	54.6	46.9	84	84.3	62.5	100	74.4	90
Arab/Middle East	51.1	36	81.1	81.4	70.8	40	61.4	60.8
Arab/Africa	47.1	33.8	83.6	82.6	73.7	100	41.2	45.2
South east Asia	59.3	39.9	71.9	65	39.1	46.7	56.5	56.1
Western	62.1	57.1	75.9	77.6	0	0	100	57.1
No nationality	83.3	36.4	100	100	0	0	0	0
Others	46.9	55.2	74.2	86.2	66.7	100	30	25
Total	58	47.8	82.1	83.4	71.7	75	68.8	74.1

Figure 7. Gender-related prevalence rates for traffic-related behaviours across the difference ethnic categories (n=6471).

The prevalence rates of active smoking among GCC adolescent migrants residing in the UAE are comparable to rates reported in Kuwait (18%) and Qatar (19%), whereas the prevalence rate of active smoking among North African adolescent migrants (19%) is slightly higher than the average rate reported for five North African countries (Egypt, Tunisia, Morocco, Algeria, Libya, and Mauritania) (17%) and the African region (17%)(WHO, 2011) (WHO, 2009). While these differences may be attributed to the slightly different age group that the GYTS targets, it may be that the social environment of the UAE promotes smoking behaviour, and more so among the male expatriate ethnic categories from Arab, Middle Eastern, and North African origins. This is particularly evident given the increased popularity of shisha or waterpipe in the Arab world, particularly among the young adolescent population. In relation to passive smoking, GYTS results report overall higher exposure rates for Europe, Africa, South East Asia, and Western Pacific World Health Organization regions; however, lower rates are reported for Eastern Mediterranean and African regions (WHO, 2009; CDC, 2007).

4.2. Substance Abuse

In relation to substance abuse, respondents were asked whether they have ever used illegal drugs such as marijuana, hashish or cocaine and whether they ever purposely smelled gasoline, glue, fumes, correctors, car exhaust, or burning black ants. These 'other' forms of substance abuse are common knowledge in the UAE adolescent population; this consists mainly of sniffing substances such as gasoline, glue, correctors, and burning black ants. While the rates of drug use in Arab and Middle Eastern countries are not generally known, there appears to be an emerging rise in substance use among the UAE adolescents over the past few years. Our results suggest that overall 1.5% of UAE adolescents experienced illegal drugs; this prevalence is higher among males (2.3%) than females (0.7%). For other forms of substance abuse, the overall prevalence among UAE adolescents is 36%. Surprisingly, female were more likely to purposely sniff these substances than males (40% versus 30%). Figure 5 compares the use of illegal and other drugs among the different ethnicities. Migrant adolescents from North Africa were most likely to experience illegal drugs, whereas those from South East Asia were most likely to experience other substance abuse, with higher prevalence rates among South East Asian females (45%) than males (38%). While migrant adolescents from Arab or Middle Eastern origins had the highest rates of active and passive smoking, they had the lowest of illegal drug use. On the other hand, migrant adolescents from South East Asia had the lowest rate of smoking but the highest rate of other forms of substance abuse. Comparatively, both the use of illegal and other substance abuse are relatively low in the host Emirati adolescent population.

Multivariate analysis reveals that gender (male) and property ownership are significant predictors of illegal drug use (OR = 7.13 and 3.64 respectively). In relation to other substance abuse, gender (female) and property ownership emerge as significant predictors (OR = 2.27 and 1.60 respectively).

Furthermore, adolescents that reside in Ras Al Khaimah are less likely to experience other substance abuse than those that reside in UAQ (OR = 0.62).

4.3. Sedentary Habits and Physical Inactivity

Sedentary habits and physical inactivity are major risk factors for non-communicable diseases. Among the UAE adolescent population, these risk factors are examined using three main items that asked participants whether they view five or more hours of television on a regular day, use the computer or computer games for five or more hours on a regular day, and whether they participate in any form of physical activity during their leisure time. Overall, 24% of the expatriate adolescents view five or more hours of television on a regular day and 23% spent five or more hours on a regular day on the computer or playing computer games. Females showed a greater tendency to spend 5 or more hours watching televison or working on computers (26%) as compared to males (22%). Furthermore, 3.7% of the UAE adolescent population do not participate in any physical activity during their leisure time. It is important to interpret these results with caution since the level and duration of engagement in any form of physical activity is not examined in this study, rather simply whether the participant does or does not engage in any form of physical activity. Clear gender differences in physical inactivity patterns were observed among UAE adolescents, with only 2% of males never engaging in any physical activity during their leisure time compared to 5.1% of females. Figure 6 shows the prevalence rates of sedentary habits and physical inactivity across the different ethnicities. Migrants from Western countries and those from South East Asia have the lowest rates of television viewing or sitting in front of computers for five or more hours on a regular day (30.5% and 26.5% respectively). Relatively higher and comparable rates for sedentary behavior are observed for the UAE Emirati population (41.4%) and adolescent migrants from other GCC (43.1%), Arab / Africa (42%), and Arab / Middle East (36.4%) categories. Migrant adolescents that do not belong to the five main ethnic categories (GCC, Arab / Middle East, Arab / Africa, South East Asia, Western) have the highest prevalence rate for physical inactivity (7.4%) followed by the Emirati host population (4.4%). By the same token, migrant adolescents that do not belong to the five main ethnic categories have the highest rate of television viewing for five or more hours on a regular day and the lowest rate of computer / computer game use for five or more hours on a regular day.

Multivariate analysis reveals that gender and ethnicity are significantly related to sedentary habits (Table 2). Females are 1.09 times more likely to be sedentary than males. Furthermore, compared to the UAE Emirati adolescents, those from Arab / Middle East and South East Asia categories are 0.74 and 0.46 times less likely to be sedentary. In relation to physical inactivity, significant predictors include gender, Emirate, and paternal education. Females, those residing in UAQ, and those whose fathers' did not complete high school are more likely to not participate in any physical activity during their leisure time (Table 2).

4.4. Traffic-Related Behavior

Traffic-related behavior is assessed using data collected from 6 items. Respondents were asked about the frequency the vehicle they are travelling in exceeds the speed limit and the frequency of seatbelt use. Respondents were also asked whether they were involved in a car accident in the past 12 months as a driver or passenger, and if so, whether they were wearing their seatbelts. Our results suggest that overall 48.1% of UAE adolescents always or most of the time travel in a vehicle that exceeds the speed limit. This prevalence is higher among males (58%) than among females (47.8%). For seatbelt use, 82.8% of UAE adolescents do not always wear their seatbelts. Surprisingly, female were more likely to avoid wearing their seatbelts than males (83.4% versus 82.1%). Overall, 21% of the sample (n=1383) were involved in a car accident in the past 12 months as passengers (n=1053) or drivers (n=330). Overall, 49% of drivers involved in car accidents in the past 12 months were not wearing seatbelts compared to 57% of passengers involved in car accidents. Being involved in a car accident as a driver in the past 12 months is significantly related to ethnic category with lowest rates among Westerners (2.7%) and the highest rates among UAE nationals (7.3%) (Chi-square = 36.35, p = 0.02). Figure 7 compares travel-related behaviors among the different ethnic categories.

Significant predictors of traffic-related behaviors include gender, ethnic category, income, type of school attended, paternal education, and property ownership (Table 2). Predictors of speeding include being male (OR=1.49), those that attend private schools (OR=1.32), those whose fathers did not complete high school (OR=1.49), and property ownership (OR=1.27). Participants whose monthly family income is below AED15,000 are less likely to speed compared to their counterparts (OR=0.67); furthermore, those that belong to the Arab / Middle East and Others categories are less likely to speed on the road compared to the UAE Emirati category (OR = 0.68 and 0.47 respectively). In relation to seatbelt use, significant predictors include gender (male), participants from South East Asia, monthly family income below AED15,000, and property ownership (rent) (OR = 0.86, 0.38, 0.76, and 0.69 respectively).

Discussion and Conclusion

This chapter presents a comparative analysis of health risk behaviors among the UAE adolescent migrant population. The relevance of this work stems from the fact that immigrants constitute the largest segment of the UAE population. Furthermore, adolescent children that migrate to the UAE experience life in a transitioning environment while their identity and belonging is being shaped and defined. Findings reveal significant differences in health risk behaviors among the UAE adolescent population in relation to socioeconomic and demographic features. There are several implications of these findings. First, the socioeconomic profile of UAE migrants is best assessed using a number of indicators. Figure 2 shows that conventional socioeconomic measures are not closely interrelated in the UAE population. For example, attending public school and property ownership are linked to UAE Emiratis largely due to social and economic programs that the UAE government offers to its citizens. On the other hand, attending private school and parental education are linked to the migrant population due to the influx of educated workers into the country and the benefits that are provided to them by their employers. This is particularly relevant for participants from the Western category. For most of the ethnic categories, the percentage of respondents whose monthly family income is below AED 15,000 is relatively high. The high prevalence rates of parents that did not complete high school and those that are below the AED 15,000 annual income among the UAE Emirati and GCC categories are notable. In relation to the residential profile, in general, participants from the Western and Emirati category have the best residential conditions, whereas those with no nationality had the highest prevalence rates of tanker truck / well sources of water, regular exposure to pesticides or insecticides, exposure to pests in their homes, paint in their homes that is peeling flaking or chipping, and uncomfortable temperatures.

Second, when examining the health risk behaviors of the UAE adolescent population, significant socioeconomic and demographic predictors of risk behavior include gender, ethnic category, Emirate, monthly family income, school type attended, paternal education, and property tenure. In general, males are more likely to smoke, experience illegal drugs, and speed than females; females are more unlikely to participate in physical activity but more likely to use other forms of substance abuse than males. Participants from the Arab / Middle East category are more likely to smoke and be exposed to smoke, but less likely to be sedentary and to speed than UAE Emirati adolescents. Participants from Arab / Africa and Western categories are more likely to smoke tobacco than their Emirati counterparts. Those from the South East Asia category are less likely to be exposed to tobacco smoke, to be sedentary, and to not always use their seatbelts than the UAE Emirati adolescent population. Compared to UAQ, exposure to environmental tobacco smoke is more likely in Abu Dhabi, whereas the use of other forms of substance abuse is less likely in RAK; in addition, residing in UAQ is linked to not engaging in any form of physical activity during leisure times. Participants whose monthly family income is below AED 15,000 are less likely to speed and not always use their seatbelt; whereas, those that attend private high schools are more likely to speed on the roads. Furthermore, those whose fathers did not complete high schools are more likely to disengage in any form of physical activity and to speed on the roads. Property ownerships is significantly linked to use of illegal and other forms of substance abuse and speeding on the road; however, those that own their property are more likely to always wear their seatbelts.

Finally, it is important to highlight the policy implications of these results. In general, the quest for relatively higher socioeconomic status appears to come with a trade-off for health risk behaviors among the UAE migrant adolescent population. This is more notable for male migrants. Given that immigrants constitute a large proportion of the UAE population, more health behavior and promotion awareness and education programs should target young adolescents that migrate to the country. The importance of not exceeding the speed limits on UAE roads should be highlighted particularly in private school programs, which is a predictor of this health risk behavior. Furthermore, given that relatively high socioeconomic status (measured through property ownership) is linked to traffic-related health risk behaviors and substance abuse, the UAE population needs to be made aware of the dangers of providing these young adolescents with too much time on their hands and the tools (fast vehicles and finances) that may lead to detriments in health status. Policies may need to target programs that offer these adolescents skill building workshops or job training, thus slowly preparing this young vulnerable population to become a productive sector in the UAE society. This study was subject to certain limitations. First, sampling did not represent gender and ethnic categories in all of the Emirates. In addition, all data is self-reported and therefore subject to bias. Regardless, these research findings contribute to knowledge on the relationship between health risk behaviors and ethnicity in fast developing countries. Future work should compare the health of the UAE expatriate adolescents with their native counterparts; it should also examine the acculturation process over time and its effects on health risk behaviors among the different ethnic categories that reside in the UAE.

REFERENCES

Abraido-Lanza, A., Chao, M., and Florez, K. (2007). Do healthy behaviors decline with greater acculturation? Implications for Latino moratlity paradox. *Social Science and Medicine , 61* (6), 1243 - 1255.

Agarwal, M., Hughes, P., Haliga, A., Newman, P., Sheekh-Hussen, M., and Shalabi, A. (1995). Relevance of cholesterol screening in the United Arab Emirates. A preliminary study. *European Journal of Epidemiology , 11* (5), 581 - 585.

Al-Marzooqi, A. A., Badi, M., and El-Jack, A. (2010). Road Traffic Accidents in Dubai, 2002 - 2008. *Asia Pac J Public Health , 22* (3), 31S - 39S.

Al-Matroushi, M. (2005). *United Arab Emirates Global School-based Student Health Survey .* Retrieved 07 04, 2011, from World Health Organization: http://www.who.int/chp/gshs/2005_United_Arab_Emirates_GSHS_Country_Report.pdf

Babones, S. (2008). Income Inequality and Population Health: Correlation and Causality. *Social Science and Medicine , 66* (7), 1614-1626.

Barakat-Haddad, C. (2011). Factors that Influence Physical Activity among School-aged Emirati Females in Dubai, UAE. *Canadian Association of Geographers.* Calgary.

Baynouna, L., Revel, A., Nagelkerke, N., Jaber, T., Omar, A., Ahmed, N., et al. (2009). Associations of cardiovascular risk factors in Al Ain- United Arab Emirates. *Cardiovascular Diabetology , 8*, 21.

Belal AM. (2009). Nutrition-related chronic diseases Epidemic in UAE: can we stand to STOP it? *Sudanese Journal of Public Health , 4* (4), 383-392.

Bender, K., and Ioannis, T. (2009). Controlling for Endogeneity in the Health-Socioeconomic Status Relationship of the Near Retired. *The Journal of Socio-Economics , 38* (6), 977-987.

Bener, A., Berger, A., and Al-Falasi, A. (1994). Risk Taking Behavior in Road Traffic Accidents. *J. Traffic Med 22*, 67 - 70.

Bennett, S. (1993). Inequalities in risk factors and cardiovascular mortality among Australia's immigrants. *Australian Journal of Public Health , 17* (3), 251 - 261.

Braveman, P., Cabbin, C., Egerter, S., Chideya, S., Marchi, K., Metzler, M., et al. (2005). Socioeconomic status in health research: One size does not fit all. *Journal of the American Medical Association , 294* (22), 2879 - 2888.

Bundhun R. (2009, February 03). UAE monthly household income revealed. *CULTURE and SOCIETY – NEWS* p. www.arabianbusiness.com.

Cattell, V. (2001). Poor People, Poor Places, and Poor Health; 1516., the mediating role of social networks and social capita. *Social Science and Medicine , 52* (10), 1501 - 1516.

CDC. (2006). Use of Cigarettes and Other Tobacco Products Among Students Aged 13-15 Years Worldwide, 1999-2005. . Mortality and Morbidity Weekly Report. 55(20), 553-556.

CDC. (2007). Exposure to Secondhand Smoking Among Students Aged 13- 15 Years - Worldwide, 2000-2007. Morbidity and Mortality Weekly Reports. 56(20), 497-500.

Central Intelligence Agency CIA – The World Factbook. (2011). Retrieved 07 01, 2011, from https://www.cia.gov/library/publications/the-world-factbook/geos/ae.html.

Corra M, G. G. (2000). *Tobacco control country profiles.* Atlanta, GA: American Cancer Society.

Diez-Roux, A., Link, B., and Northbridge, M. (2000). A multilevel Analysis of Income Inequality and Cardiovascular disease risk factors. *Social Science and medicine , 50* (5), 673-687.

Doll, R. (1998). Uncovering the effects of smoking: historical perspective. *Statistical Methods in Medical Research , 7* (2), 87-117.

Eapen, V., Mabrouk, A., and Bin-Othman, S. (2006). Disordered eating attitudes and symptomatology among adolescent girls in the United Arab Emirates. *Eating Behaviors , 7*, 53 - 60.

El-Shahat, Y., Bakir, S., Farjou, N., Hashim, T., BoHaliga, A., Al-Hossani, H., et al. (1999). ypertension in UAE Citizens - Preliminary Results of a Prospective Study. *Saudi J Kidney Dis Transpl , 10*, 376 - 381.

Evans, G., and Kantrowitz, E. (2002). SOCIOECONOMIC STATUS AND HEALTH: The Potential Role of Environmental Risk Exposure. *Annual Review of Public Health , 23*, 303 - 331.

Galler, D., and Sher, L. (2010). Immigration and Mental Health: Stress, Psychiatric Disorders and Suicidal Behavior Among Immigrants and Refugees. New York: Nova Science Publishers.

Garcia, C., and Saewyc, E. (2007). Perceptions of mental health among recently immigrated Mexican adolescents. *Issues in mental health nursing , 28* (1), 37 - 54.

Global status report on road safety: time for action. (2009). Retrieved October 12, 2010, from World Health Organization, Geneva: http://www.who.int/violence_injury_prevention/road_safety_status/2009

Hemminki, K., and Li, X. (2002). Cancer Risks in second-generation immigrants to Sweden. *International Journal of Cancer , 99*, 229 - 237.

Kennedy, S., McDonald, J., and Biddle, N. (2006, December). The Healthy Immigrant Effect and Immigrant Selection: Evidence from Four Countries. *Social and Economic dimensions of an Aging Population Research Papers* , p. 54.

Khondker, H. (2008). Social Change in the United Arab Emirates: challanegs of Mgration and "Emiratisation. Lecture delivered at the Middle East Institute.

Lorant, V., and Bhopal, R. S. (2010). Ethnicity, socio-economic status and health research: insights from and implications of Charles Tilly's theory of Durable Inequality. *J Epidemiol Community Health* , doi:10.1136/jech.2010.116418.

Malik, M., and Bakir, A. (2007). Prevalence of overweight and obesity among children in the United Arab Emirates. *Obes Rev , 8* (1), 15 - 20.

Malik, M., Bakir, A., Saab, B., and King, H. (2007). Glucose intolerance and associated factors in the mulit-ehtnic population of the United Arab Emirates: results of a national survey. *Diabetes res Clin Pract , 78*, 369 - 377.

Mandil, A., Hussein, A., Omer, H., Turki, G., and Gaber, I. (2005). Characteristics and risk factors of tobacco consumption among University of Sharjah students. *Eastern Mediterranean Health Journal , 13* (6).

Marmot, M., and Wilkinson, R. (1999). *Social determinants of health.* Oxford University Press.

Ministry of Health Annual Statistics Report (2007). (2007). Retrieved October 12, 2010, from http://www.moh.gov.ae/AdminCP/AssetsManager/Files/Statistics/Statistics_2007/media/6-2.pdf

Murray, C., Salomon, J., Mathers, C., and Lopez, A. (2002). In *Summary measures of population helath: concepts, ethics, measurement and applications* (p. 770). Geneva: World Health Organization.

Nair, C., Nargundkar, H., Johansen, H., and Stachan, J. (1990). Canadian cardiovascular disease mortality: First generation immigrants versus Canadian-born. *Health Reports , 2* (4), 203 - 228.

Neto, F. (2009). Predictors of mental health among adolescents from immigrant families in Portugal. *Journal of family psychology , 23* (3), 375 - 385.

Popkin, B., and Udry, J. (1998). Adolescent obesity increases significantly in second and third generation US immigrants, The National Longitudinal Study of Adolescent health. *J. Nutr. , 128*, 701 - 706.

Razum, O., Zeeb, H., and Akgün, S. (1998). Low overall mortality of Turkish residents in Germany persists and extends into a second generation: merely a healthy migrant effect? *Tropical Medicine and International Health , 3* (4), 297-303.

Sexton, K., Adgate, J., Church, T., Hecht, S., Ramachandran, G., Greaves, I., et al. (2004). children Exposure to environmental Tobacco smoke : Using Diverse Exposure Metrics to document Ethnic/Racial Differences. *Environmental Health Perspectives , 112* (3), 392 - 397.

Shafey O, D. S. (2003). *Tobacco control country profiles.* Atlanta (GA): American Cancer Society.

Singh, G., Yu, S., Siahpush, M., and Kogan, M. (2008). High levels of physical inactivity and sedentary behaviors among US immigarnnt children and adolescents. *Arch Pediatr Adolesc Med , 162* (8), 756 - 763.

Smith, P., Bogin, B., Varela-Silva, M., Orden, B., and Loucky, J. (2002). Does Immigration Help or Harm Children's Health? *The Mayan Case Social Science quarterly , 83*, 994 - 1002.

Steffen, P., Smith, T., Larson, M., and Butler, L. (2006). Acculturation to Western society as a risk factor for high blood pressure: a meta-analytic review. *Psychosomatic medicine , 68* (3), 386 - 397.

Stillman, S., Gibson, J., and McKenzie, D. (2010). McKenzie report on the Impact of immigration on child health: experimental Evidence from a Migration lottery program. Western Economic Association International.

Valkonen, T., Brancker, A., and Reijo, M. (1992). Mortality differentials between three populations residents of Scandinavia, Scandinavian immigrants to Canada and Canadian born residents of Canada, 1979-1985. *Health Reports , 4* (2), 137 - 159.

WHO (2011). *Tobacco fact sheet N° 339.* Geneva: World Health Organization.

WHO (2009). *WHO Report on the Global Tobacco Epidemic.* Geneva: World Health Organization

Wilkinson, R. (1996). Unhealthy Societies: The Afflictions of Inequalities. Routledge: London.

World Development Indicators Database. (2011, 07 01). Retrieved 07 04, 2011, from The World Bank: http://siteresources.worldbank.org/DATASTATISTICS/Resources/ GNIPC. pdf

In: Socioeconomic Status and Health Implications ISBN: 978-1-62100-675-6
Editor: Sarah Reibert and Alice Jannings, pp. 111-126

Chapter 5

SOCIOECONOMIC STATUS AND HEALTH IMPLICATIONS

***I. C. Céspedes*[1], *N. R. Oliveira-Monteiro*[2], *M. C. Garcia*[1], *D. A. Ribeiro*[1] *and R. C. Spadari-Bratfisch*[1]**

[1] Department of Biosciences,
[2] Department of Health, Education and Society, Institute of Health and Society, *Campus* Baixada Santista, Federal University of Sao Paulo, Santos, SP, Brazil.

ABSTRACT

The socioeconomic status (SES) is considered a well-established risk factor for poor health, the poorer the SES the worse prospects for health outcomes. SES gradients in disease's risk are partially explained by bad health related behaviors, and partially by environmental conditions that people at lower SES are exposed to. Stressors whether they were physical or psychological, activate several neural pathways including the hypothalamus-pituitary-adrenal axis and the autonomic nervous system. The stress response aimed to create resilience and guarantee survival may, then turn in mal-adaptation, increasing vulnerability to illnesses. One of the consequences is the increase in the cortisol plasma levels that superimpose to the endogenous corticosteroids circadian rhythm which might be altered by the low SES, as well as by an adverse work or domestic environment, conditions that determine chronic psychosocial stress, and contribute to the prevalence of severe illnesses. Indeed, negative correlations between monthly income wage and salivary cortisol levels were reported. When the SES is accompanied by additional stressors, the risk for diseases is accentuated and, in some cases, stress is characterized by hypocortisolism rather than hypercortisolism. High levels of epinephrine were also associated with low SES. These stress hormones effects on the brain and peripheral organs may trigger diseases to which the individual presents some genetic predisposition. Therefore, public policies that give social support to people living in low SES may impact positively on their health.

1. INTRODUCTION

It is well known that individuals from more advantaged social classes enjoy better mental and physical health than do individuals within lower socioeconomic classes. Various mechanisms have been evoked to explain the association between socioeconomic status (SES) and health, and stress has emerged as an important risk factor for those diseases, since it has been suggested that individuals lower in SES report greater exposure to stressful life events and a greater impact of these events on their life than individuals higher in SES (Lupien *et al.,* 2001). However, there are other studies arguing that no correlation has been found between stress hormones and poor health related to low SES.

It is also well established that the impact of stress on health depends on individual vulnerability, which is determined by genetic, biological, behavioral, and environmental factors that interact over the lifespan to influence the risk trajectories, particularly through neurobiological pathways. Classically, stress has been defined as the organic response to demands that can be perceived as threatening or beneficial, depending on the availability of one's adaptive coping resources (Lazarus and Folkman, 1984; Cohen *et al.,* 2007). The biological, behavioral, and social coping strategies are orchestrated to specifically create resilience and survival (Lovallo, 2005). However, when excessive or prolonged, stress responses may turn in risk for health. Therefore, the stress impact on health can be "good" and "tolerable," or "toxic", depending on the degree to which an individual has control over a given stressor and resources for handling stressors over the lifespan (Knudsen *et al.*, 2006; Shonkoff, 2006). Accordingly, some stressful experiences can lead to proliferation of behavioral, cognitive, physiological, and neural changes that promote adaptation and resilience or lead to vulnerability and poor health (McEwen and Gianaros, 2010).

2. THE STRESS SYSTEM

The brain is the primary mediator and target of resilience and vulnerability to stress because it determines what is threatening and because it determines the behavioral and physiological stress response. The hippocampus and the amygdala (brain areas supporting memory and mood), and areas of the prefrontal cortex related to decision making and emotions, impulsivity, as well as the hypothalamus, that organizes autonomic and neuroendocrine functions, are specifically recognized as targets for the stress hormones (McEwen *et al.*, 1968; McEwen, 2007). Stressful experiences and associated changes in the blood levels of the stress hormones may produce both adaptive and maladaptive effects on these brain regions throughout life (McEwen, 2007). Early abuse, conflict-laden familial relationships, stressful life events, and adverse physical and social conditions, can modulate the structural and functional plasticity of the above cited areas. Alterations in these brain systems due to neuroplasticity can affect patterns of emotional expression and regulation, stress reactivity, recovery, and coping. Although critical, the effects of stress on the brain are not necessarily permanent and are amenable to recover. Preventative strategies and interventions that include pharmacological therapy and changes in the lifestyle (*e.g.*, regular practice of exercise, health dietary habits, and social support) can change the risk for poor health related to stress. Consequently, public and private social policies will necessarily affect people's mental and physical health and those leaving in lower SES will depend most on these policies.

As far as low SES is a potential source of poor health associated with life stress, then the stress system in the brain most plausibly include the above reported limbic brain areas (hippocampus, hypothalamus, amygdala, prefrontal cortex) that jointly support social and emotional information processing, besides regulating neuroendocrine, immune, and autonomic nervous system functions; the entire system being involved in both adaptation and maladaptation, and expressing well-characterized forms of neuroplasticity in conditions of chronic and acute stress (McEwen, 2006).

The brain not only processes inputs from the external environment, but also controls adjustments of the body engendered by behavioral states like waking, sleeping, lying, standing, exercising, and so on. These bodily adjustments promote adaptation and coping with aversive situations and discrete stimuli (such as noise, crowding, hunger, excessive heat or cold) and other more aggressive threats to safety. The peripheral systems promoting adaptation include the hypothalamic-pituitary-adrenal cortex (HPA) axis, the autonomic nervous system, the metabolic system (including the thyroid axis, insulin and other metabolic hormones), the gut, the kidney, and the immune system. The biomediators of these systems (*e.g.*, cortisol, sympathetic and parasympathetic transmitters, cytokines, metabolic hormones) operate as a nonlinear, interactive network in which mediators down- and up-regulate each other, depending on some factors such as concentration, location in the body, and sequential temporal patterning (McEwen, 2006). Importantly, the activity of these peripheral components of the stress system and its mediators are closely coupled to one's psychological and genetic background, developmental history, and behavioral state (McEwen and Gianaros, 2010).

3. Low SES and Health Outcomes

There is cumulative evidence that disparities in the income, education, occupation, and other dimensions of SES account for appreciable variance in all cause and disease-specific morbidity and mortality rates, as well as the prevalence of risk factors for chronic medical conditions (Adler *et al.*, 1993, 1999), prevalent psychopathologies of mood, and drug abuse (Kessler *et al.*, 1994; Lorant *et al.*, 2003). However, that health and longevity track a socioeconomic gradient cannot be explained entirely by material deprivation, illiteracy, or restricted availability of quality health care among those occupying a low socioeconomic position (Marmot, 2004; Sapolsky, 2004). Hence, several conceptual models of SES-related health disparities speculate that life experiences inherent to socioeconomic positions at the individual, familial, and community levels could influence well-being and disease risk through the stress-related pathways (Kelly *et al.*, 1997; Dohrenwend, 2000). So, it is proposed that the chronic experience of being at low SES at the individual level could involve enduring financial hardships, a sense of insecurity regarding future prosperity, and the possible demoralizing feelings of marginalization or social exclusion attributable to comparative social, occupational, or material disadvantage. Further, an individual's perception of his or her relative ranking in the social hierarchy, formally termed subjective social status, may affect his or her pattern of emotional, behavioral and physiological reactivity to and recovery from life stressors, and consequently enhancing risk for poor health (Adler *et al.*, 2000; Singh-Manoux *et al.*, 2003, 2005; Cohen *et al.*, 2008). These stress-related processes are mediated by and feedback to the brain, impacting its abilities to regulate peripheral functios, to engage in adaptive social and health behaviors, to experience and control emotions, and to support cognitive functioning. Therefore, according to this proposal, a person who develops, matures, and ages in a low socioeconomic position could become vulnerable to impairments in the functionality of the stress regulatory systems that are important for health and well-being. Such stress-related processes may operate not only at the individual level, but also at the level of families and communities. For example, children who develop in lower SES households, are more likely to live in unfavorable housing conditions in addition to being exposed to toxic substances and excessive noise and temperature variations, and also to be exposed to what have been termed "risky family" dynamics, characterized by conflict-laden relationships, aggressive and harsh parenting, and other forms of early life stress which may alter risk trajectories for poor health in later life (Repetti *et al.*, 2002). Individuals living in low SES neighborhoods may be more frequently exposed to stressful life events in association with higher concerns over community crime, pollution, and crowding, as well as unstable, effortful, and unrewarding employment opportunities related to persistent economic hardship (Dohrenwend, 1973; McLeod and Kessler, 1990; McEwen and Gianaros, 2010).

Adversity, including interpersonal conflicts, social instability, and other stressful experiences, can accelerate pathological processes through the stress systems, increasing vulnerability for higher morbidity and mortality rates at a population level. Therefore, the physiological responses of the autonomic nervous system, HPA axis, cardiovascular, metabolic and immune systems that have evolved to protect and adapt the organism to challenges, whether excessive may become detrimental to health. However, the process referred to as allostasis (Sterling and Eyer, 1988), which is essential for survival, and adaptation to adversity create allostatic load, defined as the wear-and-tear imposed to the body by the daily life events. When excessive, the allostatic overload resulting from chronic dysregulation (i.e., over-activity or inactivity) of the physiological systems that are normally involved in adaptation to environmental challenge may trigger diseases to which the individual has some genetic predisposition (McEwen and Stellar, 2003; McEwen and Gianaros, 2010).

4. Low SES and the Stress System Function

Theories regarding how SES might affect health through psychological pathways include stress-induced pathophysiology, negative emotional style, and mental illness (Gunnar and Vazquez, 2006). Two organic systems are the major mediators of the peripheral stress response: the autonomic nervous system, mostly the sympathetic division, and the HPA axis. However, the SES focused research has not examined how psychological stimuli or processes associated to SES could be converted into disrupted autonomic function (Seeman *et al.*, 2010).

The effect of stress on the brain function can be demonstrated by using appropriate stimuli designed to activate certain known neural areas (Lynch *et al.*, 1996). By using this method, it was observed that people in low SES positions demonstrated decreased activation in areas commonly associated to the processing of positive affective stimuli, including those regions associated with pleasure, reward, and anticipated satisfaction in comparison with subjects in the higher SES (Gunnar and Vazquez, 2006; Seeman *et al.*, 2010).

The above mentioned cerebral regions show relative down regulation in subjects leaving in low SES compared to those in higher SES. Moreover, the neural activation in the areas implicated in motivation and action differed strongly between SES groups, thus offering additional evidence to implicate stress related to the socioeconomic status as a risk factor for depression and, possibly, other mood disturbances. Alterations in the function of cortical regions associated with the reciprocal modulation of cognition, the heteromodal sensory system, limbic and autonomic systems give the support for those processes (Brindley and Rolland, 1989; Van Oijen *et al.*, 2008; Silverman *et al.*, 2009; Seeman *et al.*, 2010).

Growing evidence also suggest that SES modify brain development and function, beginning at the earliest stages of life and continuing across the entire life. Such influences in the brain development and function impact, and indeed regulate, not only upstream known interconnections between structures such as the prefrontal cortex, hippocampus and amygdala, but also downstream peripheral biology through cortico-limbic-autonomic pathways, and the hypothalamic-pituitary-adrenal (HPA) axis (Palkovits, 1987; McEwen, 2003, 2008; Gunnar and Quevedo, 2007; Seeman *et al.*, 2010). .

There is evidence linking SES to differences not only in such downstream HPA and sympathetic nervous system (SNS) activity (*e.g.*, circulating levels of cortisol, norepinephrine, and epinephrine) but also in their target systems, reflecting in altered cardiovascular, metabolic, and inflammatory parameters (Seeman *et al.*, 2010). The negative consequences for health of high blood pressure (particularly systolic blood pressure) have been recognized for decades, including higher death rates, the onset of cardiovascular diseases, and the loss of both physical and cognitive functioning (Kaplan and Keil, 1993; Seeman *et al.*., 1994; Tzourio, 1999). Several studies have also found that high resting heart rate is associated with increased risk of mortality (Zhang and Zhang, 2009). Metabolic parameters, including higher serum total and LDL cholesterol, lower HDL cholesterol, and higher relative weight, are also recognized risk factors for poor health outcomes including mortality, cardiovascular diseases, and functioning loss (Benfante and Brody 1985; Lynch *et al.*., 1996; Khaw *et al.*., 2001). Elevated glucose levels (as indexed by fasting glucose or more integrated assessments of glucose metabolism such as glycosylated hemoglobin) have also been related to risk for heart disease, to higher mortality, and to poorer cognitive and physical function (Reaven, 1988; Craft *et al.*, 1993; Seeman *et al.*, 1994; Fried *et al.*, 1998). It is important to note that even modest elevations in these biomarkers are associated with adverse outcomes, even when they do not meet accepted thresholds for clinical intervention (Park *et al.*, 1996; Van Oijen *et al.*, 2008). Dysregulations in HPA axis activity, particularly chronically elevated cortisol, have been related to increased risks for a range of health problems, including obesity, hypertension, type 2 diabetes mellitus, lipid imbalance, atherosclerosis, accelerated brain aging, hippocampal atrophy, and cognitive impairment, loss of bone mineral density, sarcopenia, and immune dysfunction (Sapolsky *et al.*, 1986; Landfield, 1987; Brindley and Rolland, 1989; Lupien *et al.*, 1994, 1998; Dhabhar and McEwen, 1997; Lamberts *et al.*, 1997; McEwen *et al.*, 1999; Reynolds *et al.*, 2005). Similarly, more chronic elevations in SNS activity can raise blood pressure and heart rate that promotes atherosclerosis, and appears to be independently associated with cancer mortality (Thomas *et al.*, 2001). Exposure to chronically elevated inflammatory mediators has also been increasingly recognized as a significant health risk with links to increased risks for osteoporosis, cardiovascular diseases and cognitive decline (Tracy *et al.*, 1997; Weaver *et al.*, 2002; Danesh *et al.*, 2004; Yun and Lee, 2004; Ginaldi *et al.*, 2005; Seeman *et al.*, 2010).

These peripheral processes also have feedback loops to the brain so that downstream physiological activity frequently has significant impacts on "brain health" as well. For example, dysregulation of metabolism as in type 2 diabetes mellitus has deleterious effects on the brain (Gold *et al.*, 2007). Elevated HPA and cardiovascular parameters have also been linked to poor cognitive functioning in many studies. Accumulating evidence also indicates that inflammatory processes in the body are associated with reductions in volume of the hippocampus as well as poor sleep quality (Seeman *et al.*, 1997, 2010; Lee *et al.*, 2007; Yaffe, 2007).

5. Biomarkers of Stress

Two biological systems are thought to be central in linking stressor exposure to disease: the sympathetic nervous system (SNS) and the hypothalamic-pituitary adrenocortical (HPA) axis (Cohen *et al.*, 1995). Primary markers of SNS activation, epinephrine and norepinephrine, are increased by stress and may cause 1) suppression of cellular immune function; 2) hemodynamic changes, including increased blood pressure and heart rate; 3) abnormal cardiac rhythms (ventricular arrhythmias) that have been linked to sudden death; and 4) neurochemical imbalances that contribute to the development of psychiatric disorders (Herd, 1978; McCubbin *et al.*, 1980; Anisman and Zacharko, 1992; Rabin, 1999). The variability of cardiac beating rate has been proposed as a marker of the balance between the effect of the sympathetic and the parasympathetic systems on the heart and can be used as a biomarker of stress. However, there are not studies on this parameter focusing SES (Cohen *et al.*, 2006b).

Similarly, elevations or chronically reduced blood levels of the primary marker of HPA activation, cortisol, have been associated with stressful situations such as care giving and work strain (Irwin *et al.*, 1997; Pike *et al.*, 1997; Steptoe *et al.*, 2000). Elevated levels of cortisol have been found to 1) suppress immune function; 2) facilitate central adiposity, a risk factor for coronary heart disease and diabetes; and 3) possibly contribute to major depression (Rabin, 1999; Andrew *et al.*, 2002; Cohen *et al.*, 2006b). Hypocortisolism, however, have been reported in subjects suffering from post traumatic stress disorder (PTSD), autoimmune and inflammatory diseases, such as fibromyalgia and endometriosis, and those with chronic stress (Petrelluzzi *et al.*, 2008).

Several studies have examined the relationship between indices of SES and diurnal cortisol using ambulatory repeated saliva collections. However, the protocols differed in timing, number of cortisol samples, and in cultural context, and were inconsistent addressing the potential confounding effects of race/ethnicity. In the British Whitehall Study, higher SES (as indicated by job grade) was associated with lower cortisol levels in working-days for 45 to 58 year-old men, whereas in women these levels were higher (Steptoe *et al.*, 2003). Increasing SES (defined as education level, and occupational, and employment status) was associated with higher morning cortisol levels in 35 to 65 year-old German men and women (Brandtstädter *et al.*, 1991). In contrast, a study of 17 to 49 year-old men from Dominica

(Decker, 2000), and the Whitehall Study (Steptoe *et al.*, 2003) found no association of SES and morning cortisol. All of these studies failed to find differences in late and end-of-the-day cortisol levels related to SES. In contrast, data from the study on Coronary Artery Risk Development in Young Adults (CARDIA), a multisite study conducted in the United States with 35 to 45 year-old men and women, indicated that lower income and education were associated with higher cortisol levels in the late afternoon and evening (Cohen *et al.*, 2006a). Moreover, elevated levels among those with lower SES could be mostly explained by differences in health practices, primarily smoking but also, to a lesser extent, by social network diversity, depression, perceived social support, and mastery. The CARDIA analysis was based on a large sample (nearly 800 subjects) and controlled for potential effects of race and other spurious factors. However, the median household year income in the CARDIA sample was US$ 77,800, and therefore, the sample represented primarily the higher stratus of the SES scale. On the other hand, the study of Cohen *et al.* (2006a) using a sample with household median year income of US$ 17,500, higher SES was associated with lower levels of salivary cortisol and urinary epinephrine and marginally lower levels of urinary norepinephrine. These associations were independent of race, age, gender, and body mass, and the association with cortisol also occurred relatively equally across time of day. In all cases, the associations were graded, with each increase in SES being associated with a decrease in hormone concentration (Cohen *et al.*, 2006b).

Although both, the CARDIA and the Cohen *et al.* (2006a) studies found elevated cortisol levels with lower SES, the former found that this association occurred only in the late afternoon and evening, whereas the other study demonstrated that the effect was fairly equal across the day. A major difference between these studies is that CARDIA sample had a higher median income. It is possible that rises at different points of the SES gradient influence cortisol levels at different times of the day, possibly due to different activity levels of higher versus lower-income jobs (Adler *et al.*, 1999). Similar results were obtained in a comparison between elementary school children in poverty with a middle class sample (Evans and English, 2002), with the poverty sample showing higher levels of cortisol and epinephrine, without any difference for norepinephrine. That the association with epinephrine is stronger than that with norepinephrine is likely due to norepinephrine being released as a neurotransmitter, as well as an adrenal hormone, and hence providing a noisier measure of its function as a "stress hormone". The associations of SES and higher levels of both of these catecholamines are consistent with the hypothesis that SNS activation plays a role in linking SES to health outcomes. This would be especially relevant for diseases where the SNS has been identified as a modulator of pathophysiology, as is the case, for example, for heart diseases or those where the immune system plays a key role, such as infectious and autoimmune diseases (Cohen *et al.*, 1994, 2006b; Rabin, 1999).

In the above cited studies, there were no correlations between cortisol and catecholamine levels, what suggests that these systems are not closely associated when measured as average response over several weeks. Even though cortisol and the catecholamines are not correlated, the data suggest that both the SNS and HPA are activated among those with lower SES and hence may each contribute separately to the dysregulation of physiological systems and consequently to disease risk.

Although all the above cited studies pointed out for stress and high blood levels of cortisol and catecholamines as the main factors linking low SES and poor health, a cross sectional study using data from the 2000 Social and Environmental Biomarkers of Aging

Study (SEBAS) do not support the hypothesis that chronic stress, via sustained activation of stress related autonomic and neuroendocrine responses, is an important mediator in the relation between SES and health outcomes. Most notably, this study, that used a representative sample of 972 men and women aged 54 and older, failed to show an association of lower SES to higher basal levels of cortisol (Dowd and Goldman, 2006). High levels of basal salivary cortisol and perceived stress index were also described by Garcia *et al.* (2008) in Brazilian men living in low SES compared to those of high SES. The awakening cortisol response or cortisol diurnal rhythm were not altered.

An analysis of 200 participants in the Whitehall study showed that resting blood pressure, heart rate, and salivary cortisol did not differ by employment grade, while average cortisol over the workday was significantly higher for lower grade men but significantly lower for lower grade women (Steptoe *et al.*, 2003). On the other hand, a study of 767 adults in Germany found positive associations between morning salivary cortisol concentrations and levels of education and occupational status (Brandtstädter *et al.*, 1991), while a study of 150 men from Lithuania and Sweden found that low social class was related to high early morning levels of salivary cortisol (Kristenson *et al.*, 2001). In a sample of 217 Canadian children, those of low SES were found to have significantly higher morning salivary cortisol levels than children with high SES (Lupien *et al.*, 2000; Dowd and Goldman, 2006).

These conflicting results could be explained by the specially selected samples, as well as the fact that there is high intraindividual variation in cortisol measured throughout the day, resulting from variation in activity and exposure to stimuli. The variability across studies may also represent actual variations across populations, which have been found for other biomarkers. Associations between SES and cardiovascular parameters may be confounded by other risk factors including poor nutrition, inactivity, and smoking, which are known to increase cardiovascular risk (Seplaki *et al.*, 2004; Dowd and Goldman, 2006).

Moreover, the association between low SES and altered cortisol may vary throughout life. In order to measure whether the development of the relationship between SES and mental health is sustained by exposure to high levels of glucocorticoids, morning salivary cortisol levels as well as cognitive function (memory, attention, and language) were measured in 307 children (from 6 to 16 years of age) from low versus high SES in the Montreal area in Canada. Significantly higher salivary cortisol levels were detected in low SES children from 6 to 10 years old when compared to children from high SES. This difference disappeared at the time of school transition, and no SES differences were observed in salivary cortisol levels during high school. However, children from low and high SES do not differ with regard to memory or to attentional and linguistic skills. Also, mothers of low SES children reported higher feelings of depression and more unhealthy behaviors, while mothers of high SES children reported higher stress related to work or family transitions. Altogether, these results show that low SES in young children is related to increased cortisol secretion, although the impact of SES on cortisol secretion is absent after transition to high school (Lupien *et al.*., 2001).

The situation is even worse when low SES is associated with additional burden. Bella *et al.* (2011) evaluated the level of salivary cortisol and perceived burden, stress and health of low SES mothers and primary caregivers of children (4-11 years of age) with cerebral palsy and those of mothers of children with no developmental problems. Data have shown that mothers of healthy children leaving in unfavorable socioeconomic conditions face high levels of perceived stress with no detected alteration in the HPA axis function. However, to the mothers of children with cerebral palsy, who live in even worse socioeconomic conditions and also have the burden of caring for a disabled child, the level of stress was overwhelming, to an extent that it impaired the HPA axis function, as well as reflecting negatively on certain aspects of their physical and psychological well-being.

6. Early Life Low SES and Future Health Outcomes

Mounting evidence suggests that early-life SES is a determinant of susceptibility to the chronic diseases of adulthood. To the extent that children spend the first years of their lives in unfavorable socioeconomic conditions, they show increased vulnerability to infectious, respiratory, and cardiovascular diseases in adulthood, as well as some forms of cancer (Cohen *et al.*, 2004; Galobardes *et al.*, 2004, 2006). These disparities are generally independent of SES in adulthood. For example, the Precursors Study followed 1,131 graduates of Johns Hopkins Medical School over 40 years and found that even among this highly educated, affluent cohort of physicians, low early-life SES conferred a 2.4-fold risk of incident coronary heart disease by age of 50 years-old (Kittleson *et al.*, 2006). These findings raise the possibility that a child's SES modulate his or her biology in a fashion that persists across multiple decades and eventually heightens susceptibility to the chronic diseases of adulthood throughout the biological programming of early social experience (Hertzman, 1999; Meaney and Szyf, 2005; Gluckman *et al.*, 2008). Indeed, it has been demonstrated that animals that received inadequate parental nurturance or experienced prolonged maternal separations showed permanent alterations in stress-related outflow of the autonomic nervous system and the HPA axis (Gunnar and Vazquez, 2001; Newport *et al.*, 2002; Levine, 2005). These effects were partially mediated by down-regulation of the glucocorticoid receptor (GR), a ligand activated transcription factor that regulates HPA outflow through a negative-feedback circuit (Szyf *et al.*, 2005). The effects of early social adversity also extend to the immune system, since adult mice that were repeatedly separated from their mothers early in life show an excessive inflammatory response and reduced viral clearance after influenza infection, an effect that is partially mediated by impaired glucocorticoid regulation of cytokine release. Collectively, these data suggest that repeated social adversity in early life can program a ''defensive'' phenotype, which is marked by exaggerated adrenocortical and inflammatory responses to challenge (Avitsur *et al.*, 2006; Zhang *et al.*, 2006; Coe and Lubach, 2007). Some evidence indicates that this phenotype involves the development of a functional resistance to GR-mediated signaling, which allows cortisol to partially escape inhibition by negative feedback and facilitates the synthesis of pro-inflammatory mediators by leukocytes. In social contexts where threats like crowding, predation, and conflict are common, these response patterns might confer a survival advantage by helping organisms to rapidly mobilize energy for fighting and fleeing and to display vigorous immune responses to infection and injury (Zhang *et al.*, 2006). However, in the context of late-life chronic illnesses, dysregulated GR signaling may enable exaggerated inflammatory responses that contribute, for example, to the pathogenesis of cardiovascular disease, some types of cancer, and respiratory conditions. If this process occurred in the hippocampal centers that regulate HPA outflow, it might enable cortisol to partially escape negative feedback inhibition, and lead to the relative increase in diurnal cortisol output seen in subjects exposed to low SES in early-life (Miller *et al.*, 2009).

Future work would benefit from looking in more detail at the relation between SES and both extremes of the distribution of neuroendocrine markers which will be useful for to direct the physiopathology studies of the people in low SES.

CONCLUSION

Many studies support data that increasing SES is associated with decreasing stress, as expressed by the levels of two of the stress hormones, cortisol and adrenaline. They also provide plausibility for the argument that at least some of the SES associations with disease may be mediated by differential levels of stress hormones. Overall, the data provide strong evidence for decreasing concentrations of stress hormones with increasing levels of SES, at least for young adults at the bottom third to half of the SES gradient. However, some authors have reported no association between SES and the levels of the stress hormones. Therefore, this issue is still a matter of investigation. On the other hand, the socioeconomic status (SES), whether measured in terms of income, education, or occupation, has been found to be negatively associated with rates of mortality and morbidity from almost every disease condition. These relationships exist across countries with different levels of state sponsored health care, suggesting that access to care is not the underlying causal mechanism. Alternatively, persons of lower SES are embedded within environments characterized by high levels of psychosocial disruption that increase the risk for disease by continuously provoking stress-elicited dysregulation of key behavioral and biological systems. Therefore, public policies that contribute to improve SES and to give some social support to those living in low socioeconomic conditions have a positive impact on these people health.

REFERENCES

Adler NE, Boyce WT, Chesney MA, Folkman S, Syme SL. Socioeconomic inequalities in health. No easy solution. *JAMA.* 1993. 269:3140–3145.

Adler NE, Marmot MM, Mcewen BS, Stewart J. *Socioeconomic Status and Health in Industrial Nations: Social, Psychological, and Biological Pathways.* New York, NY: New York Academy of Sciences. 1999. 3–15.

Adler Ne, Epel ES, Castellazzo G, Ickovics JR. Relationship of subjective and objective social status with psychological and physiological functioning: preliminary data in healthy white women. *Health Psychol.* 2000. 19:586–592.

Andrew R, Gale CR, Waler BR, Secki JR, Martyn CN. Glucocorticoid metabolism and the metabolic syndrome: association in an elderly cohort. *Exp Clin Endocrinol Diabetes.* 2002. 110:284 –90.

Anisman H and Zacharko RM. Depression as a consequence of inadequate neurochemical adaptation in response to stressors. *Br J Psychiatry.* 1992. 160:36–43.

Avitsur R, Hunzeker J, Sheridan JF. Role of early stress in the individual differences in host response to viral infection. *Brain Behav Immun.* 2006. 20:339–348.

Benfante RDR and Brody J. Biological and social predictors of health in an aging cohort. *J Chronic Dis.*1985. 38: 385–395.

Bella GP, Garcia MC, Spadari-Bratfisch RC. Salivary cortisol, stress, and health in primary caregivers (mothers) of children with cerebral palsy. *Psychoneuroendocrinology.* 2011. 36(6):834-42.

Brandtstadter J, Baltes-Go¨TZ B, Kirschbaum C, Hellhammer D. Developmental and personality correlates of adrenocortical activity as indexed by salivary cortisol: observations in the age range of 35–65 years. *J Psychosom Res.* 1991. 35:173– 85.

Brindley DN AND Rolland Y. Possible connections between stress, diabetes, obesity, hypertension and altered lipoprotein metabolism that may result in atherosclerosis. *Clin. Sci. (Lond.).* 1989. 77: 453–461.

Coe Cl AND Lubach GR. In: *Psychoneuroimmunology,* ed Ader R (Elsevier, Boston), 4th Ed. 2007. pp 455–474.

Cohen S, Kaplan JR, Manuck SB. Social support and coronary heart disease: underlying psychological and biological mechanisms. In: Shumaker SA, Czajkowski SM. *Social Support and Cardiovascular Disease: The Plenum Series in Behavioral Psychophysiology and Medicine.* New York, NY: Plenum. 1994.195–221.

Cohen S, Kessler RC, Underwood Gordon L. Strategies for measuring stress in studies of psychiatric and physical disorders. In: Cohen S, Kessler RC, Underwood Gordon L, eds. *Measuring Stress: A Guide for Health and Social Scientists.* New York, NY: Oxford Press; 1995. 3–26.

Cohen S, Doyle WJ, Turner RB, Alper CM, Skoner DP Childhood socioeconomic status and host resistance to infectious illness in adulthood. *Psychosom Med.* 2004. 66:553–558.

Cohen S, Schwartz JE, Epel E, Kirschbaum C, Sidney S, Seeman T. Socioeconomic status, race and diurnal cortisol decline in the Coronary Artery Risk Development in Young Adults (CARDIA) Study. *Psychosom Med.* 2006a. 68:41–50.

Cohen S, Doyle WJ, BAUM A. Socioeconomic Status Is Associated With Stress Hormones. *Psychosomatic Medicine.* 2006b. 68:414–420.

Cohen S, Janicki-Deverts D, Miller GE. Psychological stress and disease. JAMA. 2007. 298:1685–1687.

Cohen S, Alper CM, Doyle WJ, Adler N, Treanor JJ, Turner RB. Objective and subjective socioeconomic status and susceptibility to the common cold. *Health Psychol.* 2008. 27:268–274.

Craft S, Dagogo-Jack SE, Wiethop BV, Murphy C, Nevins RT, Fleischman S, RICE V, Newcomer JW, Cryer PE. Effects of hyperglycemia on memory and hormone levels in dementia of the Alzheimer type: a longitudinal study. *Behav. Neurosci.* 1993. 107: 926–940.

Danesh J, Wheeler JG, Hirschfield GM, Eda S, Eiriksdottir G, RUMLEY A, Lowe GD, Pepys MB, Gudnason V. C-reactive protein and other circulating markers of inflammation in the prediction of coronary heart disease. *N. Engl. J. Med.* 2004. 350: 1387–1397.

Decker S. Salivary cortisol and social status among Dominican men. *Horm Behav.* 2000. 38:29 –38.

Dhabhar FS AND Mcewen BS. Acute stress enhances while chronic stress suppresses cell-mediated immunity in vivo: a potential role for leukocyte trafficking. *Brain Behav Immunol.* 1997. 11: 286–306.

Dohrenwend BS. Social status and stressful life events. *J. Personal. Soc. Psychol.* 1973. 28:225–235.

Dohrenwend BP. The role of adversity and stress in psychopathology: some evidence and its implications for theory and research. *J. Health Soc. Behav.* 2000. 41:1–19.

Dowd JB, Goldman N. Do biomarkers of stress mediate the relation between socioeconomic status and health? *J Epidemiol Community Health.* 2006. 60:633–639.

Evans GW AND English K. *The environment of poverty: multiple stressor exposure, psychophysiological stress, and socioemotional adjustment. Child Dev.* 2002. 73:1238–48.

Fried LP, Kronmal RA, Newman AB, Bild DE, Mittelmark MB, POLAK JF, Robbins JA, Gardin JM. Risk factors for 5-year mortality in older adults: the Cardiovascular Health Study. *JAMA.* 1998. 279: 585–592.

Galobardes B, Lynch JW, Davey Smith G. Childhood socioeconomic circumstances and cause-specific mortality in adulthood: Systematic review and interpretation. *Epidemiol Rev.* 2004. 26:7–21.

Galobardes B, Smith GD, Lynch JW. Systematic review of the influence of childhood socioeconomic circumstances on risk for cardiovascular disease in adulthood. *Ann Epidemiol.* 2006. 16:91–104.

Garcia MC, DE Souza A, Bella GP, Grassi-Kassisse DM, Tacla AP, Spadari-Bratfisch RC. Salivary cortisol levels in Brazilian citizens of distinct socioeconomic and cultural levels. *Ann N Y Acad Sci.* 2008. 1148:504-8.

Ginaldi L, Benedetto MCDI, Demartinis M. *Osteoporosis, inflammation and ageing. Immun. Ageing.* 2005. 2: 14.

Gluckman PD, Hanson MA, Cooper C, Thornburg KL. Effect of in utero and early-life conditions on adult health and disease. *N Engl J Med.* 2008. 359:61–73.

Gold SM, Dziobek I, Sweat V, Tirsi A, Rogers K, Bruehl H, Tsui W, Richardson S, Javier E, Convit A. Hippocampal damage and memory impairments as possible early brain complications of type 2 diabetes. *Diabetologia* 2007. 50: 711– 719.

Gunnar MR AND Vazquez DM. Low cortisol and a flattening of expected daytime rhythm: Potential indices of risk inhumandevelopment. *Dev Psychopathol.* 2001. 13:515–538.

Gunnar M AND Vazquez D. Stress neurobiology and developmental psychopathology. In *Developmental Psychopathology: Developmental Neuroscience.* Cicchetti D and Cohen D. Ed. Wiley. New York. 2006. 533–577.

Gunnar M and Quevedo K. The neurobiology of stress and development. *Annu. Rev. Psychol.* 2007. 58: 145–173.

Herd JA. Physiological correlates of coronary-prone behavior. In: Dembroski TM, Weiss SM, Shields JL, Haynes SG, Frankels M, eds. *Coronary-Prone Behavior.* New York. NY: Springer-Verlag. 1978. 129 –36.

Hertzman C. The biological embedding of early experience and its effects on health in adulthood. *Ann NY Acad Sci.* 1999. 896:85–95.

Irwin M, Hauger R, Patterson TL, Semple S, Ziegler M, Grant I. Alzheimer caregiver stress: basal natural killer cell activity, pituitary-adrenal cortical function, and sympathetic tone. *Ann Behav Med.* 1997. 19:83–90.

Kaplan GA and Keil JE. Socioeconomic factors and cardiovascular disease: a review of the literature. *Circulation.* 1993. 88: 1973–1998.

Kelly S, Hertzman C, Daniels M. Searching for the biological pathways between stress and health. *Annu. Rev. Public Health.* 1997.18:437–462.

Kessler RC, Mcgonagle KA, Zhao S, Nelson CB, Hughes M, Eshleman S, Wittchen HU, Kendler KS. Lifetime and 12-month prevalence of DSM-III-R psychiatric disorders in the United States. Results from the National Comorbidity Survey. *Archives of General Psychiatry.* 1994. 51: 8–19.

Khaw KT, Wareham N, Luben R, Bingham S, Oakes S, Welch A, Day N. Glycated haemoglobin, diabetes, and mortality in men in Norfolk cohort of European prospective investigation of cancer and nutrition (EPIC-Norfolk). *BMJ.* 2001. 322: 15–18.

Kittleson MM, Meoni LA, Wang NY, Chu AY, Ford DE, Klag MJ. Association of childhood socioeconomic status with subsequent coronary heart disease in physicians. *Arch Intern Med.* 2006. 166:2356–2361.

Knudsen EI, Heckman JJ, Cameron JL, Shonkoff JP. Economic, neurobiological, and behavioral perspectives on building America's future workforce. *Proc. Natl. Acad. Sci.* 2006. 103:10155–10162.

Kristenson M, Kucinskiene Z, Bergdahl B, Orth-Gomér K. Risk factors for coronary heart disease in different socioeconomic groups of Lithuania and Sweden—the LiVicordia study. *Scand J Public Health.* 2001. 29:140–50.

Lamberts SW, Van Den Beld AW, Van Der Lely AJ. *The endocrinology of aging. Science.* 1997. 278: 419–424.

Landfield P.W. Modulation of brain aging correlates by long-term alterations of adrenal steroids and neurally-active peptides. 1987. *Prog. Brain Res.* 72: 279–300.

Lazarus RS AND Folkman, S. *Stress, Appraisal and Coping.* Guilford. New York: 1984.

Lee BK, Glass TA, Mcatee MJ, Wand GS, Bandeen-Roche K, BOILA KI, Schwartz BS. Associations of salivary cortisol with cognitive function in the Baltimorememory study. *Arch. Gen. Psychiatry.* 2007. 64: 810–818.

Levine S. Developmental determinants of sensitivity and resistance to stress. *Psychoneuroendocrinology.* 2005. 30:939–946.

Lorant V, Deliège D, Eaton W, Robert A, Philippot P, Ansseau M. Socioeconomic inequalities in depression: a meta-analysis. *Am. J. Epidemiol.* 2003. 157:98–112.

Lovallo WR. Stress and Health: *Biological and Psycholocial Interactions.* Sage; Thousand Oaks, CA. 2005.

Lupien S, Lecours AR, Lussier I, Schwartz G, Nair NP, MEANEY MJ. Basal cortisol levels and cognitive deficits in human aging. *J. Neurosci.* 1994. 14: 2893–2903.

Lupien SJ, DE Leon M, DE Santi S, Convit A, Tarshish C, Nair NP, Thakur M, Mcewen BS, Hauger RL, Meaney MJ. Cortisol levels during humanaging predict hippocampal atrophy and memory deficits. *Nat. Neurosci.* 1998.1: 69–73.

Lupien SJ, King S, Meaney SJ, Mcewen BS. Child's stress hormone levels correlate with mother's socioeconomic status and depressive state. *Biological Psychiatry.* 2000. 48 (10): 976-980.

Lupien SJ, King S, Meaney MJ, Mcewen BS. Can poverty get under your skin? basal cortisol levels and cognitive function in children from low and high socioeconomic status. *Dev Psychopathol.* 2001. 13(3):653-76.

Lynch JW, Kaplan GA, Cohen RD, Tuomilehto J, Salonen JT. Do cardiovascular risk factors explain the relation between socioeconomic status, risk of all-cause mortality, cardiovascular mortality, and acute myocardial infarction? *Am. J. Epidemiol.* 1996. 144: 934–942.

Marmot M. T*he Status Syndrome: How Social Standing Affects our Health And Longevity*. Henry Holt and Company. New York. 2004.

Mccubbin JA, Richardson J, Obrist PA, Kizer JS, Langer AW. *Catecholaminergic and hemodynamic responses to behavioral stress in young adult males.* Paper presented at the twentieth annual meeting of the Society for Psychophysiological Research. 1980.

Mcewen BS, Weiss J, Schwartz L. Selective retention of corticosterone by limbic structures in rat brain. *Nature.* 1968. 220:911–912.

Mcewen BS AND Stellar E. Stress and the individual. Mechanisms leading to disease. *Arch. Intern. Med.* 1993. 153:2093–2101.

Mcewen BS, DE Leon MJ, Lupien SJ, Meaney MJ. Corticosteroids, the Aging Brain and Cognition. *Trends Endocrinol.Metab.* 1999. 10: 92– 96.

Mcewen BS. Early life influences on life-long patterns of behavior and health. *Ment. Retard.Dev.Disabil.Res. Rev*. 2003. 9: 149–154.

Mcewen BS. Protective and damaging effects of stress mediators: central role of the brain. *Dial. Clin. Neurosci. Stress*. 2006. 8:367–381.

Mcewen BS. Physiology and neurobiology of stress and adaptation: central role of the brain. *Physiol. Rev.* 2007. 87:873–904.

Mcewen BS. Central effects of stress hormones in health and disease:Understanding the protective and damaging effects of stress and stress mediators. *Eur. J. Pharmacol.* 2008. 583: 174–185.

Mcewen BS AND Gianaros PJ. Central role of the brain in stress and adaptation: Links to socioeconomic status, health, and disease. *Ann N Y Acad Sci.* 2010. 1186: 190–222.

Mcleod JD AND Kessler RC. Socioeconomic status differences in vulnerability to undesirable life events. *J. Health Soc. Behav.* 1990. 31:162–172.

Meaney MJ AND Szyf M. Environmental programming of stress responses through DNA methylation: Life at the interface between a dynamic environment and a fixed genome. *Dial Clin Neurosci.* 2005. 7:103–123.

Miller GE, CHEN E, Fok AK, Walker H, Lim A, Nicholls EF, Cole S, Kobor MS. Low early-life social class leaves a biological residue manifested by decreased glucocorticoid and increased proinflammatory signaling. *PNAS*. 2009. 25 (106): 3414716–14721.

Newport DJ, Stowe ZN, Nemeroff CB. Parental depression: Animal models of na adverse life event. *Am J Psychiatry.* 2002. 159:1265–1283.

Palkovits M. Organization of the stress response at the anatomical level. In *Progress in Brain Research.* De Kloet ER, Wiegant VM., Wied D. Ed. *Elsevier Sci. Amsterdam.* 1987. 47–55.

Park S, Barrett-Connor E, Wingard DL, Shan J, Edelstein S. GHb is a better predictor of cardiovascular disease than fasting or postchallenge plasma glucose in women without diabetes. Rancho Bernardo Study. *Diabetes Care.* 1996. 19: 450–456.

Petrelluzzi KF, Garcia MC, Petta CA, Grassi-Kassisse DM, Spadari-Bratfisch RC. Salivary cortisol concentrations, stress and quality of life in women with endometriosis and chronic pelvic pain. *Stress.* 2008. 11(5):390-**7.**

Pike JL, Smith TL, Hauger RL, Nicassio PM, Patterson TL, Mcclintick J, Costlow C, Irwin MR. Chronic life stress alters sympathetic, neuroendocrine, and immune responsivity to an acute psychological stressor in humans. *Psychosom Med.* 1997. 59:447–57.

Rabin BS. Stress, *Immune Function, and Health: The Connection.* New York, NY: Wiley-Liss; 1999.

Reaven GM. Banting lecture 1988. Role of insulin resistance in human disease. *Diabetes.* 1988. 37: 1595–1607.

Repetti R, Taylor S, Seeman T. Risky families: family social environments and the mental and physical health of offspring. *Psychol. Bull.* 2002. 128:330–366.

Reynolds RM, Dennison EM, Walker BR, Syddall HE, Wood PJ, ANDREW R, Phillips DI, Cooper C. Cortisol secretion and rate of bone loss in a population-based cohort of elderly men and women. *Calcif. Tissue Int.* 2005. 77: 134–138.

Sapolsky RM, Krey LC, McEwen BS. The neuroendocrinology of stress and aging: the glucocorticoid cascade hypothesis. *Endocr. Rev.*1986. 7: 284–301.

Sapolsky R. Social status and health in humans and other animals. *Annu. Rev. Anthropol.* 2004. 33:393–418.

Seeman TE, Charpentier PA, Berkman LF, Tinetti ME, Guralnik JM, Albert M, Blazer D, Rowe JW. Predicting changes in physical performance in a high-functioning elderly cohort: MacArthur studies of successful aging. *J Gerontol.* 1994. 49(3):M97-108.

Seeman TE, mcEwen BS, Singer BH, Albert MS, Rowe JW. Increase in urinary cortisol excretion and memory declines: MacArthur studies of successful aging. *J. Clin. Endocrinol. Metab.* 1997. 82: 2458–2465.

Seeman T, Epel E, Gruenewald T, Karlamangla A, McEwen BS. Socio-economic differentials in peripheral biology: Cumulative allostatic load Ann. N.Y. *Acad. Sci.* 2010. 1186: 223–239.

Seplaki CL, Goldman N, Weinstein M, Lin YH. How are biomarkers related to physical and mental well-being? *J Gerontol A Biol Sci.* 2004. 59:201–17.

Shonkoff JP. A promising opportunity for developmental and behavioral pediatrics at the interface of neuroscience, psychology, and social policy. *Award Pediatrics.* 2006. 118:2187–2191.

Silverman ME, Muennig P, Liu X, Rosen Z, Goldstein MA. The Impact of Socioeconomic Status on the Neural Substrates Associated with Pleasure. *The Open Neuroimaging Journal.* 2009. 3: 58-63.

Singh-Manoux A, Adler NE, Marmot MG. Subjective social status: its determinants and its association with measures of ill-health in the Whitehall II study. *Soc. Sci. Med.* 2003. 56:1321–1333.

Steptoe A, Cropley M, Griffith J, Kirschbaum C. Job strain and anger expression predict early morning elevations in salivary cortisol. *Psychosom Med.* 2000. 62:286 –92.

Steptoe A, Kunz-Ebrecht S, Owen N, Feldman PJ, Willemsen G, Kirschbaum C, Marmot M. Socioeconomic status and stress-related biological responses over the working day. *Psychosom Med.* 2003. 65:461–70.

Sterling P AND Eyer J. Allostasis: a new paradigm to explain arousal pathology. In: Fisher, S.; Reason, J., editors. *Handbook of Life Stress, Cognition and Health.* John Wiley and Sons; New York. 1988. p. 629-649.

Szyf M, Weaver IC, Champagne FA, Diorio J, Meaney MJ. Maternal programming of steroid receptor expression and phenotype through DNA methylation in the rat. *Front Neuroendocrinol.* 2005. 26:139–162.

Thomas F, Guize L, Bean K, Benetos A. Pulse pressure and heart rate: independent risk factors for cancer? *J. Clin. Epidemiol.* 2001. 4: 735–740.

Tracy RP, Lemaitre RN, Psaty BM, Ives DG, Evans RW, Cushman M, Meilahn EN, Kuller LH. Relationship of C-reactive protein to risk of cardiovascular disease in the elderly. Results from the Cardiovascular Health Study and the Rural Health Promotion Project. *Arterioscler. Thromb. Vasc. Biol.* 1997. 17: 1121–1127.

Tzourio C, Dufouil C, Ducimetière P, Alpérovitch A. Cognitive decline in individuals with high blood pressure: a longitudinal study in the elderly. EVA Study Group. *Epidemiol. Vascular Aging. Neurology.* 1999. 53: 1948–1952.

Van Oijen M, Okereke OI, Kang JH, Pollak MN, Hu FB, Hankinson SE, Grodstein F. Fasting insulin levels and cognitive decline in older women without diabetes. *Neuroepidemiology*. 2008. 30: 174–179.

Weaver JD, Huang MH, Albert M, Harris T, Rowe JW, Seeman TE. Interleukin-6 and risk of cognitive decline: MacArthur studies of successful aging. *Neurology.* 2002. 59: 371–378.

Yaffe K. Metabolic syndrome and cognitive disorders: is the sum greater than its parts? *Alzheimer Dis. Assoc. Disord.* 2007. 21: 167–171.

Yun AJ AND Lee PY. Maldaptation of the link between inflammation and bone turnover may be a key determinant of osteoporosis. *Med. Hypotheses* 2004.63: 532–537.

Zhang TY, Bagot R, Parent C, Nesbitt C, Bredy TW, Caldji C, Fish E, Anisman H, Szyf M, Meaney MJ. Maternal programming of defensive responses through sustained effects on gene expression. *Biol Psychol.* 2006. 73:72–89.

Zhang GQ AND ZHaNG W. Heart rate, lifespan, and mortality risk. *Ageing Res Rev.* 2009. 8: 52–60.

In: Socioeconomic Status and Health Implications
Editor: Sarah Reibert and Alice Jannings, pp. 127-143
ISBN: 978-1-62100-675-6

Chapter 6

SOCIOECONOMIC STATUS AND INDIVIDUAL ADJUSTMENT IN EARLY ADOLESCENCE[11]

Massimo Santinello and Alessio Vieno*
University of Padova, Italy.

ABSTRACT

Socioeconomic status (SES) has been shown to play an important role in socialization. In the present study three indicators of socioeconomic status were examined in terms of their relations with each other and three areas of social adjustment. The three measures of SES were: father occupation, Family Affluence Scale, and a single question regarding the individual's subjective evaluation of the family's SES. The social adjustment measures included school adjustment, parental support, psychosocial well-being, and two related behaviors health habits (physical activity, and dietary habits). The sample was composed of 3,168 Italian middle school students (47.3% girls). Bivariate correlations among the three measures of SES were weak, and only one of those measures (the subjective evaluation) was consistently correlated with adjustment. Using Structural Equation Models, however, showed that the different measures of SES could be used to create a latent construct of SES, which demonstrated a reliable relation with four of the five social adjustment constructs (school adjustment, parental support, and two health habits). Our results suggest that, in the study of social inequalities during adolescence, we need to consider indicators that could have a strong effect during the rest of the life. Moreover, comparing different type of analysis, the study offered a rationale for use SES in terms of a latent construct.

Keywords: Early Adolescence, SES, Individual Adjustment, SEM.

---

[11] The HBSC study in Veneto is funded by Regione Veneto (D.G.R. n° 203 of April, 4, 2000). HBSC is a cross-national study co-ordinated from the European Office of WHO. International co-ordinator for the 1997/99 study: Candace Currie, University of Edinburg; Data Bank Manager: Bente Wold, University of Bergen; National co-ordinator: Franco Cavallo, University of Torino.

* Address correspondence to: Alessio Vieno. Department of Developmental and Social Psychology, Via Belzoni 80, 35131 Padova, Tel. ++39 049 8278479; Fax. ++39 0498278451. E-mail: alessio.vieno@unipd.it; Socioeconomic Status and Individual Adjustment in Early Adolescence.

INTRODUCTION

The development of health promotion programs needs valid information on the determinants and covariates of physical and psychological health and well being. Such information can lead to a systematic match between prevention efforts and the natural sequencing of mechanisms related to exacerbation of, or protection against, maladjustment. Past research has underlined the importance of social contextual variables such as socioeconomic status (SES) for understanding individual adjustment. Many demographic, medical and epidemiological studies have highlighted how general health (including physical, emotional and social well-being) is correlated to socioeconomic factors (Blane, 1996; Cohen *et al.*, 1999; Conger *et al.*, 1999; Currie *et al.*, 1997). Other research has shown that adolescents who come from a high socioeconomic background reach the highest levels of education (Erikson and Jonsson, 1996), receive more support from the parents (Conger *et al.*, 1999), and exhibit less problem behavior such as smoking and unhealthy life styles (Argyle, 1994). However, because of limitation linked to measurement strategies (Dutton and Levine, 1989), to the disagreement about the definition of SES (Rose *et al.*, 2001), and to methodological approach (Adler *et al.*, 1994), we still have an incomplete understanding of the relation between SES and individual adjustment, in particular during adolescence.

For example, SES has been frequently treated as a control variable and has not been systematically studied as an important etiologic factor in its own right. On the other hand, of those studies that have examined the health effects of SES, most have compared the health of individuals at the very bottom of the SES hierarchy either with those above the poverty level or with those at the top of the hierarchy (see Adler et al., 1994).

DIFFERENT APPROACHES TO MEASURING SES

Although the concept of SES is central to the social sciences, theorists have not agreed on definition. As a result, researchers have rarely relied on explicit theory to operationalize the construct (Rose *et al.*, 2001). SES measurement relies almost entirely on data from occupational position, education, and/or income (Oakes and Rossi, 2003). Stemming from a 1949 community study, Hollingshead's measurement effort evolved into a three-factor scale for use in mental health epidemiological studies. The scale was subsequently modified (Hollingshead, 1975) for more general use and became the widely known two-factor Index of Social Prestige, which is based upon occupation and education. This scale has been severely criticized on methodological grounds, for its lack of validity and practicality. Hauser and Warren (1997) argue that the relative rank of particular professions seemed to be a "combination of his rating of specific individuals in New Haven and of his perception of the general social standing of occupations" (p. 197). Moreover, Haug (1977) characterizes Hollingshead's classification of occupations as both outdated and incomplete because only occupations reported by his New Haven sample were included on his occupational ranking lists.

Using youth reports of SES presents unique problems and several approaches have been used. First of all, information supplied by children or adolescents is frequently incomplete or even absent and it does not allow exact definition of their parents' SES. For example, the children are frequently not aware of their parent's profession or income. In the 1986 Scottish HBSC survey over 20% of responses (early adolescents) to these questions could not to be coded to give occupational categories (Currie *et al.,* 1997). To deal with this problem, researchers propose to use more simple measures to which children and adolescents could respond more easily and accurately. For example, whether the family owns their house, whether they own a car or multiple cars, whether a telephone is installed, as well as the characteristics of the area of residence (Currie *et al.,* 1997; Eames, 1993; Goldbatt, 1997; Townsend, 1990; Wardle *et al.*, 2002). Currie and colleagues (1997), compared the number of missing data of occupational indicators (22%) and non-occupational indicators (1%), and concluded that the non-occupational indicators were easier for children and adolescents to answer.

Another approach is based on the individual perception of the "family's financial well-being" (Piko and Fitzpatrick, 2001). The results presented by Piko and Fitzpatrick (2001) show that SES self-perception prove to be better predictor than 'classic' indicators (e.g., parents' education, occupational class, etc.) of adolescent's psychosocial health. For this reason Piko and Fitzpatrick concluded that self perceived SES seems to be a more valid indicator of ones 'true' family position in the social hierarchy.

Because of the lack of studies comparing different measure of SES, in the present study we use multiple indicators of the construct with the aim of evaluating 3 measures of SES according to adolescent self-report. In sum, the aim is not to discard the parental occupation measures but rather to compare a range of measures with children and adolescents as respondents. Specifically we will examine how, when using adolescent informants, non-occupational based measures of SES compare to occupation based measures of SES, in terms of missing data generated, and their association with measures of adolescent well-being and health behavior.

SES and Well-being in Early-Adolescence

A great deal of research indicates that economic hardship has an adverse influence on health status and health behavior during all the life stages (Anderson and Armstead, 1995; Link and Pelan, 1995; Marmot *et al.*, 1997). However, according to West (1997) during adolescence conditions arise in which socioeconomic factors do not have the same influence on mental and physical health that they do in childhood and adulthood. For example, West (1988) found that the relation between social class and death rates and chronic illness differed across different ages. SES affects on mortality rates and chronic illness were present during childhood (age 1-4 and 5-9 years), were virtually absent in early adolescence (age 10-14 years) and "re-emerge" in adulthood. Later, in an extensive literature review, West (1997) suggested that youth (10-19 years of age) might be experiencing a period of "relative SES equality" with respect to their health. He concluded that youth, particularly during their secondary education years, exhibit fewer SES-related health problems than at any other point in the life cycle. The fact that some health problems seem to be un-sensitive to SES was explained by West (1997), and more recently by Chen and colleagues (2002), in terms of a combination of diminishing effects of the family, and neighborhood, together with the increasing effects of school, peer group and youth culture. West (1997) and Chen and colleagues (2002) consider this as a general SES equality that should be found across domains of well being and adjustment.

Consistent with this hypothesis, others research has shown a lack of relation between SES and individual health status for a variety of variables such as chronic illness (Hendry *et al.*, 1993), and rates of depression, anxiety and general psychosocial well-being (Currie *et al.*, 1997; Mann *et al.,* 1983). Moreover, several authors have failed to confirm the socioeconomic differences in eating and physical habits among adolescents (Donato *et al.*, 1997; Tuinstra *et al.*, 1998).

There have been several important criticisms of the hypothesis that adolescence is characterized by relative SES equality in health outcomes. For example, Judge and Benzeval (1993) have suggested that this SES equality will be specific to a limited number of domains, and that the lack of significant effects may be attributable to poor measurement, sampling problems, or other methodological issues such as the use of just one measure of SES.

In fact, other variables have been shown to be sensitive to SES during adolescence such as, school achievement (Argyle, 1994; Duncan and Brooks-Gunn, 1997; Erikson and Jonsson, 1996; Koivusilta *et al.*, 2003), and family relations (Barrera *et al.*, 2002; Conger *et al.*, 1999; McLoyd, 1998). These studies have shown that adolescents from wealthy families are likely to reach a higher education level and establish positive and constructive relationships with their parents. Moreover, according to several studies (Koivusilta *et al.*, 1999; Mullan and Currie, 2000), family wealth is associated to health behaviors, such as regular physical exercise and eating well, but also to feelings of happiness and security. Other studies (Garcia *et al.*, 1998) have highlighted that giving up physical exercise is linked to low SES, both because of lack of time and lack of money.

Finally, low SES is often associated with poor psychosocial adjustment and an increased likelihood of depression (McLoyd, 1998). McLeod and Nonnemaker (2000) have found that adolescents belonging to higher socioeconomic levels report higher self-esteem. However, from a very different prospective, Rutter and Smith (1995), in their extensive review of psychosocial problems in young people (age 11-19 years), contrast the lack of a relationship between social class and "psychosocial disorders" in youth with the evidence for such a relationship in the case of physical illness. These results were confirmed in several other prominent studies of adolescents (Bradley and Corwyn, 2001; McLoyd *et al.*, 1994).

The incomplete understanding of the relation between SES and individual adjustment (West, 1997; Chen *et al.*, 2002; Tuinstra *et al.*, 1998; Koivulsita *et al.*, 1999; Piko and Fitzpatrick, 2001) should be explained in two ways. The first is related to the choice of outcomes considered (Goldbatt, 1997; Judge and Benzeval, 1993). Therefore in present study we use multiple indicators of well-being in early adolescence. The second possible explanations is related to the analytic approach (Adler *et al.*, 1994; Eames, 1993). For this reason we use two different approaches to analyze the data: using bivariate correlations and using latent constructs within Structural Equations Models (SEM).

Objectives and Hypotheses

Considering the lack of studies comparing different measures of SES, the first aim of the present study was to examine the correlations among three self-report measures of SES: one based on the occupation of the parents, one related to the affluence of the family, and one to the adolescents' subjective perception of family economic well-being. Because they are indicators of the same construct, we expected these measures to be correlated (Currie *et al.*, 1997).

Because the contrasting findings regarding the effects of SES during adolescence may be related to the choice of outcomes (Judge and Benzeval, 1993), or to the analytic approach used (Adler *et al.*, 1994), in this study we investigate both issues. First, by using different outcomes, and second, by using different analytic approaches. Because SES may function most powerfully in terms of "latent construct" (Adler *et al.*, 1994), we expected that, using latent constructs in the context of SEM, SES would likely show stronger associations with measures of psychosocial adjustment.

A variety of mechanisms linking SES to adolescent well-being have been proposed (see Bradley and Corwyn, 2002), with most involving differences in social resources. In particular, different studies provide substantial support for the path linking low SES to lower competence and maladaptive behavior via harsh or neglectful parenting and compromised parent-child relationships (Conger et al., 1999). For that reason, we expected that, when using SEM, SES would be positively related to family relations. On the other hand, children from poor families have less access to a wide variety of different recreational and learning materials from infancy to adolescence. They are less likely to go on trips, visit library or museum, attend a theatrical performance, or be given lessons directed at enhancing their skills (Bradley and Corwyn, 2002). Therefore, we expect a positive relation between SES and academic achievement.

It is not easy to isolate what process accounts for the SES effects on adolescent psychosocial well-being, because SES frequently co-occurs with other socio-cultural conditions (such as minority or immigrant status, single parenthood, and hazardous environmental condition). In any case, direct biological damage may contribute to SES differences: mental illness or depressive symptoms can result from trauma or exposure to pathogens, both of which are more common among individuals who are low SES. On the other hand, low-SES children are more often the victims of child abuse or harsh or neglectful parenting (Garbarino, 1992). According to the literature (see McLeod and Nonnemaker, 2000) we expected lower SES adolescents to express feelings such as sadness, loneliness, irritability and feeling down more frequently than adolescents with a more favorable economic background.

Among the most oft-cited linkages between SES and well-being is access to resources. According to the model that identifies inadequate dietary intake as a key pathway to poor health (see Bradley and Corwyn, 2002), inadequate diet results in defective nutrient absorption but also in a les healthy diet. With regards to health behavior, we expected family SES to be positively related to their inclination to consume a healthier diet (Garcia *et al.*, 1998).

As children move towards adolescence, their own health-relevant behaviors become conduits for adaptive functioning. Families coming from high-SES background are likely to purchase an array of goods and service that directly benefit healthy development: for example, the possibility of their children to access to physical activities (see Garcia *et al.*, 1998). For this reason, we expected adolescents from wealthier families to spend more time in healthier lifestyles such as engaging in sports.

METHOD

Procedures

This study was carried out in the Veneto region of Italy. The region is composed by 4,540,853 citizens with 351 middle schools serving 120,419 students. The Veneto region is situated in the north east of Italy, and is the wealthiest region in the country: the incidence of families living below the poverty level in this region is 5.7 %, as compared to a national average of 12.3%. The data presented in this study are part of the "Health Behaviour in School-aged Children" (HBSC) project, a transnational study carried out in collaboration with the European office of the World Health Organization (Wold *et al.*, 1993).

Participants

Participants were chosen through the "sample clustering" approach: first, the schools were randomly selected from the Regional School Office's data base (82 from 351), then in each school one class for each age group was selected randomly.

The questionnaire was filled out by a total of 3,168 student, and the average age of the two age groups considered (11 years N = 1,637; 13 years N = 1,531) is 10.93 and 12.99 respectively. The sample is made up of 1,669 boys (52.7%) and 1,499 girls (47.3%).

Measures

Data were collected through a self-report questionnaire, devised in 1997-1998 by the HBSC international group, in which early adolescents' and adolescents' main health behaviors are investigated. Only data related to SES indicators, school adjustment, parental support, psychosocial well-being and some behavioral styles will be analyzed for the present study.

Socioeconomic Status

Three measures of SES were considered. All three measures were recoded to have 4 levels. This was done to be consistent with the international protocol used also by the other research sites and thus facilitating comparability across studies. We also analyzed the data using the original scales and obtained the same pattern of results.

The first measure of SES was the youths' self-report of their father's occupation (OCC, Wold *et al.*, 1993; Currie *et al.*, 1997). Despite the difficulties with parental occupation-based indicators of SES, it is useful as a contributor to an overall assessment of SES, and was therefore included in the study. Participants were asked simply to respond to these questions: "What is your fathers' job?". According to the international protocol, using the occupations provided by the participants the professional categories were sub-divided into four groups (1=low to 4=high) created considering the social prestige associated with them: unskilled manual (1), skilled manual and clerks (2), teacher and self-employed (3), professional and managerial (4). This coding scheme is based on the main occupational classification system used in Italy in the national census.

The second measure was "Family Affluence Scale" (Wardle *et al.*, 2002; WHO, 1998). For this measure, participants were asked to respond to three questions. The first was: "Does your family have a car or a van?". Responses were given on a 3-point scale ranging from "no" (0), "yes, one" (1) and "yes, two or more" (2). The second was: "Do you have your own bedroom for yourself?" ("no"=0 and "yes"=1). The last one was: "During the past year, how many times did you travel away on holiday (vacation) with your family?". Responses were given using a 4-point scale ranging from "not at all" (0) to "more than twice" (4). In accordance with the research protocol FAS was computed summing the three indices and four groups were created (1=low to 4=high): (1) corresponding to 0, 1 and 2; (2) to 3; (3) to 4; (4) to 5.

The third measure of SES assessed the individual's subjective perception of family economic well-being "Family Well Off" (FWO) (Mullan and Currie, 2000). Responses to the question "How well off do you think your family is?" were given on a 4-point ordinal scale (1="not very well-off" to 4="very well off").

School Adjustment

The individual's relationship in the school was measured using two questions, one regarding academic achievement and one regarding school liking (Samdal *et al.*, 2000). The first question was: "In your opinion what do yours teachers think about your school performance compared to your classmates?". Responses were given on a 4-point scale ranging from "below average" (1) to "very good" (4). The second question was: "What do you feel about the school at the present time?". Responses were given on a 4-point scale ranging from "I don't like it at all" (1) to "I like it a lot" (4). The correlation (Spearmans) between these two questions was $r = .39$ ($p < .001$).

Parental Support

Parental support was measured using one question repeated for the mother and the father (King *et al.*, 1996). This question was: "How easy is it for you to talk with your father/mother about things that really bother you?". Responses were given on a 4-point scale ranging from "very difficult" (1) to "very easy" (4). The correlation between the two questions was $r = .46$ ($p < .001$).

Psychosocial Well-being

Four questions were used as a measure of psychosocial well-being (Haugland *et al.*, 2001). One was related to happiness: "In general, how do you feel about your life at present?". The second was related to loneliness (reverse code): "Do you ever feel lonely?". For these two questions responses were given on a four point scale, respectively ranging from "I'm not happy at all" (1) to "I feel very happy" (4), and from "yes, very often" (1) to "no" (4). The third item was related to "feeling low" (reverse code): "In the last six months how often have you felt low?". The final question related to "feeling irritable" (reverse code) was: "In the last six months how often have you felt irritable or in a bad mood?". Responses to the last two questions were given on a 5-point scale ranging from "about every day" (1) to "rarely or never" (5). Cronbachs' alpha for these four items was good ($\alpha = .73$).

Sports Activity

To measure participation in sports activities participants were asked two questions (WHO, 1998). These were: "Outside school hours: how often do you usually exercise in your free time so much that you get out of breath or sweat?" and " Outside school hours: how many hours a week do you usually exercise in your free time so much that you get out of breath or sweat?". For the first question answers were given on a 7-point scale ranging from "never" (1) to "every day" (7) and for the second question on a 6-point scale ranging from "none" (1) to "7 hours or more" (6). The correlation between the two questions was $r = .60$ ($p < .001$).

Diet

As a measure of diet two questions were asked (WHO, 1998). These were: "How often do you eat vegetables?" and "How often do you eat fruits?". Answer were given on a 5-point scale ranging from "never" (1) to "more than once a day" (5). The correlation between these two questions was $r = .35$ ($p < .001$).

Although some of the correlations among scale items are not high (ranging from .35 to .46) we feel justified using of these scales for three reasons. First, the items included in each scale are conceptually related (school liking and school achievement; eating fruits and eating vegetables; communication with mother and communication with the father). Second, by using latent constructs we are able to examine the correlated variance among the items within each scale, and how this is related to the other latent constructs. Moreover, if low reliability were to create problems, the result would be attenuated effects. Thus, the likely consequence will be an underestimate of the relations among latent constructs, rather than an overestimate.

RESULTS

Descriptive Statistics

Descriptive statistics regarding the distributions of the three SES measures, across the two age groups are presented in table 1. The first thing that is shown in table 1 is the very low percentage of participants for whom it is not possible to define the socioeconomic level by considering the three indicators. The indicator that has produced the highest level of missing data regards father occupation. However, the percent of missing data is relatively low (5%) as compared to other studies (Currie *et al.*, 1997) in which about 20% of the sample had missing data.

Observing the distributions of the three measures it can be seen that the OCC measure results in fewer high SES and more low SES participants than the FAS and FWO measures. The more subjective measure (FWO) resulted in the most families with high SES. One possible explanation for this, according to Goodman and colleagues (2000), is the possibility that adolescents seem to overestimate their SES when using subjective measures.

Table 1. Number (%) of early adolescents categorized according to SES indicators by age group

SES indicator	Category	age 11 (%)	age 13 (%)
OCC	I (low)	256 (15.6)	237 (15.5)
	II (low-middle)	625 (38.2)	581 (37.9)
	III (high-middle)	536 (32.7)	513 (33.5)
	IV (high)	146 (8.9)	127 (8.3)
	Unclassifiable/Missing	74 (4.5)	73 (4.8)
FAS	I (low)	199 (12.2)	213 (13.9)
	II (low-middle)	340 (20.8)	377 (24.6)
	III (high-middle)	609 (37.2)	544 (35.5)
	IV (high)	477 (29.1)	384 (25.1)
	Unclassifiable/Missing	12 (0.7)	13 (0.8)
FWO	I (low)	68 (4.2)	81 (5.3)
	II (low-middle)	440 (26.9)	692 (45.2)
	III (high-middle)	589 (36.0)	542 (35.4)
	IV (high)	531 (32.4)	202 (13.2)
	Unclassifiable/Missing	9 (0.5)	14 (0.9)

Table 2. Cross tables between the SES indicators (OCC, FAS and FWO)

		OCC			
		I (%)	II (%)	III (%)	IV (%)
FAS	I	104 (21.2)	177 (14.8)	92 (8.8)	7 (2.6)
	II	125 (25.5)	308 (25.7)	213 (20.4)	35 (12.8)
	III	166 (33.9)	426 (35.6)	412 (39.5)	102 (37.4)
	IV	95 (19.4)	287 (24.0)	327 (31.3)	129 (47.3)
FWO	I	27 (5.5)	45 (3.7)	53 (5.1)	9 (3.3)
	II	200 (40.7)	459 (38.2)	363 (34.8)	51 (18.8)
	III	167 (34.0)	444 (37.0)	375 (36.0)	111 (40.8)
	IV	97 (19.8)	253 (21.1)	251 (24.1)	101 (37.1)
		FAS			
		I (%)	II (%)	III (%)	IV (%)
FWO	I	55 (13.5)	44 (6.1)	41 (3.6)	8 (0.9)
	II	182 (44.6)	323 (45.0)	413 (35.9)	213 (24.8)
	III	110 (27.0)	233 (32.5)	448 (39.0)	334 (38.9)
	IV	61 (15.0)	117 (16.3)	248 (21.6)	303 (35.3)

Table 3. Correlation between indicators of SES and indicators of "well-being"

	OCC	FAS	FWO
School Adjustment			
Academic achievement	.11**	.08**	.07**
Liking school	.09**	.10**	.12**
Parental Support			
Father	.05**	.10**	.18**
Mother	.02	.07**	.16**
Psychosocial well-being			
Feel happy	.03	.09**	.24**
Feel lonely (reverse code)	.02	.09**	.16**
Feel low (reverse code)	.01	.07**	.19**
Feel irritable (reverse code)	.04*	.05*	.17**
Sports activity			
Weekly activity	.07**	.17**	.05**
Hour activity	.08**	.12**	.01
Diet			
Fruit	.05**	.10**	.07**
Vegetable	.09**	.06**	.01

**. p< .01. *. p< .05.

Correlation between Measures of SES

To examine the relationship between the different measures of SES we conducted correlations between the three measures of SES included in the study. The correlations were as follows: FAS and OCC $r = .21$ ($p < .05$), FAS and FWO $r = .26$ ($p < .01$) and OCC and FWO $r = .10$ ($p < .05$). These correlations range from weak to moderate, but do suggest common variance across measures.

To better understand the relation between the three measures of SES we also examine the contingency tables obtained by crossing the three indicators (Tab. 2). Looking at the diagonals, which indicate a correspondence across measures, we can observe that lower levels of agreement are predominant at the lower levels of SES.

SES and Early Adolescents' Well-being

Table 3 shows the correlation coefficients between the three indicators of SES and individual well-being. It is clear that the relation between the two objective indicators (OCC and FAS) and the indices of well-being considered are very low, even if statistically significant. With regards to FWO, the correlations are noticeably stronger although still weak: the stronger correlations here may be the result of correlating subjective measures which share a mono-method bias. From an overall examination of the table 3 we can conclude that participants do not seem to be particularly affected by the family socioeconomic background.

Assuming that all three measures of SES included measurement error, it is likely that the relations between SES and well-being were attenuated.

Therefore we tested the hypothesized relations using latent construct models. By utilizing structural equation models (SEM) we were able to create a latent construct for the family's SES including the occupational indicator (OCC), the family affluence scale (FAS), and family well-off (FWO). The same procedure was then used for the dependent variables and three different models were tested: one regarding school and family relations (see Figure 1), one regarding psychosocial adjustment (see Figure 2), and one regarding health behavior (sport and diet, see Figure 3).

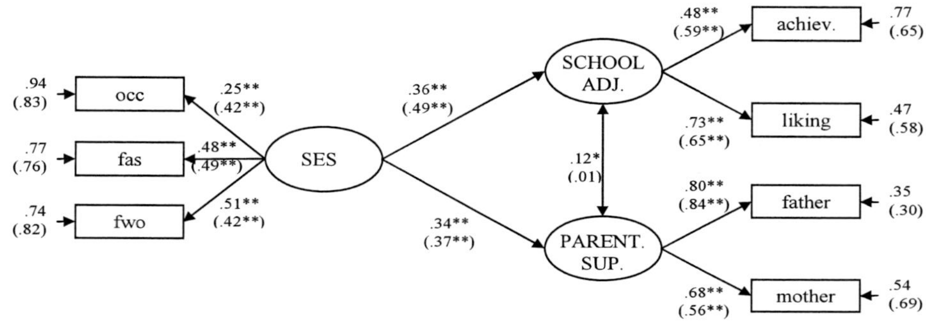

χ^2=60.98, D.F.=12, p=.01, GFI=.99, AGFI=.98, NFI=.95, RMSEA=.05
(χ^2=82.11, D.F.=12, p=.01, GFI=.98, AGFI=.96, NFI=.92, RMSEA=.06)

Figure 1. Model showing standardized path coefficients for boys and girls (girls are reported in parenthesis). Latent construct of SES include the occupational indicator (occ), the family affluence scale (fas), and family well-off (fwo); school adjustment include achievement and liking; parental support include difficulty to speak with mother and father.

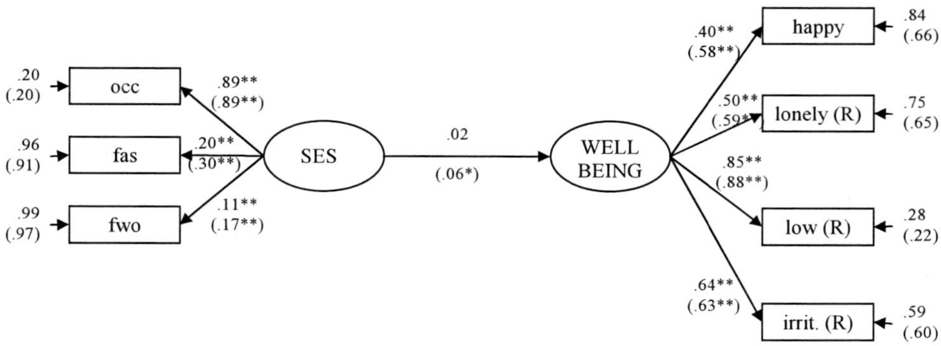

χ^2=248.21, D.F.=14, p=.01, GFI=.96, AGFI=.92, NFI=.83, RMSEA=.10
(χ^2=229.69, D.F.=14, p=.01, GFI=.96, AGFI=.92, NFI=.88, RMSEA=.10)

Figure 2. Model showing standardized path coefficients for boys and girls (girls are reported in parenthesis). Latent construct of SES include the occupational indicator (occ), the family affluence scale (fas), and family well-off (fwo); psychosocial well being include happiness, loneliness (Reverse code), feel low (Reverse code) and irritable (Reverse code).

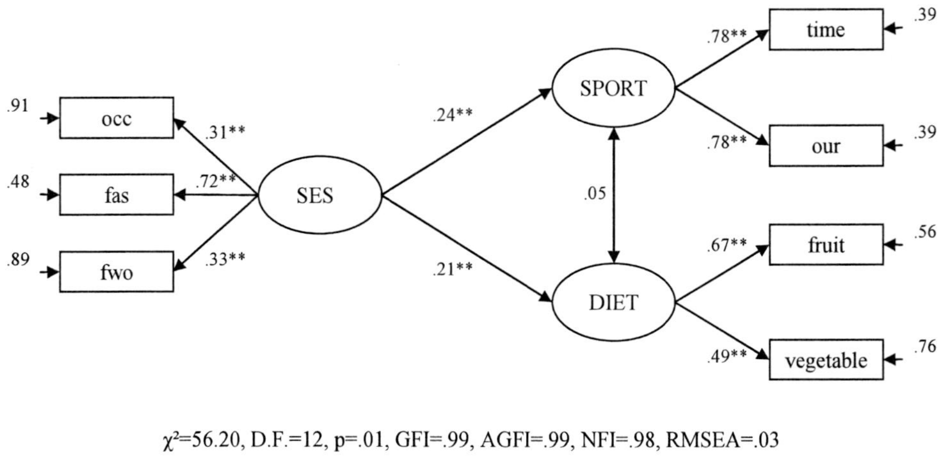

Figure 3. Model showing standardized path coefficients (all sample). Latent construct of SES include the occupational indicator (occ), the family affluence scale (fas), and family well-off (fwo); sports habits include time and hour spent in sports activity; diet habits include eat fruit and vegetable.

To test for differences between the covariance matrices for males and females the procedures proposed by Byrne (1989) were used. Analyses shows significant differences in the covariance matrices between males and females when considering family/school (χ^2 = 52.91, p = .01) and psychosocial well-being (χ^2 = 99.00, p = .01), but not for sport activity and diet (χ^2 = 29.90, p = .37). For that reason two separate models (boys and girl separately) are presented for family/school relation, and psychosocial well-being, and one model (all sample) for sport activity and diet.

Figure 1 shows the relations between SES, parental support and school adjustment, both for boys and girls (girls standardized path coefficients are presented inside parenthesis). The first thing that can be observed is that the model fits the data well (see fit indices) nearly identically for boys and girls. Note that, although χ^2 is significant in the two models, the very large sample size (n = 1,665 for boys, 1495 girls) is likely to result in a significant χ^2 even trough the data fit well. Therefore a better test is obtained from GFI =.99 (.98), AGFI = .98 (.96), NFI= .95 (.92) and RMSEA = .05 (.06), showing the good fit of both models. In particular, examining the standardized path coefficients it is clear that SES latent construct is a good predictor of school (γ = .36 for boys, γ = .49 for girls) and family (γ = .34 for boys, γ = .37 for girl) relations. The model accounted for 13% (boys) and 24% (girls) of the variance in school adjustment and 12% (boys) and 14% (girls) of variance in parental support. This data confirms our hypotheses on the relationship between SES and school adjustment, and parental support for both boys and girls.

The model predicting psychosocial well-being fit the data not as well as the previous model (see Figure 2). Moreover, looking at the relations between variables, the path going from SES to well being was not different from zero for boys and very low for girls. Although the significant relationship between SES and psychosocial adjustment for girls, the fit index seems to suggest that the data doesn't fit the hypothesized model.

The model predicting sports activity and diet (all sample) is presented in figure 3. The fit indices indicate that the model provided a good fit with the data (χ^2 = 56.20, p = .01; GFI = .99; AGFI = .99; NFI = .98; RMSEA = .02). Moreover, the path coefficients (γ = .24 and γ =

.21) indicated that SES is significantly related to both outcome variables (explaining 6% of the variance of sports activity and 5% of diet). These results confirm our hypothesis that SES is related to healthy living habits.

DISCUSSION

Research has amply documented the relations between SES and individual health during adulthood and childhood. However, during adolescence this relation appears to be less robust (West, 1997; Chen *et al.*, 2002; Tuinstra *et al.*, 1998; Koivusilta *et al.*, 1999; Piko and Fitzpatrick, 2001). The two possible explanations proposed in the literature are related to the choice of individual adjustment outcomes considered (Goldbatt, 1997; Judge and Benzeval, 1993), and to the analytic approach used (Adler *et al.*, 1994; Eames, 1993). The current study provides evidence in favor of these explanations. First of all, the relation between SES and adolescent adjustment depends on the type of outcome variable that is considered (such as school adjustment and family support or healthier habits like eating and sports behavior). Second, the relation between SES and adolescent adjustment depends on the type of analysis that is used: the expected relations were found only using latent construct.

The first objective of the study was to test for relations among different SES measures considered. The bivariate correlations among the three SES measures were all significant but ranging from very weak to moderately weak ($r = .10$ to $r = .21$). These correlations are lower than what would be expected by measures of the same construct. There are three possible explanations for these weak relations. First, the measures that were used may simply be poor indicators of SES. For example, the number of cars, rooms, vacations and the type of job may not be good indicators of an underlying construct. A second possibility is that these measures are appropriate indicators of SES, but that there is a large amount error variance and variance attributable to other causes. For example, differently from high SES adolescent's, a week-end outside the house could be interpreted as vacation by an adolescents from low SES. Similarly, a family with few economic resources could have a home with many small rooms even though the home itself may not have a high economic value. The third possible explanation is that we are measuring different, but related, aspects of SES. For example, the type of job could capture social prestige that may not be strictly related to the real economic position of the family. Results regarding the relations between these measures of SES and individual adjustment shed light on this and will be discussed below.

One main goal of the study was to test for the relation between SES and measures of lifestyle and well-being during adolescence. Considering the results obtained, the zero order correlations seem to suggest that no relations exist between SES and adolescent adjustment. However, using structural equation models the results were remarkably different. In particular, results showed that children belonging to the higher socioeconomic levels demonstrated better school adjustment, more parental support, and healthier eating and sports behavior. These clear relations between SES and adolescent adjustment obtained using SEM suggest that a latent construct of SES considering multiple indicators is the most sensitive and valid approach for testing for SES effects. Moreover, the fact that when using bivariate correlations, no relations were found between SES and adjustment, but were found using SEM, suggests that the individual measures include a great deal of variance not attributable to the latent construct of SES. Therefore, the finding provide a strong rational for using multiple indicator of SES to create a composite measure of SES in future research to capture different aspects of this construct.

At a theoretical level this study provides a valid and sensitive test of the relations between SES and the various measures of individual adjustment. This finding suggests that adolescence is not a phase of "social equalization" when considering indicators of well-being such as school adjustment, parental support, and health behavior measures (sports activity and eating habits). These results suggest that, during adolescence, social inequalities may have important implications for health behavior and personal life-style decisions that are likely to impact the individual's life for many years to follow.

On the other hand, our data did not show a relation between psychosocial well-being and SES. This null-effects of SES could be explained as a combination of the diminishing effects of the family, home background, and neighborhood, together with increasing effects of the school, peer group, and youth culture (West, 1997). Another, with particular relevance for psychological well-being derives from school - parental expectations for educational success which, as a stressor (McLeod and Nonnemaker, 2000), might impact more in high SES adolescents, equilibrating SES gradients. In this perspective, great importance has to be attributed to the confirmed relationship between SES and the specific health behaviors studied here.

Although the current work provides answers to several questions, it also has limitations of its own. The principal limitation was related to the informant: in this research we use only adolescents as informants. Future research is needed using different informants, such as parents and teachers, to compare with adolescents and to have a more detailed picture of adolescent's life. From a methodological point of view we have to underline the lack of number of indicators of SES included in the survey: educational level, for example could be helpful to better define the correct position of the family on the socioeconomic scale. Further research is required to better understand the way in which different elements of inequality is related to the adolescent adjustment. In conclusion, the study gives evidence of the association between SES and health related behavior. However, the effects in the individual's future life, and the stability of these findings from adolescence to adult life, needs to be tested by longitudinal study design.

In conclusion, we maintain that a science oriented to the prevention of health problems need to be based on empirically verified models of how individuals develop over time. This information may then lead to the clear identification of specific mechanisms and determinants that explain behavioral problems related to health, at particular points in the life course, which may be amenable to preventive intervention. For that reason more attention should be focused on socioeconomic inequality, especially in a particular phase like adolescence where, for several reason discussed above, the relation between SES and health may be attenuated.

REFERENCES

Adler, N.E., Boyce, T., Chesney, M.A., Cohen, S., Folkman, S., Kahn, R.L., and Syme, S.L. (1994). Socioeconomic status and health. *Am. Psychol.* 49: 15-24.

Anderson, N.B., and Armstead, C.A. (1995). Toward understanding the association of socioeconomic status and health: a new challenge for the biopsychoscocial approach. *Psychosom. Med.* 52: 213-225.

Argyle, M. (1994). *The psychology of social class,* Routledge, London.

Barrera, M., Prelow, H.M., Dumka, L.E., Gonzales, N. A., Knight, G.P., Michaels, M.L., Roosa, M. W., and Tein, J.Y. (2002). Pathways from family economic conditions to adolescents' distress: Supportive parenting, stressors outside the family and deviant peers. *J. Community Psychol.* 30: 135-152.

Blane, D. (1996). *Health and social organization towards a health policy for the 21st century.* Routledge, London.

Bradley, R.H., and Corwyn, R.F. (2001). Socioeconomic status and child development. *Annu. Rev. Psychol.* 53: 371-399.

Byrne, B.M. (1989). Multigroup comparison and the assumption of equivalent construct validity across groups: methodological and substantive issues. *Multivariate Behav. Res.* 24: 503-523.

Chen, E., Matthews, K.A., and Boyce, W.T. (2002). Socioeconomic differences in children's health: How and why do these relationships change with age? *Psychol. Bull.* 128: 295-329.

Cohen, S., Kaplan, G., and Salonen, J. (1999). The role of psychological characteristics in the relation between socioeconomic status and perceived health. *J. Appl. Soc. Psychol.* 29: 445-468.

Conger, R.D., Conger, K.J., Matthews, L.S., and Elder Jr., J.H. (1999). Pathways of economic influence on adolescent adjustment. *Am. J. Community Psychol.* 27: 519-541.

Currie, C.E., Elton, R.A., Todd J., and Platt, S. (1997). Indicators of socioeconomic status for adolescent: the WHO Health Behaviour in School-aged Children Survey. *Health Educ. Res.* 12: 385-397.

Donato, F., Assanelli, D., Chiesa, R., Poeta, M.L., Tomasoni, V. and Turla, C. (1997). Cigarette smoking and sports participation in adolescents: A cross-sectional survey among high student in Italy. *Subst. Use Misuse* 32: 1555-1572.

Duncan, G.J., and Brooks-Gunn, J. (1997). Consequences of growing up poor. Russel Sage Foundation, New York.

Dutton, D.B., and Levine, S. (1989). Overview, methodological critique, and reformulation. In Bunker, J.P., Gomby, D.S., and Kehrer B.H. (eds.), *Pathways to health.* The Henry J. Kaiser Family Foundation, Menlo Park, CA, pp. 29-69.

Eames, J. (1993). Social relationship and health. *Science* 241: 540-545.

Erikson, R., and Jonsson, J.O. (1996). Introduction. explaining class inequality in education: the Swedish test case. In Erikson R., and Jonsson, J.O. (eds), *Can Education be Equalized? The Swedish Case in Comparative Perspective.* Westview Press, Oxford, pp. 1-64.

Garbarino, J. (1992). The meaning of poverty in the world of children. *Am. Behav. Sci.* 35: 220-237.

Garcia, A.W., Pendler, N., Antonakos, C.L., and Ronis, D.L. (1998). Changes in physical activity beliefs and behaviour of boy and girl across the transition of junior high school. *J. Adolesc. Health* 22: 394-402.

Goldblatt, P.B. (1997). The relationship of income inequality to mortality: does the choice of indicator matter? *Soc. Sci. Med.* 54: 1121-1127.

Goodman, E., Amick, B.C., Rezendes, M.O., Levine, S., Kagan, J., Rogers, W.H., and Tarlov, A.R. (2000). Adolescents' Understanding of Social Class: a comparison of white upper middle class and working class youth. *J. Adolesc. Health* 27: 80-83.

Haug, M. R. (1977). Measurement in social stratification. *Annu. Rev. Sociol. 3*: 51-77.

Haugland, S., Wold, B., Stevenson, J., Aaro, L.E., and Woynarowska, B. (2001). Subjective health complaints in adolescence – a cross-national comparison of prevalence and dimensionality. *Eur. J. Public Health* 11: 4-10.

Hauser, R., and Warren, J. (1997). Socioeconomic indexes for occupations: A review, update, and critique. *Sociol. Methodol.* 27:177-298.

Hendry, L., Shucksmith, J., Love, J., and Glendinning, A. (1993). *Young peoples' leisure and lifestyle*. Routledge, London.

Hollingshead, A.B. (1975). *Four factors index of social status. Working Paper.* Yale University, Department of Sociology, New Haven.

Judge, K., and Benzeval, M. (1993). Health inequalities: new concerns about the children of single mothers. *BMJ* 306: 677-680.

Koivusilta, L.K., Rimpela, A.H., and Andrei, V. (2003). Health behaviours and health in adolescence as predictors of educational level in adulthood: A follow-up study from Finland. *Soc. Sci. Med.* 57: 577-593.

Koivusilta, L.K., Rimpela, A.H., and Rimpela, M.K. (1999). Health-related lifestyle in adolescence. Origin of social class differences in health? *Health Educ. Res.* 14: 339-355.

King, A., Wold, B., and Smith, C.T. (1996). *The health of youth. A cross-national survey.* WHO Regional Publications, Europeans Series, N° 69.

Link, B.G., and Pelan, J. (1995). Social condition as fundamental causes of disease. *J. Health Soc. Behav.* 36: 80-94.

Mann, A.H., Wakeling, A., Wood, K., Monck, E., Dobbs, R., and Szmakler, G. (1983). Screening for abnormal eating attitudes and psychiatric morbidity in an unselected population of 15 year old school-girls. *Psychol. Med.* 13: 573-580.

Marmot, M.G., Ryff, C.D., Bumpass, L.L., Shipley, M., and Marks, N.F. (1997). Social inequalities in health: next questions and converging evidence. *Soc. Sci. Med.* 44: 901-910.

McLeod, J.D., and Nonnemaker, J.M. (2000). Poverty and child emotional and behavioral problems: Racial/ethnic differences in processes and effects. *J. Health Soc. Behav.* 41: 137-161.

McLoyd, V.C. (1998). Socioeconomic disadvantage and child development. *Am. Psychol.* 53: 185-204.

McLoyd, V.C., Jayaratne, T.E., Ceballo, R., and Borquez, J. (1994). Unemployment and work interruption among African American single mothers: Effects on parenting and adolescent socioemotional functioning. *Child Dev.* 65, 562-589.

Mullan, E., and Currie, C. (2000). Socioeconomic inequalities in adolescent health. In WHO (eds.), *Health and health behaviour among young people*. World Health Organisation, Copenhagen, pp. 65-68.

Oakes, J.M., and Rossi, P.H. (2003). The measurement of SES in health research: Current practice and steps toward a new approach. *Soc. Sci. Med.* 56: 769-784.

Piko, B., and Fitzpatrick, K.M. (2001). Does class matter? SES and psychosocial among Hungarian adolescents. *Soc. Sci. Med.* 53: 817-830.

Rose, D., Pevalin, D., and Elias, P. (2001). *Towards a European socio-economic classification: Final report to Eurostat of the export group*. University of Essex, Institute for Social and Economic Research, Colchester.

Rutter, M., and Smith, D.J. (1995). *Psychosocial disorders in young people: Time trend and their causes*. Wiley, Chichester.

Samdal, O., Wold, B., and Torsheim, T. (2000). The relationship between students' perception of school and their reported health and quality of life. In WHO (eds), Health and health behaviour among young people. WHO Policies series 2000, 1 [On Line]: www.who.dk/hbsc.

Townsend, P. (1990). Deprivation. *J. Soc. Policy* 16: 125-146.

Tuinstra, J., Groothoff, J.W., Van Den Heuvel, W.J.A., and Post, D. (1998). Socio-economic differences in health risk behaviour in adolescence: Do they exist? *Soc. Sci. Med.* 47: 67-74.

Wardle, J., Robb, K., and Johnson, F. (2002). Assessing socio-economic status in adolescents: the validity of a home affluence scale. *Journal Epidemiol. Community Health* 56: 595-599.

West, P. (1997). Health inequalities in the early years: is there equalisation in youth? *Soc. Sci. Med.* 44: 833-858.

West, P. (1988). Inequalities? Social class differentials in health in British youth. *Soc. Sci. Med.* 27: 291-296.

WHO (1998). *Health behaviour in school-aged children: A WHO cross national study. Research protocol for the 1997-98 Survey.* University of Edinburg, Edinburg.

Wold, B., Aaro, L., and Smith, C. (1993). *Health behaviour in school-aged children (HBSC): a WHO cross national survey: research protocol for the 1993-1994.* University of Bergen, Research Center for Health Promotion, Bergen.

In: Socioeconomic Status and Health Implications ISBN: 978-1-62100-675-6
Editor: Sarah Reibert and Alice Jannings, pp. 145-161

Chapter 7

How Deprivation Affects Life Expectancy in France and Italy: Comparative Evidence from a Factorial Analysis

Riccardo Soliani, Alessia Di Gennaro and Enrico Ivaldi *
University of Genoa, Department of Economy and Quantitative Methods, Genoa, Italy.

Abstract

This paper intends to investigate how some elements of material and social deprivation affect standard of living and life expectancy in the Italian and French regions. Literature suggests that forty indicators from Eurostat databases have a significant influence on them; thus a study with a set of comparable data on deprivation in Italy and France (a couple of quite similar countries according to their social and economic structure) is likely to yield interesting results. Our analysis aims at highlighting the difference between the two countries and also the different parts of them.

The research has been carried out following the factorial analysis methodology on those database collections.

The factorial analysis has been used to choose the deprivation variables, which were utilised to create two distinct condition indexes referring to material and social, respectively. The index of the social and material condition (SMCI) consists of the sum of the two indices.

Both indexes are positively correlated with life expectancy; the material index, however, correlates more highly than the social index.

Our choice of putting together Italy and France is due to the comparable history, culture, institutions of both countries and the structure of their economies, as several authors maintain and the Governor of the Bank of Italy has remarked recently (May 2011) in his report on the Italian economy, citing social and economic indicators.

1. Introduction

The history, culture, institutions of France and Italy and the structure of their economies do give sense to our approach, as the Governor of the Bank of Italy remarked in May 2011 in his report on the Italian economy, comparing productivity, foreign direct investment, industrial structure, growth of GDP, wages and consumption and other indicators in both countries (*Considerazioni* ..., 2011). In France and Italy population, GDP per capita in PPS and its rate of growth, have been very similar in the last decade. Moreover, they have the same model of capitalism, namely coordinated market economy (Soskice 1999). The social problems, particularly the sustainability of the welfare state, are almost the same in France, Italy and Germany (Esping – Andersen 1990; Smith 2004). Furthermore, in 2007 life expectancy and rate of mortality were almost the same in France (77 and 84 years for men and women and 9 ‰) and in Italy (78 and 84; 10 ‰) (*Tableaux* ..., 2011). Thus the comparison based upon the respective importance of material and social elements of deprivation in France and Italy may be interesting.

The difference between "material" and "social" is nuanced: we assume that income and employment concern "material", whereas age, family structure and opportunity of communication concern rather "social" conditions. Indeed, according to Townsend (1987), the material form of deprivation "entails the lack of goods, services, resources, amenities and physical environment which are customary, or at least widely approved in the society under consideration", while its social form "is non-participation in the roles, relationships, customs, functions, rights and responsibilities implied by a member of a society and its sub-groups". Material deprivation is likely to be a major cause of social deprivation (although the latter can be rooted also in different grounds, e. g. racial discrimination), as Sen shows by his concept of "empowerment": the possession of commodities is valuable only to the extent that it enables people to do or be a range of things (Sen 1987).

Since both countries are marked by significant territorial differences, we adopted macro-regions as our geographical scale. The availability of Eurostat data at NUTS1 level has made this analysis possible, which in this manner is more effective to single out the (dis)similarities between the countries. As Heidenreich maintained a few years ago (but it is true also today), regional disparities in Europe are persistent, indicating a relatively stable division of labour and are a challenge to the EU, which implements the enhancement of education, infrastructures and communication (Heidenreich 2003). However, the regional scale of analysis of deprivation has almost remained neglected in Europe (remarkable exceptions: Callens, Croux 2009; Reinstadler, Ray 2009), whilst most of studies focus on the urban or national dimension, so that some scholars speak of "disciplinary impasse" (Labao et al. 2008).

2. Material and Methods

We considered appropriate to construct an index based on currently available data, which do not require *ad hoc* surveys, with the double result of avoiding the creation of additional costs and of being allowed to update indexes in a simple and continuous manner, basing decisions on objective and transparent data coming directly from certified sources (Jarman 1983; Gordon and Pantazis 1997).

A classification nomenclature of territorial units for statistics has been used. NUTS is the acronym (from the French nomenclature des Unités territoriales statistiques), created in 1988 by Eurostat taking as a benchmark the size of the resident population in each local administrative area, going from a minimum of three million inhabitants to a maximum of seven million inhabitants (Eurostat 2003). The NUTS 1 level used is one which includes the geographical areas shown in Table 1a and b.

The analysis of literature offers several solutions to deduce in advance what should be the most appropriate variables to be included within an index, even if the choice is influenced by both the availability of data and the purpose of the indicator (Jarman 1983; Carstairs, Morris 1991; Cadum et al. 1999; Valerio, Vitullo 2000; Grasso 2002; Noble et al. 2003; Testi et al. 2005; Brenna 2007; Guio 2009; Whelan et al. 2010; Ivaldi, Testi 2011; Testi, Ivaldi 2011).

Defining the material and social deprivation indexes as a proxy for the socio-economic conditions of a Nuts 1 area requires the choice of variables to utilise, and secondly how to deal with them on a statistical basis (Ivaldi, Testi 2010).

The literature suggests that forty indicators have a significant influence on life expectancy, so we have selected six potential indicators on the basis of their significant correlation (Pearson Correlation Coefficient ρ) to life expectancy. An exploratory factor analysis was carried out in order to provide insight into the underlying data structure (Dillon, Goldstein 1984; Hogan, Tchernis 2004).

Table 1a. NUTS 1 Classification (France)

Île-de-France	Île-de-France
Parisian basin	Champagne-Ardenne, Picardie, Haute-Normandie, Centre, Basse-Normandie, Bourgogne
Nord-Pas-de-Calais	Nord-Pas-de-Calais
East	Lorraine, Alsace, Franche-Comté
West	Pays de la Loire, Brittany, Poitou-Charentes
South West	Aquitaine, Midi-Pyrénées, Limousin
Centre East	Rhône-Alpes, Auvergne
Mediterranean	Languedoc-Roussillon, Provence-Alpes-Côte d'Azur, Corse
Overseas departments*	Guadeloupe, Martinique, French Guiana, Réunion

* Not included in the analysis.

Table 1b. NUTS 1 Classification (Italy)

North West	Valle d'Aosta, Liguria, Lombardia, Piemonte
North East	Emilia-Romagna, Friuli-Venezia Giulia, Trentino-Alto Adige/Südtirol, Veneto
Centre	Lazio, Marche, Toscana, Umbria
South	Abruzzo, Puglia, Basilicata, Calabria, Campania, Molise
Islands	Sardegna, Sicilia

Factor analysis aims to summarizing information contained in a matrix of correlation or variance / covariance, and tries to statistically identify their latent and not directly observable dimensions (Stevens 1986). If two variables are highly correlated to the same factor, a significant proportion of the correlation between the two variables is explained by the fact that they have common factors (Dillon, Goldstein 1984). Therefore, by providing a principle of identification of these common factors, the factor analysis sets out a description in a simple form of the complex web of interpolations existing within a set of associated variables (Johnson, Wichen 2002).

As for the present case, subsequent tests with different algorithms for extraction and rotation showed real stability in the extracted factors (Kaiser 1958). We have applied the rotation QUARTIMAX that maximizes the variance of the saturation per line (Carroll 1953), in order to concentrate as much variance as possible for each variable on a single factor. The Quartimax reduces the presence of the variables among the factors, obtaining the minimum number of factors, where the single variable has significant weights (Neuhaus, Wrigley 1954).

We have found two subsets of variables, each of them reflecting a latent data dimension, which validates our expectations in that the two kinds of variables, direct and indirect, should be kept separate.

The second step is to detect the best way of aggregating together the partial indicators to describe socio-economic conditions in each area with a single number and to allow comparing them.

In both cases, the commonly adopted z-score technique was used to solve the problem of aggregating variables into an overall index.

Therefore two indexes were made, the *Material Condition Index (MCI)* and the *Social Condition Index (SCI).* In both cases, to solve the problem of aggregation, the commonly adopted z-score technique was used. This procedure was suggested by the differences found out in the scales of the variables. Standardisation allows one to obtain the same weight for items with longer and shorter scales in the overall score. Finally we have summarized the two indexes found in an overall index, the *Social and Material Condition Index (SMCI)* . The additive index is rather simple, consisting in summing the partial indicators. The only difficulty is that the partial indicators are usually quantified in different units of measure. This therefore requires standardizing them before summing up, to avoid that some of them have more importance compared to the others (Jarman 1983; Jarman 1984; Townsend 1987; Townsend et al. 1988; Carstairs, Morris 1991; Forrest, Gordon 1993; Bartley, Blane 1994, DETR 2000, Testi, Ivaldi 2009, Ivaldi, Testi 2010).

In order to solve the problem of aggregating variables into an overall index, following the literature, the variables have been standardized through the Box Cox method (Box, Cox 1964), to transform the original non-normal distribution into an approximate, normal distribution for each variable (Bland, Altman 1996). After this transformation, z-scores were calculated for each observation, obtained by subtracting the means of the distribution from the observed, transformed value and dividing the result by the standard deviation of the distribution (Osborne 2002). Therefore, both indexes result from the sum of three z-scores.

Lastly, the index distributions were obtained, where values may be either negative or positive, going from the most deprived areas (larger negative values) to the most affluent ones (larger positive values).

Two indexes were therefore constructed, MCI and SCI. The first one includes: Gross domestic product (GDP) at current market prices, Employment by sex and age from 25 to 64 years, Income of households; the second one includes: Not single-parent households, People aged 25-64 with higher secondary education attainment, (%), Households with access to the Internet at home.

Finally, after being sure that the partial indicators had been correctly aggregated, the most important thing is to also be sure that the proposed indexes are good predictors of health status. The most appropriate synthetic measure of health is, in our opinion, the life expectancy at birth, that is the expected (in the statistical sense) number of years remaining to live.

The final step is grouping the values of *SMCI* index into categories to identify groups of areas with similar socio-economic conditions.

We have selected the areas following the parameters of the distribution (means and variance), in order to retain the discriminatory features of the distribution (Carstairs, Morris, 1991; Carstairs 2000).

3. The Model

We have based our analysis on a set of variables in line with most of literature. Also Serge Paugam, member of the *Observatoire Sociologique du Changement,* founded his analysis of the "spiral of precariousness" on indicators such as job, family structure, poverty, social relations. Indeed Paugam's "precariousness" is synonymous of our material and social "deprivation": as poverty, as social deprivation are likely to trigger a vicious circle leading to "social disqualification", that is unemployment, dependency, lack of self-esteem (Paugam 1995).

More recently in France public authorities (the *Haut commissaire aux solidarités actives contrela pauvreté*), unsatisfied of the monetary definition of poverty are setting up complementary indicators of poverty, which consider education, health, home, employment and so on (Lambert 2008a).

Even Michel Foucault, whose methodological approach was utterly different from ours, in a lecture in 1970 held in Tokyo put forward three forms of exclusion, or "existential marginality", concerning the poor: job, family and language (cited in Gueslin 2006, p. 374), that roughly correspond to our data on employment, one parent families, and education and Internet access.

Generally speaking, our groups of variables describe the individual and social condition of people. GDP and employment are standard macroeconomic indicators of the level of economic activity and the effectiveness of the system in creating jobs; the income of households has the prominent role regarding the material deprivation. On the other hand, single-parent households indicate a situation that is relevant to quantify social deprivation, and they are much more at risk of unemployment, as shown by long-period data[12]; education and access to the Internet allow better participation in social life[13]. In France people aged 25-64 who accomplished the 2° cycle are 70.4%; in Italy 54.3% (UE 27 72%). Only Spain, Portugal and Malta have a level of education lower than Italy (*Tableaux* ..., 2011). This is a significant difference that can not be easily represented by our analysis, but that must be kept in mind when interpreting it.

[12] In the period 1975-2002 the percentage of one parent families without a job had soared from 9.6 to 25.8% (*La France* ... 2006) and they are classified as a deprived social group (Gueslin 2004).

[13] According to some authors, since "social exclusion" concerns life expectancy, social links, education, job, family, and so on, "exclusion" and "poverty" must be distinguished: the poor can be not excluded and, on the other hand, excluded people not always are poor (CESIS, 1997; IDS 1997; Iorio 2001: pp. 92-93; Freguja, Pannuzi 2007).

We have not examined data relating to the housing property, since the very higher amount of public housing in France would take away the sense of such a comparison. In France in 2008 only 57.9% of households owned their home; 6.6 m. households paid rent on the free market; 5.1 m. lived in public housing. In the same year, households paying rent on the free market whose cost of housing (net of any sort of public aid) is 40% or more of disposable income, are only 10% of total households in France (that is the lowest percentage in EU 27) and 27.4% in Italy (EU 27: 25.6%) (*Tableaux* ... 2011). This wide gap suggests that the structure of housing is different in Italy and France. Gender, immigration and ethnic differences have been excluded as well: data are not available or gives rise to distortion, since, for example, the female life expectancy is always longer. However the distinction between material and social deprivation, and their respective weight in the macro-regions, are depicted; this is quite a satisfying result, taking into account that the world of French poverty is made up of heterogeneous groups difficult to aggregate on the social and cultural level (Gueslin 2004, Paugam 1995); also Italian evidence, as it appears from a few inquiries in the Nineties, has shown an important territorial dimension and the progressive multidimensional pathway towards marginality and exclusion, confirmed by our study (Mingione 1997; Iorio 2001).

In the material index, the labour market trends play a key role. Here the emerging difference deserves some further reflection: it is due to structural elements and to the reactions to the current crisis as well (see Cochard and Heyer 2010). In 2009 in France the rate of activity (70.7%) and employment (64.2%) were significantly higher than in Italy (62.4% and 57.5% respectively), and have recently risen; the difference in the rate of female employment is remarkable: 60.1% compared with 46.4%. However the upturn of the active population and the crisis have increased the rate of unemployment, which is 9.1% (in Italy 6.9%), with a significant share of long term unemployment (*Tableaux* ..., 2011). In France the drop in GDP and employment, caused by the crisis, has been lower than in Italy, but at the same time the rate of unemployment is higher, so mirroring the different structure of the labour market, namely the lower rate of participation in Italy.

All this, together with the economic policies to cope with the crisis, also influences poverty. Allègre and Cochard forecast a rise of 1.4% in the rate of poverty between unemployed and a slight drop in it (- 0.2%) between labourers in the period 2007 – 2011, the final effect being a small rise (0.4%)[14] (Allègre, Cochard 2010). However, in France political action is more effective than in Italy: the rate of poverty in France is 25% before and 13% after social transfers; in Italy the data are 24% and 20% respectively. Poverty affects the two countries almost in the same measure, but the French social net expenditure (about 30% of GDP in 2006) is more efficacious in reducing it. The effectiveness of France is near that of Northern countries, whereas Italy belongs to the less effective Mediterranean group (Italy, Spain, Greece). In Europe, French are the most frightened by poverty: 86% of them think that everybody might fall below the poverty line and lose his home. This can be explained by the multidimensional character of poverty, difficult to grasp by statistics (Lambert 2008b). In 2009 the disposable income of households rose (+1.0%), even though the income deriving from activities and wealth decreased; this may be explained by the drop in taxation (-4.4% on

[14] Under the hypothesis of constant social and fiscal policies, they reckon 42 more poor out of 100 more unemployed, the total being 297,000 new poor from 2007 to 2011. The line of poverty is defined as less than 60% of the median GDP per head. See also Lambert 2008a, where the relationship between relative poverty and inequality is briefly discussed from the point of view of their measurement.

income and wealth taxes) and the rise in public aid. Total wages decreased, due to the fall in employment and in unitary wages as well and social aid, which soared (+4.7%) between 2008 and 2009, is now 27.8% of primary household incomes. Nevertheless, the rate of poverty after social transfers is 13.3% (in Italy the same indicator is higher: 18.7%). Since the beginning of the crisis, the upturn of the subsidies to the unemployed (+10.8%) and the extension of the public aid (+22.7%) has coped with the deterioration of the labour market and the risk of poverty. In 2009 the global social aid *Prestations de protection sociale* was 36.7% of the gross disposable income of households (34.7% in 2000; 32.8% in 1990) (*Tableaux* ..., 2011).

On these basis six variables from Eurostat have been chosen among about forty of those affecting socio-economic conditions (Table 2).

Exploratory factorial analysis on the selected variables has been carried out to detect if we can individuate two subsets of variables, each one reflecting a latent data dimension. The variables are distributed on two principal components. Figure 1 and Table 3 point out how social and material variables are significantly loaded on the first and on the second factor respectively, thus empirically validating the conceptual distinction.

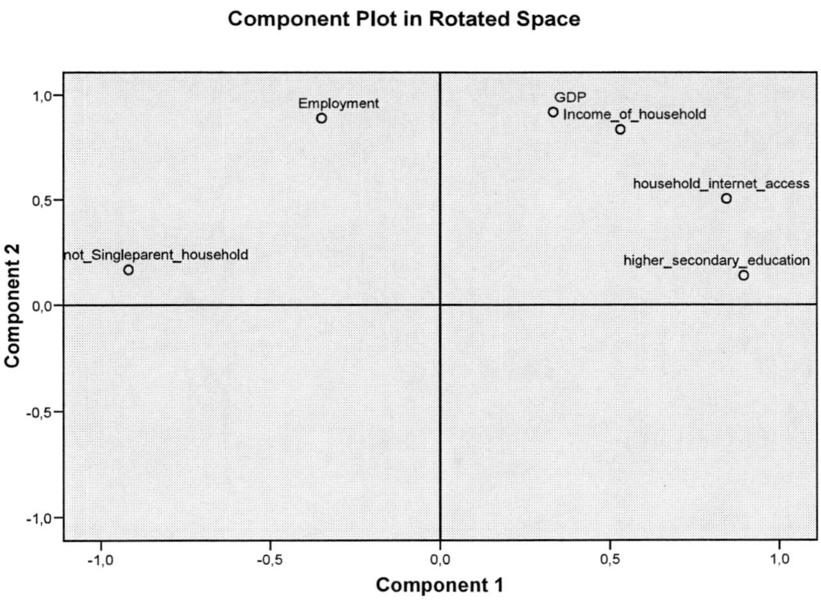

Figure 1. Factorial Analysis Plot.

Table 2. Variables description

Variable
Gross domestic product (GDP) at current market prices
Employment by sex and age from 25 to 64 years
Income of households
Not Single-parent household
Persons aged 25-64 with higher secondary education attainment
Households with access to the Internet at home

Table 3. Factorial Analysis: Rotated Component Matrix

	Component	
	1	2
Not Single-parent household	**-0,919**	0,168
Persons aged 25-64 with higher secondary education attainment (%)	**0,895**	0,140
Households with access to the Internet at home	**0,845**	0,504
Gross domestic product (GDP) at current market prices (Purchasing Power Standard per inhabitant)	0,333	**0,916**
Employment by sex and age from 25 to 64 years	-0,350	**0,887**
Income of households. Balance of primary income, net (uses)	0,531	**0,833**

Extraction Method: Principal Component Analysis.
Rotation Method: Quartimax with Kaiser Normalization.
a Rotation converged in 3 iterations.

Table 4. Social, Material and Social-Material Conditions Indexes

GEO/TIME	SCI	MCI	SMCI
Île-de-France (F)	1,9	5,9	7,8
North West (I)	-0,1	3,9	3,8
North East (I)	0,6	2,4	3,1
Centre (I)	0,7	1,5	2,2
Centre East (F)	1,1	0,0	1,1
West (F)	1,0	-0,7	0,3
Parisian basin (F)	0,2	0,0	0,1
South West (F)	0,7	-0,9	-0,2
East (F)	0,6	-1,4	-0,8
Mediterranean (F)	-0,7	-1,0	-1,7
Nord - Pas-de-Calais (F)	-0,8	-2,7	-3,5
South (I)	-2,3	-2,7	-5,0
Islands (I)	-2,9	-4,2	-7,1

With the selected variables, three indexes have been calculated: *SCI, MCI* and *SMCI.* SCI is the sum of the z-scores referred to in the variables disposed on the first factor: Not Single-parent household, Persons aged 25-64 with higher secondary education attainment, (%), Households with access to the Internet at home; MCI is the sum of the z-scores referred to in the variables disposed on the second factor: Gross domestic product (GDP) at current market prices, Employment by sex and age from 25 to 64 years, Income of households (Table 3). The SMCI index is the sum of the two indexes.

Finally, to assess which index is able to better take into account health inequalities as measured by Life Expectancy, the parametric correlation (Pearson) was tested (Table 5).

MCI is the most correlated with life expectancy, but we have to take into account also the social aspects that affect life expectancy, although to a lesser extent.

The final step is grouping the values of indexes into categories to identify the areas with similar socio-economic conditions.

Table 5. Values of Pearson's ρ coefficient

Indexes	Life Expectancy
SCI	0,398
MCI	0,605
SMCI	0,579

Table 6a. Classes homogeneous with respect to the SCI index

Class	Country
1	Île-de-France (F)
2	North East (I), Centre (I), Centre East (F), West (F), Parisian basin (F), South West (F), East (F),
3	North West (I) Mediterranean (F), Nord-Pas-de-Calais (F)
4	South (I), Islands (I)

Table 6b. Classes homogeneous with respect to the MCI index

Class	Country
1	Île-de-France (F), North West (I)
2	North East (I), Centre (I), Centre East (F), Parisian basin (F)
3	West (F), South West (F) Mediterranean (F), East (F), South (I), Nord-Pas-de-Calais (F)
4	Islands (I)

Table 6c. Classes homogeneous with respect to the SMCI index

Class	Country
1	Île-de-France (F), North West (I)
2	North East (I), Centre (I), Centre East (F), West (F), Parisian basin (F)
3	South West (F), East (F), Mediterranean (F), Nord-Pas-de-Calais (F)
4	South (I), Islands (I)

We have selected the areas following the parameters of the distribution (means and variance), in order to retain its discriminatory features (Carstairs, Morris 1991; Carstairs 2000).

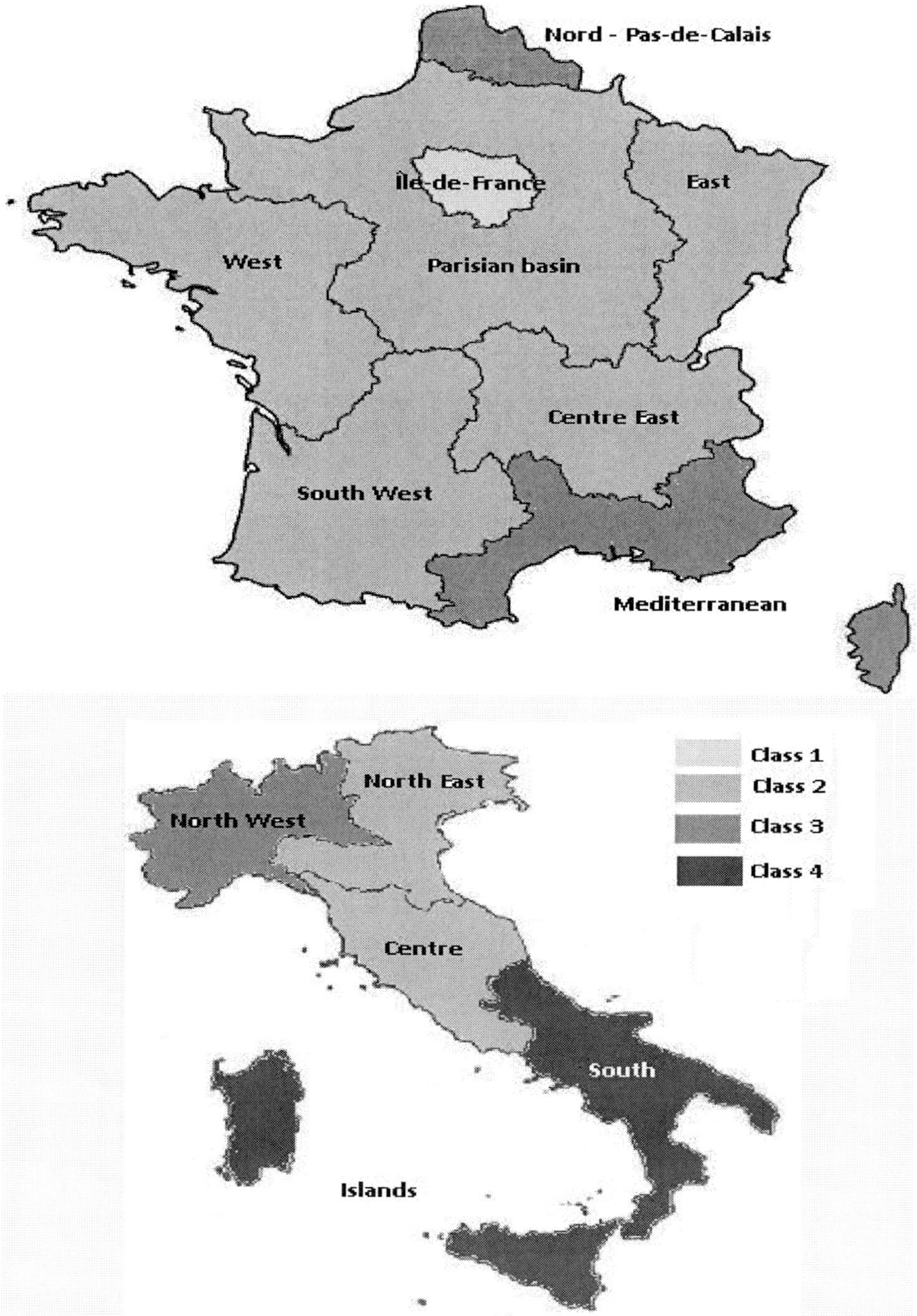

Figure 2a. Maps of social deprivation.

In Figures 2a-c the four classes are highlighted with decreasing colour gradient.

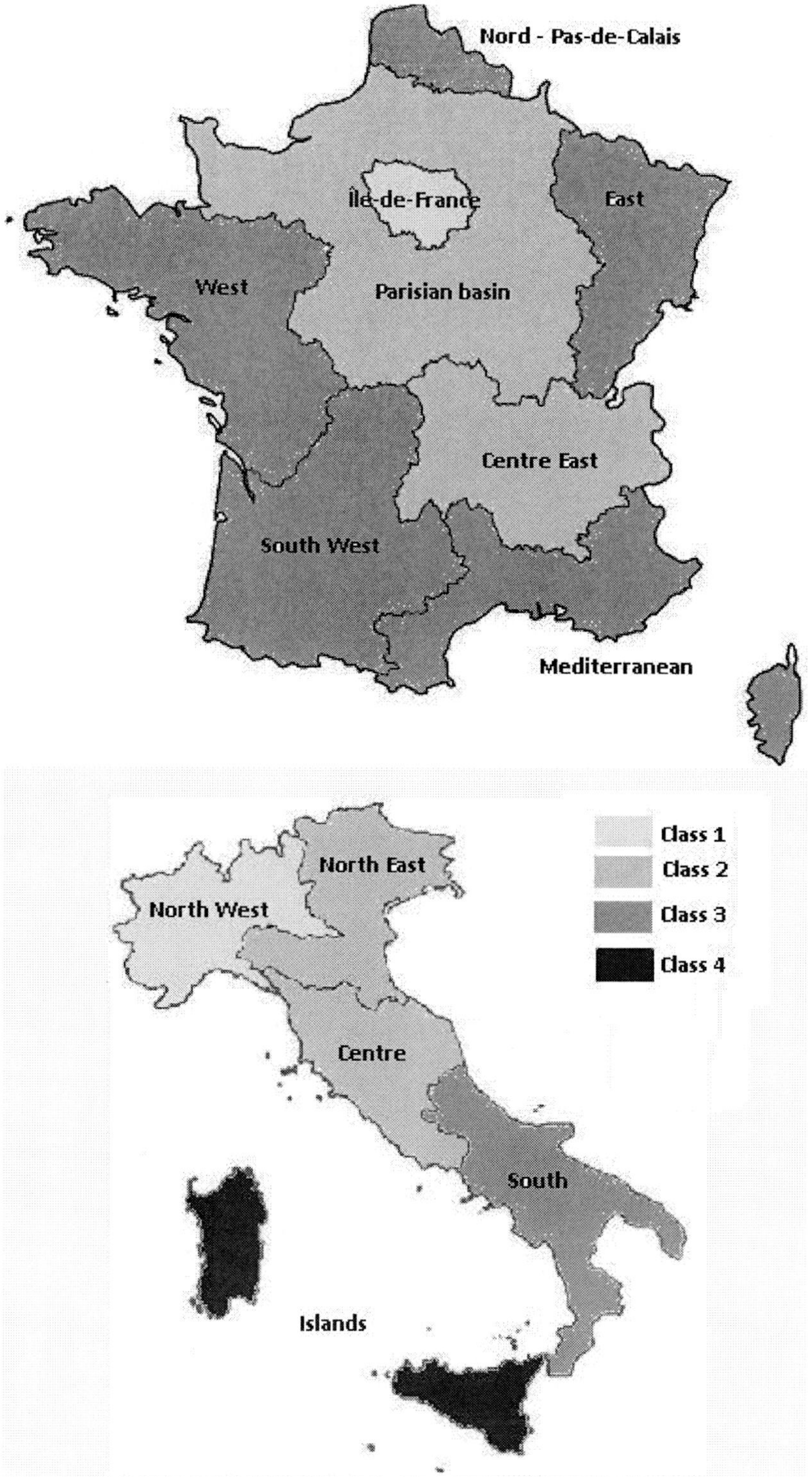

Figure 2b. Maps of material deprivation.

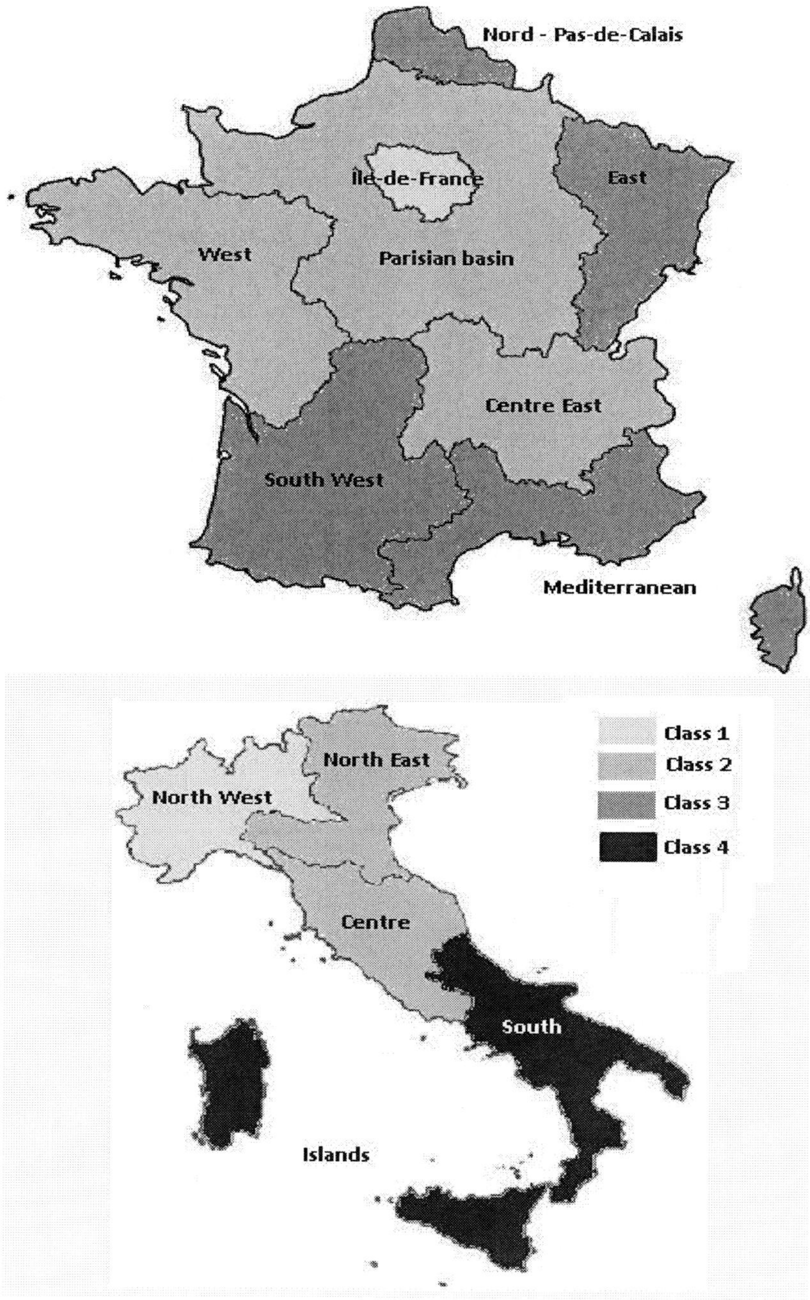

Figure 2c. Maps of social and material deprivation.

The distribution of the index has been divided into four classes: class 1 identifies the countries with the best socio-economic conditions, while class 4 contains, on the contrary, countries characterized by the lowest index value (Table 6a-c). In order to identify homogeneous areas the values of 0 and $\pm 1/2\sigma$ have been used as a cut off. The patterns appear quite different, suggesting a theoretical distinction between material and social deprivation.

4. Discussion

The analysis of the ranks of the two additional components in the indicator (SCI and MCI) reveals the peculiarities of the different regions. First of all we can observe that no substantial differences between SCI and MCI exist in these areas: Île-de-France (F), North East (I), Parisian basin (F), Centre (I), Centre East (F), Mediterranean (F), Nord-Pas-de-Calais (F) and Islands (I).

Secondly, West (F), South West (F) and East (F) have a better SCI rank compared to MCI, due to above average education, whereas employment is lower than average. North West is the only Italian region that shows a marked difference between the two components of the SMCI index, being 2nd place in the MCI, and only 5th place in the SCI. This is due to the fact that the variables that make up MCI are all above average - especially employment - whilst two SCI variables are below average and the third is on average with the other geographical areas.

From the results obtained through the SMCI indicator it can be noted that there are differences in the distribution of the index in the two countries: in particular, from Figure 2c we see that in France deprivation increases moving away from the capital, according to a concentric structure while in Italy deprivation increases with the passage from North to South (Benassi, Colombini 2007). Indeed a few French researches have shown that the various forms of territorial development influence standard of living and poverty differently. In some French areas the economic activity is exposed to international competition; elsewhere pensions and public wages, or tourism, are the main source of income. The more dynamic regions are less affected by poverty (adjustment costs of crises are likely to be borne by the upper and middle classes), but there it remains constant, whilst in the areas where the income derives from public expenditure the initially high rate of poverty decreases. The evolution of the human geography of poverty, from retirees to workers, is mirrored well in its spatial dimension, since the urban character of poverty has grown in last years, especially in Nord-Pas-de-Calais (Davezies 2004; Noyé 2008).

We also note (Table 4) that the value of the Île-de-France is much higher than other geographical areas concerned, thus giving evidence to a situation of well-being and classifying the area at the first place for both the SCI and MCI, even though other studies demonstrate that inequality is marked in that region and France has no NUTS1 areas in the last class (Noyé 2008). Finally the Italian situation presents higher variability, as shown by the lack of areas in Class 3 in SMCI.

Conclusions

Our index of deprivation is a flexible set of few data, quite easy to find, which offers information about social and material deprivation, in the wake of the concepts of capabilities, empowerment, entitlement proposed by Sen (Sen 1987). This approach highlights the fact that what people can or can not afford is the core point of deprivation; poverty is important, but it is only one component of deprivation, because social exclusion is multidimensional, so its quantitative evidence is difficult to find (Iorio 2001). Our indicator sets in this field of analysis and shows that the distinction between "social" and "material" can be tested and holds well. Whilst general demand-sided macroeconomic policies financed by progressive taxation can improve material conditions, social deprivation must be faced by fine-tuned public policies (education and access to the web) aiming at the equality of capabilities and/or "endowments" (*dotations*: see Bourguignon 2008), or by specific welfare programmes: this current distinction of economic policy suits our analysis perfectly.

Social and material deprivation are considered separately, to grasp the territorial specificity of the standard of living, and then they are put together, to come to a synthesis and a comparison between different macro-regions. Our benchmark is life expectancy, insofar as it is a "neutral", appropriate and synthetic measure of health. The material index is more correlated, as expected. However, social aspects also express a significantly high correlation, although in less proportion, and our empirical analysis suggests that income and "capabilities" are significantly linked (Bourguignon 2008) This is a consequence of our social complexity and stratification: apparently one can hardly maintain that, e.g., the connection to the Internet has a direct influence on life expectancy, but the groups marked by social deprivation (which difficult communication is an element of) have a worse quality of living and their shorter life expectancy bears witness to it.

The resulting geographical distribution of deprivation is consistent with many other indicators of social and economic conditions. However, immediately a couple of hints emerge: first, inequality in Italy is stronger even on territorial basis, with the wide gap of Southern Italy and the Islands; secondly, the case of the Île-de-France, where the geographical polarization is to be considered as the aftermath of the role of Paris. Indeed our results about the geography of deprivation can be compared with some regional demographic trends, showing interesting analogies. In France the higher demographic rise takes place in the Southern and Western regions, where also the balance of immigration is positive (inflow higher than outflow); on the contrary it is negative for the North and the North-East. The Île-de-France has net outflow of population, but its dwellers are particularly young (*Tableaux* ..., 2011): presumably Paris attracts the young, while old Parisiens prefer to move towards smaller towns or to the countryside. In Italy, where the natural demographic trend is negative, the small rise in the population (about 0.5%), due to immigration, is higher in the North and also in the Centre, thanks to the attractiveness of Rome.

REFERENCES

Allègre G., Cochard M. (2010) "Quel impact de la crise sur la pauvreté?", in OFCE 2010, ch. IV, pp. 86-93.

Bartley M., Blane D. (1994), "Commentary: Appropriateness of deprivation indices must be ensured", *British Medical Journal*, 309, p. 1479.

Benassi D., Colombini S. (2007) "Caratteristiche e distribuzione territoriale della povertà e della disuguaglianza sulla base dei dati dell'archivio Disrel", in Brandolini A., Saraceno C. 2007.

Bland J., Altman D. (1996) "Statistics Notes: Transforming data", *British Medical Journal*, 312, p. 770.

Bourguignon F. (2008), "Du revenu aux dotations : le renouvellement des conceptions de la pauvreté", *Regards croisés sur l'économie*, n° 4, pp. 34-42.

Box G., Cox D. (1964) "An analysis of transformations (with discussion)", *Journal of the Royal Statistic Society*, 26, pp. 211-252.

Brandolini A., Saraceno C. (a cura di) *Povertà e benessere. Una geografia delle disuguaglianza in Italia*, Bologna, Il Mulino.

Brenna E. (2007), "The weighting of capitation on the basis of deprivation factors. Tips for Italy from the Scottish", *Politiche Sanitarie*, n°2, pp. 65-76.

Cadum E, Costa F, Biggeri A, Martuzzi M. (1999), "Deprivation and mortality: a deprivation index for the analysis of geographically-based inequalities", *Epidemiologia e Prevenzione*, 23, pp. 175-187.

Callens M., Croux C. (2009) "Poverty Dynamics in Europe: A Multilevel Recurrent Discrete-Time Hazard", *International Sociology*, 24, pp. 368-396.

Carroll J. B. (1953) "An analytical solution for approximating simple structure in factor analysis", *Psychometrika*, 18, pp. 23-38.

Carstairs V. (2000) "Socio-economic factors at area level and their relationship with health", in Elliott P., Wakefield J., Best N., Briggs D. (eds.) *Spatial Epidemiology methods and applications*, Oxford University Press, pp. 51-68.

Carstairs V., Morris R. (1991) *Deprivation and Health in Scotland*, Aberdeen University Press.

CESIS (1997), "Non Monetary Indicators of Poverty and Social Exclusion", Working paper presented at a seminar in Lisbon, March.

Cochard M., Heyer E., "L'adjustement de l'emploi dans la crise", in OFCE 2010, ch. VI, pp. 102-109.

Considerazioni finali del Governatore della Banca d'Italia, Roma, 31 maggio 2011.

Davezies L. (2004), "Formes de développement des territoires et pauvreté", in *Les travaux de l'Observatoire national de la pauvreté et de l'exclusion sociale*, Paris, La Documentation française, pp. 415-435.

Department of Environment, Transport and the Regions (DETR) (2000), "Indices of Deprivation 2000", *Regeneration Research Summary,* Vol. 31, pp. 3-42.

Dillon W., Goldstein M. (1984), *Multivariate analysis method and application*, New York, Wiley.

Esping – Andersen G. (1990), *Social Foundations of Post-industrial Economies*, Oxford, Oxford University Press.

Eurostat (2003), *European and social statistics: income, poverty and social exclusion*, Luxembourg.

Forrest R., Gordon D. (1993) *People and Places: a 1991 Census atlas of England*, SAUS, University of Bristol.

Freguja C., Pannuzi N. (2007) "La povertà in Italia: che cosa sappiamo dalle varie fonti?" in Brandolini A., Saraceno C. 2007.

Gordon D., Pantazis C. (1997) *Breadline Britain in the 1990s*, Ashgate, Ashgate Publishing Limited.

Grasso M. (2002) "A measurement of welfare in the Italian regions" (original in Italian), *Politica Economica*, a. XVIII, sez. 2, pp. 261-292.

Gueslin A., (2004) *Les gens de rien. Une histoire de la grande pauvreté dans la France du XXe siècle*, Paris, Fayard.

Guio A.C. (2009), "What can be learned from deprivation indicators in Europe?" European Commission, Methodologies and Working Papers, ISBN 9789279123085.

Heidenreich M. (2003) "Regional inequalities in the enlarged Europe", *Journal of European Social Policy*, 4, pp. 313-333.

Hogan J., Tchernis R. (2004) "Bayesian Factor Analysis for Spatially Correlated Data, with Application to Summarizing Area-Level Material Deprivation from Census Data", *Journal of the American Statistical Association*, 466, pp. 314-324.

IDS (1997), "Poverty and Social Exclusion in North and South", Working paper n. 55, Brighton.

Iorio G. (2001) *La povertà. Analisi storico-sociologica dei processi di deprivazione* Roma, Armando.

Ivaldi E., Testi A. (2011) "Socio-Economic Conditions and Health in Europe: A Comparison among the 27 EU Countries", in Rowsen J. D., Eliot A. P. (eds.) *Social Inequalities*, New York, Nova Publisher (forthcoming).

Ivaldi, E., Testi A. (2010) "Genoa Index of Deprivation (GDI): An Index of Material Deprivation for Geographical Areas", in Baird C. M. (ed.) *Social Indicators: Statistics, Trends and Policy Development*, New York, Nova Publisher.

Jarman B. (1983) "Identification of underprivileged areas", *British Medical Journal*, 286, pp. 1705-09.

Jarman B. (1984) "Underprivileged areas: validation and distribution of scores", *British Medical Journal*, 289, pp. 1587-1592.

Johnson R.A., Wichern D.W. (2002) *Applied Multivariate Statistical Analysis*, 5th Edn., Englewood Cliffs, Prentice-Hall.

Kaiser H. F. (1958) "The varimax criterion for analytic rotation in factor analysis", *Psychometrika*, 23, pp. 187–200.

La France invisible (2006), sous la direction de Beaud S., Confavreux J. et Lindgaard J., Paris, La Découverte.

Labao L. M., Hooks G., Tickamyer R. A. (2008) "Poverty and inequality across space: sociological reflection on the missing-middle subnational scale", *Cambridge Journal of regions, economy and society*, 1, pp. 89-113.

Lambert A. (2008a) "Quelle mesure officielle pour la pauvreté?", *Regards croisés sur l'économie*, n° 4, pp. 30-33.

Lambert A. (2008b) "Pauvreté: où se situe la France par rapport au reste de l'Union européenne ?", *Regards croisés sur l'économie*, n° 4, pp. 178-181.

Mingione T. (1997) "La povertà estrema. La questione della identificazione dei soggetti in Italia", in Guidicini G., Pieretti G., Bergamaschi M. (eds.), *Gli esclusi dal territorio*, Milano, Angeli.

Neuhaus J. O., Wrigley C. (1954) "The quartimax method: an analytical approach to orthogonal simple structure", *British Journal of Statistical Psychology*, 7, pp. 81-91.

Noble M., Smith G., Wright G., Dibben C., Loyd M., Ratcliffe A., McLellan D., Sigala M., Anttila C. (2003) *Scottish indices of deprivation 2003*, Edinburgh, Scottish Executive.

Noyé C. (2008) "Territoires de la pauvreté : les dynamiques de fragilisation des espaces", *Regards croisés sur l'économie*, n° 4, pp. 62-69.

OFCE (2010), *L'économie française 2011*, Paris, La Découverte.

Osborne J. (2002) "Notes on the use of data transformations. Practical Assessment", *Research and Evaluation*, 8, pp. 912-935.

Paugam S. (1995), "The Spiral of Precariousness", in Room G. (ed.), *Beyond the threshold. The measurement and analysis of social exclusion*, Bristol, Policy Press.

Reinstadler A., Ray, J. C. (2010) *Macro determinants of individual income poverty in 93 regions of Europe*. Methodologies and working papers, Eurostat.

Sen, A. (1987) *On ethics and economics*, Oxford, Basil Blackwell.

Smith T. B. (2006) *La France injuste*, Paris, Éditions Autrement.

Soskice D. (1999) "Divergent Production Regimes: Coordinated and Uncoordinated Market Economies in the 1980s and 1990s", in Kitschelt H., Lange P., Marks G., Stephens, J. D. (eds.), *Continuity and Change in Contemporary Capitalism*, Cambridge (UK), Cambridge University Press, pp. 101–134.

Stevens J. (1986), *Applied multivariate statistics for the social sciences*, Hillsdale, Lawrence Erlbaum Associates.

Tableaux de l'économie française. Édition 2011 (2011), Paris, INSEE.

Testi A., Ivaldi E. (2011) "Measuring Progress in Health through Deprivation Indexes", *Review of Economics and Finance*.

Testi A., Ivaldi E. (2009) "Material versus social deprivation and health: a case study of an urban area", *The European Journal of Health Economics*, 3, pp. 323–328.

Testi A., Ivaldi E., Busi A. (2005) "Features and information potential of the indices of deprivation" (original in Italian), *Tendenze nuove*, 2.

Townsend P. (1987) "Deprivation", *Journal of Social Policy*, 2, pp. 125-146.

Townsend P., Phillimore P., Beattie A. (1988). *Health and deprivation: inequality and the North*. London, Croom Helm.

Valerio M., Vitullo F. (2000) "Testing of an index of social disadvantage in Basilicata", *Epidemiologia e Prevenzione*, 24, pp. 219-223.

Whelan C.T., Lucchini M., Pisati M., Maître B. (2010) "Understanding the socio-economic distribution of multiple deprivation: An application of self-organising maps", *Research in Social Stratification and Mobility*, 3, pp. 325-342.

Reviewed by Alain Clément, Université "F. Rabelais", Tours, France.

In: Socioeconomic Status and Health Implications ISBN: 978-1-62100-675-6
Editor: Sarah Reibert and Alice Jannings, pp. 163-174

Chapter 8

JAPANESE WOMEN'S HEALTH RELATED TO JOB STRESS: A REVIEW FOCUSING ON GENDER ROLE

Kumi Hirokawa
Baika Women's University

ABSTRACT

The Japanese average life expectancy has continued to increase during the periods of high economic growth in Japan after World War II. Indeed, it is widely acknowledged that economic growth has an impact on health inequality. However, these changes occur alongside the facts that Japanese women have unstable job statuses, and encounter large wage differences compared with men, low promotion rates, low access to child-rearing services and high burdens of aged people's care. Despite this, their life expectancy is longer than those in other countries. Gender differences in physical health should be clarified with consideration of not only biological and physical factors, but also social, psychological and cultural factors. In this chapter, Japanese women's physical health related to socioeconomic factors, specifically job stress, will be discussed with data from Japanese cohort studies, to indicate how the study gender not only contributes to, but is central to, a wider social analysis.

EMPLOYMENT STATUS AND HEALTH

One of the most reproducible demographic findings in modern societies is the inverse association between socioeconomic status and mortality (Davey Smith, Carroll, and Rankin, 1992; Davey Smith, Hart et al., 1998). Several different indicators of socioeconomic status have been investigated, including educational attainment, occupational class or employment status, income level, and indices based on the characteristics of residential areas (Davey Smith, Shipley, and Rose, 1990; Davey Smith, Blane, and Bartley, 1994; Liberatos, Link, and Kelsey, 1988). Recent geographical analyses in Japan have shown that socioeconomic status in municipalities is strongly related to regional variations in health levels, indicating higher mortality from all causes in areas of lower socioeconomic status (Fukuda, Nakamura, and

Takano, 2004). Hirokawa, Tsutsumi, and Kayaba (2006) investigated the associations between employment status and mortality in Japanese community people. According to the results of their cohort study, unemployed men showed increased mortality from all causes compared with white-collar workers, whereas unemployed women did not show a significant difference in all-cause mortality compared with white-collar workers. The majority of unemployed women were homemakers in their cohort study because traditional ways of thinking, such as the idea that men should go to work while women should stay at home, are still common in Japan. It is assumed that the husband's socioeconomic status may have an influence on the health of female homemakers. Japanese women's health is possibly dependent on their partner's socioeconomic status.

Therefore, what are the effects of socioeconomic status on health in Japanese working women? As the society's workforce requirements increase, the workforce participation rates of Japanese women have been increasing. On the other hand, it has been pointed out that Japanese women have unstable job statuses, and encounter large wage differences compared with men, low promotion rates, low access to child-rearing services and high burdens of aged people's care (Kawakami, Haratani, Kobayashi et al., 2004). There are only a few studies have investigated the effects of occupational status on Japanese working women's health. Sekine, Chandola, Martikainen et al. (2009) revealed that women with lower occupational status (i.e., without administrative titles) were more likely to report poor physical functioning than those with higher occupational status (i.e., with administrative titles). Hirokawa, Tsutsumi, and Kayaba (2009) examined the associations between socioeconomic status and fibrinogen levels as one of the risk factors for cardiovascular diseases. Their results revealed that, among white-collar women, those in non-managerial positions showed higher levels of fibrinogen than those in managerial positions, whereas there was no such difference among blue-collar women.

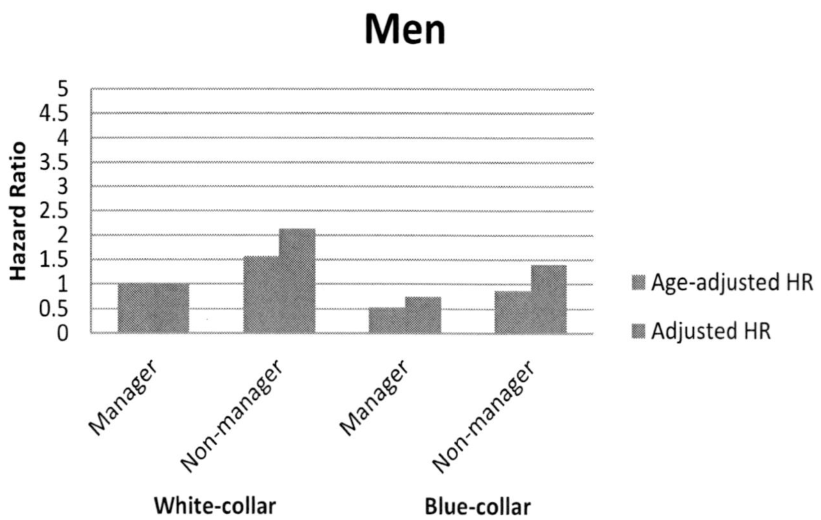

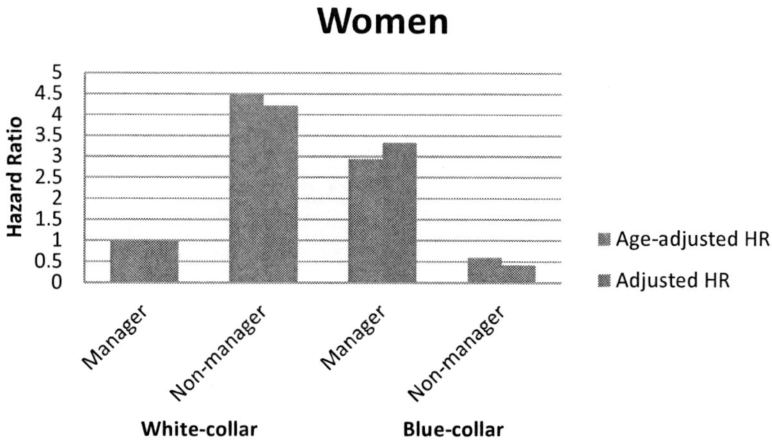

Figure 1. Occupational status and all CVD mortality: JMS cohort study (Hirokawa et al., 2008a).

Hirokawa, Tsutsumi, and Kayaba (2008a) subsequently investigated the impacts of occupational status on health in Japanese working men and women. Their results indicated that men in non-managerial positions had an increased mortality risk compared with men in managerial positions, whereas no significant association was found among Japanese working women. Although the results did not reach statistical significance, among white-collar women, those in non-managerial positions showed about a four-fold higher risk of cardiovascular mortality than those in managerial positions, whereas among blue-collar women, those in non-managerial positions showed low mortality risks compared with those in managerial positions (Figure 1). One of the reasons why the associations between occupational status and mortality of cardiovascular diseases were not significant may be the small sample of women in managerial positions in their cohort. Japanese women in managerial positions comprised only 6.9% of the total managerial positions in 2006 (Ministry of Health, Labour, and Welfare, 2007). Greater inclusion of women in managerial positions is necessary to investigate the associations between occupational status and mortality risks of cardiovascular diseases in future studies.

Gender Differences in Associations between Job Stress and Health

Environmental factors, health behavior, individual traits, physiological responses, and pathological changes are hypothesized to mediate the effects of socioeconomic status on individuals' health problems (Kristensen, 2005). As an environmental factor, especially a psychosocial factor, job stress has been widely investigated in relation to mortality and incidence of cardiovascular diseases. Regarding the assessment of work stress, the job strain model (Karaseck, 1979) is the dominant work stress theory, which defines that health risk arises from high job demands and low job control and their combination, referred to as job strain. In this model, job control was defined as skill discretion and decision authority. Job demands involved psychological pressure to work fast, work hard, and work excessively. The scores for each index were categorized using the median, and the two categorical variables were used to determine the four-level rank-ordered job strain variables corresponding to Karasek's model of job demand-control, with low job demand and high job control representing a low-strain job, high job demand and high job control representing an active job, low job demand and low job control representing a passive job, and high job demand and low job control representing a high-strain job.

The model posits that workers who face high psychological demands and have little control over their work (i.e., job strain) are at greater risk of becoming ill. Many prospective studies have supported this hypothesis using cardiovascular disease outcomes (Alterman, Shekelle, Vernon et al., 1994; Bosma, Peter, Siegrist et al., 1998; de Bacquer, Pelfrene, Clays et al., 2005; Kivimäki, Leino-Arjas, Luukkonen et al., 2002; Kuper and Marmot, 2003).

According to a review by Kawakami and Tsutsumi (2004), among 25 studies conducted in European countries and the United States, 19 studies revealed that the prevalence and incidence rates of ischemic heart disease were high in the high-strain job group. Kawakami and Tsutsumi (2004) reported that job control was consistently associated with physiological health in men, and that low job control increased mortality in men. On the other hand, although there were no consistent findings of associations between job stress and health in women, a few studies revealed that women in the active job group had increased mortality from cardiovascular diseases (Eaker, Sullivan, Kelly Hayes et al, 2004; Rosvall, Ostergren, Hedblad et al, 2002).

There are not many studies on the associations between job stress and health in Japan. Tsutsumi, Kayaba, Hirokawa et al. (2006) found that men in the active job group had reduced mortality, especially for mortality of cancer, while no association was found in women. This finding in Japanese men shows the opposite trend to previous findings in Western women (Eaker et al, 2004; Rosvall, et al, 2002). For the associations between job stress and chronic diseases and health problems, high job demands were associated with high cholesterol and high job stress was associated with high prevalence of hypertension in Japanese men (Tsutsumi, Kayaba, Tsutsumi et al., 2001; Tsutsumi, Kayaba, Ishikawa et al., 2003). Fibrinogen is considered to be one of the indicators of cardiovascular diseases and has been investigated (Folsom, Wu, Rosamond et al., 1997; Kannel, Wolf, Castelli et al., 1987; Woodward, Lowe, Rumley et al., 1998). High job demands and high job stress were associated with high fibrinogen levels in Japanese men (Ishizaki, Martikainen, Nakagawa et al., 2001; Hirokawa, Tsutsumi, and Kayaba, 2008b). On the other hand, no association was found in Japanese women. These findings for the associations between job stress and fibrinogen levels, i.e., that high job stress was associated with high fibrinogen levels in men but not in women, are consistent with Western data (Kittel, Leynen, Stam et al., 2002; Tsutsumi, Theorell, Hallqvist et al., 1999).

WOMEN'S HEALTH AND STRESS

It has been discussed that there are many potential factors for the associations between women's health and job stress (Hirokawa, 2011). Women were supposed to have stronger effects for home-related stress such as marriage, parenting, and care-giving than for job stress (Hirokawa, 2005). There are some data indicating that life stress (i.e., non-specific stress felt from daily life) was associated with physical health in Japanese women. Higher levels of life stress for Japanese women increased the mortality from cardiovascular diseases (Iso, Date, Yamamoto et al., 2007), and showed a marginally positive association with mortality from colon cancer (Kojima, Wakai, Tokudome et al., 2005). On the other hand, associations between life stress levels and these mortality risks were not found in Japanese men. It was supposed that, in Japan, job stress for men and home-related stress for women may have effects on the health status.

For data in English women, low control at home appeared to increase the incidence rate of cardiovascular diseases (Chandola, Kuper, Singh-Manoux et al., 2004). It was also revealed that care-giving and parenting predicted low control at home in women, while low job control did so in men. Therefore, among home-related stresses, care-giving and parenting could be the main stress factors for women.

WOMEN'S MULTIPLE ROLES AND HEALTH

Among the many home-related stresses, what effects of care-giving and parenting on Japanese women's health have been shown? Takeda, Kawachi, Yamagata et al. (2006) examined the associations between multiple roles, such as marital role, employment role, parenting role, and care-giving role, and health problems in a cross-sectional study. Their results showed that younger (20–39 years) women benefited from multiple roles with less smoking, whereas middle-aged (40–59 years) women reported less health maintenance behaviors including less exercise and fewer health check-ups. Although there was no statistical significance, the risks for reporting health problems in no-role women were two-fold higher than those in single-role women. Honjo, Iso, Inoue et al. (2008) examined the impact of educational levels on the risk of stroke and the modification effect of multiple roles at work and at home in middle-aged Japanese women. In their results, women with a single role in the household (having a partner, parent, or child) at college levels (i.e., high education levels) showed a higher risk of stroke than those in high school levels (i.e., references). They discussed that the potential benefit that multiple roles were protective against stroke risk among highly educated working women.

Martikainen (1995) examined the impact of multiple roles on mortality risks in Finnish women. Finnish women with a marital role, a parenting role, and an employment role had low mortality, and an increased number of children also showed a reduction of mortality. Parenting and care-giving may not have adverse effects on women's health. For working mothers, in particular, parenting may help them to reduce their stress levels. For example, employed Japanese mothers showed a lower level of child-related stress than housewife mothers (Hirokawa, Asano, Masuno et al., 2007).

WORK AND FAMILY CONFLICT

In recent years, studies on "work and family conflict" have been conducted. Chandola, Martikainen, Bartley, et al. (2004) conducted a comparative cross-sectional study of Finland, Japan, and the United Kingdom to examine the effects of multiple roles and the combination of work and family roles on mental health. In their results, both work-to family and family-to-work conflicts had adverse effects on the mental health of men and women in the three countries. They discussed that work and family roles and the balance between the two may be important for the mental health of men and women. Interestingly, single fathers in the three countries and single mothers in Finland showed poor mental health, and these results were partly explained by their higher levels of family-to-work conflict. Furthermore, Japanese women had the greatest conflict and poorest mental health, while Helsinki women had the lowest conflict and best mental health.

Gender differences in mental health in Japanese men and women may be attributed to gender differences in the family structure and work-to family conflicts rather than gender differences in work characteristics including job demands, job control, support at work, work hours, and shift work (Sekine, Chandola, Martikainen et al., 2010). Sekine et al. (2010) pointed out that, in Japan, while men were able to concentrate on their work with relative freedom from their family tasks and responsibilities, women should maintain their work-life balances, because women are expected to be much more involved in household chores and taking care of their family members.

Furthermore, a partner's job stress can lead to work-to-family conflicts (Shimazu, Bakker, Demerouti et al., 2009). In that study, work-to-family conflicts caused by the partner's high job stress damaged the relationships with their partner, and then led to poor mental health. The husband's job stress could spill over to the wife's life stress, which could also have an effect on her health. However, these results were not specific to women, and work-to-family conflicts were common problems for working men and women.

Social Support

From the data for spillover of work-to-family conflicts between a married couple (Shimazu et al., 2009), women's life stress seemed to be increased by their partner. However, a marital role may improve women's health, as well as a parenting role and a care-giving role, as reviewed in studies on multiple roles and women's health. This is because the partner, children, and aged parent(s) could be resources of social support for women.

Social support has been thought to ameliorate the effects of perceived stress on physical and mental health (LaRocco, House, and French, 1980; Karasek, Trantis, and Chudhry, 1982). Johnson and Hall (1988) focused on the moderating effect of social support, by expanding the demand-control model of job strain (Karasek, 1979) to include a social support dimension called the demand-control-support model. Support from supervisors and colleagues at work has been shown to be protective for depressive symptoms and insomnia, and to facilitate job satisfaction (Dormann and Zapf, 1999; Nakata, Haratani, Takahashi et al., 2001; McCalister, Dolbier, Webster et al., 2006).

Odagiri, Ohya, and Shimomitsu (2005) investigated gender differences in social support, including support at work and support from partner, family, and friends. They revealed that men received more support from their supervisor than women, that men and women received almost the same amount of support from colleagues, and that women received more support from their partner, family, and friends than men. Their results suggested that working women's health might not be so reliant on the job as that of men. The circle of connections as resources for social support should be broader in women than in men.

Among the stress factors, most Japanese working women reported that they felt stress from interpersonal relationships at work (Koyama, Morikawa, Torii et al., 2006). Recent studies have focused on workplace bullying, which includes psychological, physical, and sexual abuse or harassment (MacIntosh, Wuest, Gray et al., 2010). Participants among Canadian working women reported mainly psychological bullying (MacIntosh, Wuest, Gray et al., 2010). In a study in the United States, the vast majority of sex-based harassment victims reported experiencing low victimization or gender harassment (Leskinen, Cortina, Kabat, 2011). Women who experienced gender harassment showed significant decrements in their professional and psychological well-being (Leskinen et al., 2011). Both men and women who experienced workplace bullying were more likely to report sleep problems (Lallukka, Rahkonen, and Lahelma, 2010; Niedhammer, David, Degioanni et al., 2009). In a Japanese study, workplace bullying mediated associations between job stress and sleep problems, implying that a stressful work environment causes worsened interpersonal relationships and then leads to workplace bullying, which causes sleep problems and depressive symptoms (Takaki, Taniguchi, Fukuoka et al., 2010). When workplace social support was adjusted for, the mediation effects were decreased, especially in women (Takaki et al. 2010). Social support at work was expected to be protective against causes of workplace bullying (Quine, 1999). Social support may be an important factor for working women to maintain good relationships at work.

Cultural Factor for Working Women

A study on the actual situation of Japanese working women's stress found that Japanese working women during childrearing were exposed to high stress of balancing work and family, and consequently felt further stress of not saving time for themselves (Japan Association for The Advancement of Working Women, 2006). Why should Japanese working women take a great deal of the burden of balancing work and family?

According to Esping-Andersen (1990; 1999), Japan belongs to a conservative welfare regime or a hybrid welfare regime. In a conservative welfare regime, which is clustered in Southern European countries such as Spain, Italy, and Germany, family is expected to play an important role. A hybrid welfare regime is a mixed type of conservative and liberal welfare regimes. In a liberal welfare regime, which is clustered in Anglo-Saxon countries such as the United Kingdom and United States, the free market plays an important role. This 'welfare regime' approach includes points of view of culture, which could have an effect on the basic principles on which welfare state policies are founded (Pfau-Effinger, 2005). Esping-Andersen (1990; 1999) focused on different policies in the role of the family, the welfare state, and the market, which should assume a larger role in a society.

According to a well-known ecological study by Hofstede (2001), Japan was grouped as a collective society and found to be the most masculine society, implying a high orientation toward stereotypical gender differentiations, among 53 countries and areas (Hofstede, 2001). In Japanese society, the traditional gender-role attitude of "Men go to work and women stay at home" has been strong (Otake, 1977). Markus and Kitayama (1991) suggested that cultural differences may have effects on individuals' cognition, behavior, and motivation. Therefore, as Sekine et al. (2010) pointed out, while men were able to concentrate on their work with relative freedom from their family tasks and responsibilities, women should maintain their work-life balance in Japan.

Today, many Japanese women participate in economic activities for reasons such as individuals' financial situations and social demands of facilitating women's economic participation. Desirable support factors for Japanese working women may be those that facilitate them to balance work and family, and then to secure sufficient time for themselves. It may be necessary to consider how to connect support resources at work and support resources in a living community. In particular, support resources for child-care and aged-person's care, including family members and public and/or private services in the market, are required for women. Workplaces that collaborate with living communities should assume an effective role in the construction of a social network for working women's health with consideration of Japanese culture.

References

Alterman, T., Shekelle, R. B., Vernon, S. W., and Burau, K. D. (1994) Decision latitude, psychologic demand, job strain, and coronary heart disease in the Western Electric Study. *American Journal of Epidemiology,* 139(6), 620-627.

Bosma, H., Peter, R., Siegrist, J., and Marmot, M. (1998) Two alternative job stress models and the risk of coronary heart disease. *American Journal of Public Health,* 88(1), 68-74.

Chandola, T., Kuper, H., Singh-Manoux, A., Bartley, M., and Marmot, M. (2004a) The effect of control at home on CHD events in the Whitehall II study: Gender differences in psychosocial domestic pathways to social inequalities in CHD. *Social Science and Medicine,* 58(8), 1501-1509.

Chandola, T., Martikainen, P., Bartley, M., Lahelma, E., Marmot, M., Sekine, M., et al. (2004b) Does conflict between home and work explain the effect of multiple roles on mental health? A comparative study of Finland, Japan, and the UK. International *Journal of Epidemiology,* 33, 884-893.

Davey Smith, G., Blane, D., and Bartley, M. (1994) Explanations for socioeconomic differentials in mortality: evidence from Britain and elsewhere. *European Journal of Public Health,* 4, 131-144.

Davey Smith, G., Carroll, D., and Rankin, S. (1992) Socio-economic differentials in mortality: evidence form Glasgow graveyards. *BMJ,* 305, 1554-1557.

Davey Smith, G., Hart, C., Hole, D., MacKinnon, P., Gillis, C., Watt, G., et al. (1998) Education and occupational social class: which is the more important indicator of mortality risk? *Journal of Epidemiology and Community Health,* 52, 153-160.

Davey Smith, G., Shipley, M. J., and Rose, G. (1990) The magnitude and causes of socio-economic differentials in mortality: further evidence from the Whitehall study. J Epidemiol Community Health, 44, 260-265.

de Bacquer, D., Pelfrene, E., Clays, E., Mak, R., Moreau, M., de Smet, P. et al. (2005) Perceived job stress and incidence of coronary events: 3-year follow-up of the Belgian Job Stress Project cohort. *American Journal of Epidemiology,* 161(5), 434-441.

Dormann, C., and Zapf, D. (1999) Social support, social stressors at work, and depressive symptoms: testing for main and moderating effects with structural equations in a three-wave longitudinal study. *Journal of Applied Psychology,* 84(6), 874-884.

Eaker, E., Sullivan, L., Kelly Hayes, M., D'Agostino, R. S., and Benjamin, E. (2004) Does job strain increase the risk for coronary heart disease or death in men and women? The Framingham offspring study. *American Journal of Epidemiology,* 159(10), 950-958.

Esping-Andersen, G. (1990) *The three worlds of welfare capitalism.* Cambridge: Polity Press.

Esping-Andersen, G. (1999) *Social foundations of postindustrial economies.* Oxford: Oxford University Press.

Folsom, A., Wu, K., Rosamond, W., Sharrett, A. R., and Chambless, L. E. (1997) Prospective study of hemostatic factors and incidence of coronary heart disease: the Arteriosclerosis Risk in Communities (ARIC) Study. *Circulation,* 96, 1102-8.

Fukuda, Y., Nakamura, K., Takano, T. (2004) Municipal socioeconomic status and mortality in Japan: sex and age differences, and trends in 1973-1998. *Social Science and Medicine,* 59, 2435-2445.

Hirokawa, K. (2005) Stressor to sei-sa - kekkon to kenko: evidence based marriage kenkyu wo mezasite. [Gender differences in stressor: Focusing on marriage and health] *Gender and Sex Specific Medicine,* 2(11), 21-25.

Hirokawa, K. (2011) Gender differences in physical health related to psycho-social factors. Baika Women's University Faculty of Nursing Bulletin, 1, 61-72.

Hirokawa, K., Asano, J., Masuno, M., Usui, Y., Yoshida, I., and Shimizu, H. (2007). Child-Related Strain for Mothers in a Japanese Community. *The Family Journal, January,* 1, 15(1), 16-23.

Hirokawa, K., Tsutsumi, A., and Kayaba, K. (2006) Impacts of educational level and employment status on mortality for Japanese women and men: the Jichi Medical School cohort study. *European Journal of Epidemiology,* 21, 641-651.

Hirokawa, K., Tsutsumi, A., Kayaba, K. (2008a) Socio-economic inequality in health among Japanese working population: Jichi Medical Cohort Study. Paper presented at 10th International Congress of Behavioral Medicine, Tokyo, Japan.

Hirokawa, K., Tsutsumi, A., Kayaba, K. (2008b) Psychosocial job characteristics and plasma fibrinogen in Japanese male and female workers: the Jichi Medical School cohort study. *Atherosclerosis,* 198, 468-476.

Hirokawa, K., Tsutsumi, A., and Kayaba, K. (2009) Occupation and plasma fibrinogen in Japanese male and female workers: The Jichi Medical School cohort study. *Social Science and Medicine,* 68, 1091-1097.

Hofstede, G. (2001) *Culture's consequences Second Edition: Comparing values, behaviors, institutions, and organization across nations.* Thousand Oaks: Sage Publications.

Honjo, K., Iso, H., Inoue, M., and Tsgane, S. (2008) Education, social roles, and the risk of cardiovascular disease among middle-aged Japanese women: the JPHC study cohort I. *Stroke,* 39, 2886-2890.

Ishizaki, M., Martikainen, P., Nakagawa, H., and Marmot, M. (2001) Socioeconomic status, workplace characteristics and plasma fibrinogen level of Japanese male employees. *Scandinavian Journal of Work and Environmental Health,* 27, 287-291.

Iso, H., Date, C., Yamamoto, A., Toyoshima, H., Tanabe, N., Kikuchi, S. et al. (2007) Perceived mental stress and mortality from cardiovascular disease among Japanese men and women: The Japan collaborative cohort study for evaluation of cancer risk sponsored by monbusho (JACC study). *Circulation,* 106, 1229-1236.

Japan Association for The Advancement of Working Women (2006) Ninshin-ki kosidate-ki no josei rodousya no stress ni kansuru chosa houkoku syo. [A report on working women's stress during pregnancy and childrearing] http://www.jaaww.or.jp/about/pdf/document_pdf/health_stress.pdf

Johnson, J. V., and Hall, E. M. (1988) Job strain, work place social support, and cardiovascular disease: A cross-sectional study of a random sample of the Swedish working population. *American Journal of Public Health,* 78, 1336-1342.

Kannel, W. B., Wolf, P. A., Castelli, W. P., D'Agostino, R. B. (1987) Fibrinogen and risk of cardiovascular disease. The Framingham study. *JAMA,* 258, 1183-1186.

Karasek, R., (1979) Job demands, job decision latitude and mental strain: Implications for job redesign. Administrative Science Quarterly, 24, 285-306.

Karasek, R. A., Triantis, K., and Chaudhry, S. (1982) Co-worker and supervisor support as moderators of associations between task characteristics and mental strain. *Journal of Occupational Behavior,* 3, 147-160.

Kawakami, N., Haratani, T., Kobayashi, F., Izhizaki, M., Hayashi, T., Fujita, O. et al. (2004) Occupational class and exposure to job stressors among employed men and women in Japan. *Journal of Epidemiology,* 14, 204-210.

Kawakami, N., and Tsutsumi, A. (2004) Shokuba no mental health: sosetsu 2000-2003. [Occupational mental health: review paper 2000-2003] *Kyoshu Eisei,* 4, Supplement, 301-305.

Kittel, F., Leynen, F., Stam, M., Dramaix, M., de Smet, P., Mak, R. et al. (2002) Job conditions and fibrinogen in 14226 Belgian workers. The Belstress study. *European Heart Journal,* 23, 1841-1848.

Kivimäki, M., Leino-Arjas, P., Luukkonen, R., Riihimäki, H., Vahtera, J., and Kirjonen, J. (2002) Work stress and risk of cardiovascular mortality: prospective cohort study of industrial employees. *BMJ,* 325(7369), 857-860.

Kojima, M., Wakai, K., Tokudome, S., Tamakoshi, K., Toyoshima, H., Watanabe, Y. et al. (2005) Perceived psychologic stress and colorectal cancer mortality: Findings from the Japan collaborative cohort study. *Psychosomatic Medicine,* 67, 72-77.

Koyama, Y., Morikawa, Y., Torii, H., Shiroto, T., and Sato, T. (2006) Syurou josei no mental health ni oyobosu syokuba stress ni kansuru chosa kenkyu. [Survey on stress at work related to working women's mental health] Ishikawa Occupational Health Promotion Center. http://www.ishikawa-sanpo.jp/ishikawa/chousa/h18_syuuroujosei.pdf

Kristensen, T. S. (2005) The changing nature of work and its implications for cardiovascular disease. Paper presented at the fourth international conference on work environment and cardiovascular diseases. Southern California.

Kuper, H., and Marmot, M. (2003) Job strain, job demands, decision latitude, and risk of coronary heart disease within the Whitehall II study. *Journal of Epidemiology and Community Health,* 257(2), 147-153.

Lallukka, T., Rahkonen, O., and Lahelma, E. (2011) Workplace bullying and subsequent sleep problems - the Helsinki Health Study. *Scandinavian Journal of Work and Environmental Health*, 37(3), 204-212.

LaRocco, J., House, J., and French, J. (1980) Social support, occupational stress and health. Journal of Health and Social Behavior, 21, 202-218.

Leskinen, E. A., Cortina, L. M., and Kabat, D. B. (2011) Gender harassment: broadening our understanding of sex-based harassment at work. *Law and Human Behavior,* 35(1), 25-39.

Liberatos, P., Link, B. G., and Kelsey, J. L. (1988) The measurement of social class in epidemiology. *Epidemiologic Review,* 10, 87-121.

MacIntosh, J., Wuest, J., Gray, M. M., and Aldous, S. (2010) Effects of workplace bullying on how women work. *Western Journal of Nursing Research,* 32(7), 910-931.

Markus, H. R., and Kitayama, S. (1991) Culture and the self: Implication for cognition, emotion, and motivation. *Psychological Review,* 98, 224-253.

Martikainen P. (1995) Women's employment, marriage, motherhood and mortality: a test of the multiple role and role accumulation hypotheses. *Social Science and Medicine,* 40(2), 199-212

McCalister, K. T., Dolbier, C. L., Webster, J. A., Mallon, M. W., and Steinhardt, M. A. (2006) Hardiness and support at work as predictors of work stress and job satisfaction. *American Journal of Health Promotion,* 20(3), 183-191.

Ministry of Health, Labour, and Welfare (2007) Heisei 18 nendo josei koyou kanri kihon chosa. [Basic Survey of Gender Equality in Employment Management in the fiscal year of 2006] http://www.mhlw.go.jp/toukei/list/dl/71-18b.pdf

Nakata, A., Haratani, T., Takahashi, M., Kawakami, N., Arito, H., Fujioka, Y. et al. (2001) Job stress, social support at work, and insomnia in Japanese shift workers. *Journal of Human Ergology,* 30(1-2), 203-209.

Niedhammer, I., David, S., Degioanni, S., Drummond, A., Philip, P., Acquarone, D. et al. (2009) Workplace bullying and sleep disturbances: findings from a large scale cross-sectional survey in the French working population. *Sleep,* 32(9), 1211-1219.

Odagiri, Y., Ohya, Y., and Shimomitsu, T. (2005) Shokuba stress chosa ni miru seisa [Gender differences in work related stress at the workplace] *Gender and Sex Specific Medicine,* 2(11), 43-48.

Otake,S. (1977) *"Ie" to josei no rekishi* [History of "ie" and women]. Tokyo: Kogundo.

Pfau-Effinger, B. (2005) Culture and welfare state policies: reflections on a complex interrelation. *Journal of Social Policy,* 34, 3-20.

Quine, L. (1999) Workplace bullying in NHS community trust: staff questionnaire survey. *BMJ,* 228-232.

Rosvall, M., Ostergren, P. O., Hedblad, B., Isacsson, S. O., Janzon, L., and Berglund, G. (2002) Work-related psychosocial factors and carotid atherosclerosis. *International Journal of Epidemiology,* 31(6), 1169-1178.

Shimazu, A., Bakker A. B., and Demerouti, E. (2009) How job demands affect and intimate partner: a test of the spillover-crossover model in Japan. *Journal of Occupational Health,* 51, 239-248.

Sekine, M., Chandola, T., Martikainen, P., Marmot, M., and Kagaminori, S. (2006)

Socioeconomic inequalities in physical and mental functioning of Japanese civil servants: explanations from work and family characteristics. *Social Science and Medicine,* 63, 430-445.

Sekine, M., Chandola, T., Martikainen, P., Marmot, M., and Kagaminori, S. (2009)

Socioeconomic inequalities in physical and mental functioning of British, Finnish, and Japanese civil servants: role of job demand, control, and work hours. *Social Science and Medicine,* 69, 1417-1425.

Sekine, M., Chandola, T., Martikainen, P., Marmot, M., and Kagaminori, S. (2010) Sex differences in physical and mental functioning of Japanese civil servants: explanations from work and family characteristics. *Social Science and Medicine,* 71, 2091-2099.

Takaki, J., Taniguchi, T., Fukuoka, E., Fujii, Y., Tsutsumi, A., Nakajima, K. et al., (2010). Workplace bullying could play important roles in the relationships between job strain and symptoms of depression and sleep disturbance. *Journal of Occupational Health,* 52, 367-374.

Takeda, Y., Kawachi, I., Yamagata, Z., Hashimoto, S., Matsumura, Y., Oguri, S., and Okayama, A. (2006) The impact of multiple role occupancy on health-related behaviours in Japan: differences by gender and age. *Public Health,* 120, 966-975.

Tsutsumi, A., Kayaba, K. Hirokawa, K., Ishikawa, S. and The Jichi Medical School Cohort.

Study Group (2006) Psychosocial job characteristics and risk of mortality in a Japanese community-based working population: The Jichi Medical School Cohort Study. *Social Science and Medicine,* 63, 1276-1288.

Tsutsumi, A., Kayaba, K., Ishikawa, S., Gotoh, T., Nago, N., Yamada, S. et al., (2003) Job characteristics and serum lipid profile in Japanese rural workers: The Jichi Medical School Cohort study. *Journal of Epidemiology,* 13(2), 63-71.

Tsutsumi, A., Kayaba, K., Tsutsumi, K., and Igarashi, M. (2001) Association between job strain and prevalence of hypertension: a cross-sectional analysis in a Japanese working population encompassing a wide range of occupations: The Jichi Medical School Cohort Study. *Occupation and Environmental Medicine,* 58, 367-373.

Tsutsumi, A., Theorell, T., Hallqvist, J., Reuterwall, C., and de Faire, U. (1999) Association between job characteristics and plasma fibrinogen in a normal working population; A cross-sectional analysis in referents of the SHEEP study. *Journal of Epidemiology and Community Health,* 53, 348-354.

Woodward, M., Lowe, G. D. O., Rumley, A., and Tunstall-Pedoe, H. (1998). Fibrinogen as a risk factor for coronary heart disease and mortality n middle-aged men and women. *European Heart Journal,* 19, 55-62.

In: Socioeconomic Status and Health Implications ISBN: 978-1-62100-675-6
Editor: Sarah Reibert and Alice Jannings, pp. 175-182

Chapter 9

HIDDEN COSTS INCURRED BY FAMILY AND FRIENDS OF PATIENTS WITH LOW HEALTH LITERACY

Timothy V. Johnson**, Ammara Abbasi,
Michael D. Bryant, Samantha S. Ehrlich, Renee Kleris,
Evan D. Schoenberg and Viraj A. Master
Department of Urology, Emory University.

ABSTRACT

Introduction: Low written and numerical literacy significantly impact patient outcomes. However, no research has focused on the impact of low health literacy on a patient's friends and family. Moreover, the costs of health literacy have not addressed the extended costs to family and friends. We prospectively conducted a cross-sectional study using validated instruments and structured patient interviews to assess the impact of this guidance.

Methods: This cross-sectional study consisted of face-to-face interviews of 356 patients. Patients were asked questions assessing their demographics and socioeconomic status and the status of a possible companion to the visit. Finally, patients were asked how many times per month they required accompaniment to the physician. In addition to this interview, patient literacy, numeracy, and educational status were assessed. Frequency analysis and descriptive statistics were performed to examine the distribution of demographic and clinical characteristics of these groups. Univariate analysis was conducted to compare patients with and without accompaniment. Chi-squared analysis and Whitney-Mann U-test was used for categorical variables and the t-test for continuous variables.

Results: Of the cohort, 199 patients (56%) were accompanied by a friend or relative. Patients with accompaniment tended to be more likely female ($p=0.001$), have a lower educational attainment ($p<0.001$), and have lower health literacy ($p=0.048$). Patients with accompaniment reported on average (SD) 1.3 (1.7) doctor appointments per month, which was significantly higher than the 0.9 (0.9) visits reported by patients without accompaniment ($p=0.031$). According to the patient, these appointments lasted an

* Corresponding author: Timothy Van Johnson, 1365 N Clifton Rd NE. Atlanta, GA 30322. 205-792-0263. timothyvjohnson@gmail.com

average (SD) of 1.5 (1.5) hours, though some lasted up to four hours. Of the variables examined, only educational attainment and health literacy were significant predictors.

Conclusions: Navigation of the US healthcare system often requires accompaniment. This accompaniment incurs significant expense and dramatically increases the costs of low socioeconomic status.

INTRODUCTION

Health literacy consists of prose, document, and quantitative literacy and represents a patient's ability to obtain, process, and understand basic health information to make appropriate health decisions.[1-4] Nearly 90 million American adults have inadequate written health literacy.[1, 5] While the average American adult reads below the 9th grade level, 21% of adults read below the 6th grade reading level.[1, 5] Of Medicare enrollees with low health literacy, 42% could not understand medication directions, 22% could not understand their appointment slips, and 62% could not understand an informed consent form.[6] Additionally, both county hospital patients and Medicare enrollees with low health literacy are more likely to be hospitalized compared to patients with adequate health literacy [7, 8].

Low written and numerical literacy significantly impact patient outcomes.[9, 10] First, low health literacy impacts access to medical care. Patients with low health literacy are 30-50% less likely to have received a pap smear, mammogram, influenza vaccine, or pneumococcal vaccine [11, 12] Low health literacy also impacts medical compliance. Patients with low health literacy and diabetes maintain higher blood glucose and hemoglobin A1C levels [13] Consequently, low written health literacy has been firmly linked to increased costs of healthcare.[1, 9].

Finally, in a large study of 653 patients, Gazmararian and colleagues demonstrated a significant inverse relationship between low health literacy and mortality, after controlling for other variables.[14] While the literature remains incomplete, numerical literacy may contribute even more to morbidity and mortality given its higher prevalence [15].

Low health literacy also significantly adds to healthcare costs in the United States. In part, these increased costs arise from increased risk of hospitalization. For example, Kuh and Stirling reported a two-fold increased risk of hospitalization for diseases of the female genital system among patients with the least educated compared.[16] Baker and colleagues also demonstrated in several studies that patients with lower health literacy are more likely to be hospitalized.[17-19] This increased hospitalization can be attributed to poorer health and decreased use of preventive health services.[6, 20] As a result of these factors, Vernon and colleagues estimated the increased costs of care because of health illiteracy to range from $106 billion to $238 billion [21].

Recent years have seen a flurry of research detailing the scope of the low health literacy epidemic. This research has illuminated low health literacy's significant medical and financial impact on patients and the medical community. During prior literacy studies, we anecdotally noticed that friends or family members to help them navigate the healthcare system accompanied many patients with low health literacy [15, 22-24]. However, no research has focused on the impact of low health literacy on a patient's friends and family. Moreover, the costs of health literacy have not addressed the extended costs to family and friends. We prospectively conducted a cross-sectional study using validated instruments and structured patient interviews to assess the impact of this guidance. We hypothesized that patients with low health literacy will more often be accompanied by a friend or family member, increasing the hidden costs of low health literacy.

METHODS

Study Setting and Population

This IRB approved cross-sectional study enrolled 356 patients who visited the urology clinic urology clinics of Grady Memorial Hospital and Emory University Hospital. Grady Memorial Hospital, located in downtown Atlanta, is a tertiary-care facility serving the needs of a primarily underserved urban patient population and Emory University's urology department is a tertiary urological center. Exclusion criteria consisted of an inability to speak English and active, untreated psychiatric illness.

Data Collection

In face-to-face interviews, patients were asked a series of questions assessing their demographics and socioeconomic status. Additionally, patients were asked about the demographics and socioeconomic status of a possible companion to the visit. Finally, patients were asked how many times per month they required accompaniment to the physician. In addition to this interview, patient literacy, numeracy, and educational status were assessed. Patient literacy was assessed using the following Single Item Literacy Screening question, a robust, validated screening tool designed by Chew and colleagues: [25, 26] "How confident are you filling out medical forms by yourself?" Possible answer choices consisted of: "Extremely", "Quite a bit", "Somewhat", "A little bit", and "Not at all". Numeracy was assessed using the Schwartz-Woloshin 3-item numeracy tool [27].

Outcome Measures

The main outcome measured in this study was the difference in the necessity of a companion among patients with varying health literacy, numeracy, and education levels.

Statistical Analysis

Patients were categorized by whether they were accompanied to their appointment. Frequency analysis and descriptive statistics were performed to examine the distribution of demographic and clinical characteristics of these groups. Univariate analysis was conducted to compare patients with and without accompaniment. Chi-squared analysis and Whitney-Mann U-test was used for categorical variables and the t-test for continuous variables. All analyses were conducted using SPSS version 18.0.

RESULTS

Patient Characteristics

This cross-sectional study enrolled 356 patients at the Emory University urology clinic. Of these patients, 199 (56%) were accompanied by a friend or relative (Table 1).

Table 1. Patient characteristics among patients who are and are not accompanied by a friend or relative

	Status of Patient Accompaniment		Univariate Analysis
Variables	Unaccompanied (n=157)	Accompanied (n=199)	p-value
Age (years) – Mean (SD)	53.9 (16.6)	50.4 (18.6)	0.064
Sex			0.001
% Male	73.7%	47.5%	
Race			0.420
% White	66.7%	63.3%	
% Black	27.2%	32.7%	
% Other	6.1%	4.0%	
Hispanic Ethnicity			0.180
% Hispanic	5.7%	2.0%	
Educational Attainment (years) – Mean (SD)	16.3 (3.1)	14.6 (3.0)	<0.001
Health Literacy – "Confidence with Forms" Question			0.048
Extremely Confident	5.0%	2.4%	
Quite a bit	1.3%	3.0%	
Somewhat	1.3%	8.5%	
A little bit	18.8%	21.3%	
Not at all	73.8%	64.6%	
Numeracy Scale			0.399
0 – Low Health Numeracy	17.2%	13.6%	
1	29.3%	37.2%	
2	28.0%	27.6%	
3 – High Health Numeracy	25.5%	21.6%	
Number of Doctor Appointments per Month – Mean (SD)	0.9 (0.9)	1.3 (1.7)	0.031

Patients with accompaniment tended to be more likely female (p=0.001), have a lower educational attainment (p<0.001), and have lower health literacy (p=0.048). These groups did not significantly differ by age (p=0.064), race (p=0.420), Hispanic ethnicity (p=0.180), or numeracy (p=0.399). Patients with accompaniment reported on average (SD) 1.3 (1.7) doctor appointments per month, which was significantly higher than the 0.9 (0.9) visits reported by patients without accompaniment (p=0.031).

Characteristics of Accompaniment

The majority of patients (56%) in our study were accompanied by a friend or family member.

According to the patient, these appointments lasted an average (SD) of 1.5 (1.5) hours, though some lasted up to four hours. Of the patients with accompaniment, 17.0% reported that they are not regularly accompanied to doctor appointments. However, 46.8% were accompanied to all and 36.2% were accompanied to some of their doctor appointments (Figure 1).

However, this difference depended on the patient's education level. Patients with a high school education or greater reported a mean (SD) education level of 15.7 (2.8) years, and were accompanied by individuals with a mean (SD) education level of 14.6 (2.4) years, though this difference was not significant ($p=0.607$). Alternatively, patients with less than a high school education reported a mean (SD) education level of 8.4 (3.0) years, and were accompanied by individuals with a mean (SD) education level of 11.1 (5.9) year, a significant difference in increased education ($p<0.001$).

While patients brought accompaniment for many reasons, patients most commonly asked friends or relatives to accompany them to doctor appointments for help understanding. As a whole, 24% of patients asked for accompaniment to help them read forms or understand the doctor. However, this difference also varied by patient education level. Of patients with a high school education or greater, 22.4% asked for accompaniment to help with understanding. Alternatively, 35.7% of patients with less than a high school education asked for accompaniment to increase understanding, which is an increase of almost 60%.

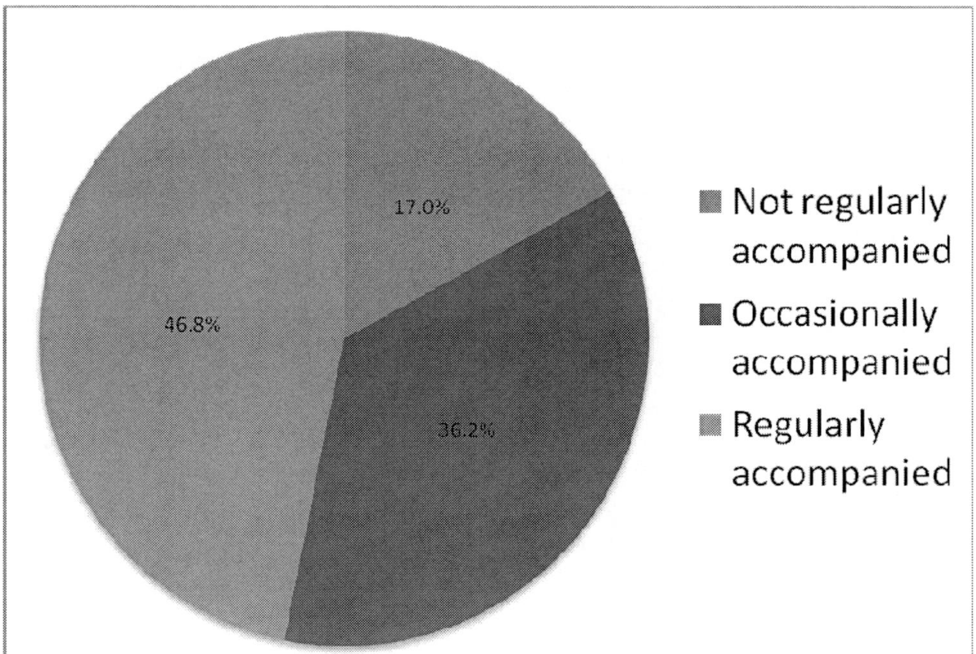

Figure 1. Frequency of patient accompaniment to physician visits.

Discussion

Low Health Literacy Costs Traditionally Focus on Patients

The impact of inadequate health literacy is extensive. Studies have demonstrated that low health literacy results in poorer health outcomes, including higher rates of hospitalization, along with higher morbidity and mortality [10, 16-19, 21]. These factors account for the significant costs attributed to inadequate health literacy [21] As a result of these factors, Vernon and colleagues estimated the cost to range from $106 billion to $238 billion.[21] These estimates were based on per capita medical expenditures, average cost increase attributed to inadequate health literacy, and the frequency of inadequate health literacy among the American population.[21] Based on these input variables, this provides provocative data regarding the personal costs of inadequate health literacy.

Anecdotally, however, we have observed significant costs to inadequate health literacy extending beyond individual patients. Specifically, friends or relatives accompany many patients. In informal interviews, many patients reported bringing accompaniment to help interpret medical forms, discuss findings with physicians, etc. In these interviews, these friends and relatives often missed work to help their patient navigate the healthcare system. Therefore we conducted this study to probe the hidden costs of inadequate health literacy, extending beyond the patient.

Low Health Literacy Extends Costs to Friends and Relatives

More than half of our cohort was accompanied by a friend or relative (Table 1). These findings suggest that patients request accompaniment to help navigate the healthcare system. In interviews, approximately one quarter of patients confirmed this finding. This percentage increased to 35% in patients with less than a high school education. Overall, the patient population reported approximately one doctor appointment per month. Interestingly, patients with accompaniment had significantly more appointments per month, on average about 0.5 an appointment more per month. Each appointment lasted about 1.5 hours, up to 4 hours.

Study Considerations

To our knowledge, this study is the first explore the costs of low health literacy hidden in the sacrifice of friends and family who accompany patients. As such, these data broaden the scope of low health literacy's economic impact. However, this study has not explored these costs to completion. To conduct a quantitative survey of these costs, this study interviewed patients regarding their accompaniment. Future qualitative studies might interview patients and their accompaniment to validate these findings and explore the sacrifice and cost underlying this accompaniment.

Additionally, this study was conducted at the Emory University urology clinic. This clinic is a tertiary urological center, treating primarily a referral population of patients with health insurance and advanced disease. However, the ramifications of this population remain unclear. A more indigent population might conceivably see higher rates of accompaniment. Alternatively, a primary center addressing non-specialist visit diseases might require less accompaniment. Finally, this study consisted solely of urology patients. Though unlikely, perhaps different specialty populations differ in their outcomes.

Further studies might also validate our findings using alternative measures of health literacy. This study relied on a single item literacy screening question to define health literacy. This question, proposed by Chew in 2004, has been well validated [25, 26]. Receiver Operating Characteristic curves in the original study demonstrated an Area Under Curve of 0.8, defined by the Short Test of Functional Health Literacy in Adults [25]. Despite its validation, further studies might confirm our findings using different measures.

References

[1] Davis TC, W. M.: Health Literacy: Implications for Family Medicine. *Fam. Med.*, 36: 595, 2004.

[2] Wilson, F. L.: Are patient information materials too difficult to read? *Home Healthc Nurse*, 18: 107, 2000.

[3] Medicine, I.O.: Health literacy: a prescription to end confusion. Washington, DC.: National Academies Press, 2004.

[4] Rudd, R. E.: Improving Americans' health literacy. *N. Engl. J. Med.,* 363: 2283, 2010.

[5] Kirsch I, J. A., Jenkins L, Kolstad A: Adult literacy in America: a first look at the findings of the national adult literacy survey. Washington, DC: National Center for Education Statistics, U.S. Department of Education, vol. 2007, 1993.

[6] Schillinger D, G. K., Piette J, Wang F, Osmond D, Daher C, Palacios J, Sullivan GD, Bindman AB.: Association of health literacy with diabetes outcomes. *JAMA,* 288: 475, 2002.

[7] Dewalt DA, B. N., Sheridan S, Lohr KN, Pignone MP.: Literacy and health outcomes: a systematic review of the literature. *J. Gen. Intern. Med.,* 19: 1228, 2004.

[8] Howard, D. H., Gazmararian, J., Parker, R. M.: The impact of low health literacy on the medical costs of Medicare managed care enrollees. *Am. J. Med.*, 118: 371, 2005.

[9] Safeer RS, K. J.: Health literacy: the gap between physicians and patients. *Am. Fam. Physician.*, 72: 463, 2005.

[10] Baker, D. W., Wolf, M. S., Feinglass, J. et al.: Health literacy and mortality among elderly persons. *Arch. Intern. Med.,* 167: 1503, 2007.

[11] Lindau ST, T. C., Lyons T, Langseth L, Bennett CL, Garcia P.: The association of health literacy with cervical cancer prevention knowledge and health behaviors in a multiethnic cohort of women. *Am. J. Obstet Gynecol.*, 186: 938, 2002.

[12] Scott, T. L., Gazmararian, J. A., Williams, M. V. et al.: Health literacy and preventive health care use among Medicare enrollees in a managed care organization. *Med. Care*, 40: 395, 2002.

[13] Ackermann, R. T., Carroll, A. E.: Support for national health insurance among U.S. physicians: a national survey. *Ann. Intern Med.*, 139: 795, 2003.

[14] Gazmararian, J. A., Williams, M. V., Peel, J. et al.: Health literacy and knowledge of chronic disease. *Patient Educ Couns*, 51: 267, 2003.

[15] Master, V. A., Johnson, T. V., Abbasi, A. et al.: Poorly numerate patients in an inner city hospital misunderstand the American Urological Association symptom score. *Urology*, 75: 148, 2010.

[16] Kuh, D., Stirling, S.: Socioeconomic variation in admission for diseases of female genital system and breast in a national cohort aged 15-43. *BMJ*, 311: 840, 1995.

[17] Baker, D. W., Parker, R. M., Williams, M. V. et al.: The relationship of patient reading ability to self-reported health and use of health services. *Am. J. Public Health*, 87: 1027, 1997.

[18] Baker, D. W., Parker, R. M., Williams, M. V. et al.: Health literacy and the risk of hospital admission. *J. Gen. Intern. Med.,* 13: 791, 1998.

[19] Baker, D. W., Gazmararian, J. A., Williams, M. V. et al.: Functional health literacy and the risk of hospital admission among Medicare managed care enrollees. *Am. J. Public Health*, 92: 1278, 2002.

[20] Nielsen-Bohlman L, P. A., Kindig D.: *Health Literacy: A Prescription to End Confusion.* Washington, D.C., 2004.

[21] Vernon, J., Trujillo, A., Rosenbaum, S. et al.: Low Health Literacy: Implications for National Health Policy: University of Connecticut, 2007.

[22] Johnson, T., Abbasi, A., Ehrlich, S. et al.: Patient misunderstanding of the individual questions of the American Urological Association Symptom Score. *J. Urol.*, 179: 2291, 2008.

[23] Johnson, T. V., Goodman, M., Master, V. A.: The efficacy of written screening tools in an inner city hospital: literacy based limitations on patient access to appropriate care. *J. Urol.,* 178: 623, 2007.

[24] Johnson, T. V., Schoenberg, E. D., Abbasi, A. et al.: Assessment of the performance of the American Urological Association symptom score in 2 distinct patient populations. *J. Urol.*, 181: 230, 2009.

[25] Chew, L. D., Bradley, K. A., Boyko, E. J.: Brief questions to identify patients with inadequate health literacy. *Fam. Med.*, 36: 588, 2004.

[26] Chew, L. D., Griffin, J. M., Partin, M. R. et al.: Validation of screening questions for limited health literacy in a large VA outpatient population. *J. Gen. Intern Med.,* 23: 561, 2008.

[27] Schwartz, L. M., Woloshin, S., Black, W. C. et al.: The role of numeracy in understanding the benefit of screening mammography. *Ann. Intern. Med.*, 127: 966, 1997.

In: Socioeconomic Status and Health Implications ISBN: 978-1-62100-675-6
Editor: Sarah Reibert and Alice Jannings, pp. 183-202

Chapter 10

CULTURAL AND SOCIOECONOMIC CONTEXTS AND NUTRITIONAL TRANSITIONS: THE ANTHROPOLOGY OF GLOBAL OVERWEIGHT AND OBESITY TRENDS OF OLDER ADULTS

***Gillian H. Ice*[1*]*, Aalyia F.A. Sadruddin*[1] *and Sharon R. Williams*[2]**
[1] Ohio University Heritage College of Osteopathic Medicine, Athens, OH, U.S.A.
[2] Purdue University, Department of Anthropology, West Lafayette, IN, U.S.A.

ABSTRACT

Although the undernourished still outnumber the over-fed, global rates of obesity are increasing, especially among older adults. While overweight and obesity is inversely proportional to socioeconomic status in the developed world, the reverse has historically been true for the developing world. Labeled the "nutrition transition" by (Popkin 1994, 2004) and initially described in Latin American urban populations, this phenomenon appears to be spreading rapidly across the developing world. As overweight and obesity increase, a concomitant increase in prevalence of chronic diseases (e.g., cardiovascular disease and diabetes) is likely. Recent epidemiological studies report rates of overweight and obesity exceeding 70% for U.S. and South African older adults (National Social Life Health and Aging Project; WHO Study of Global Aging and Adult Health), and near 15% for the aged in India (WHO/SAGE). However, less is known about the cultural and socioeconomic context of this nutritional transition. This paper combines in-depth anthropological data from field work in western Kenya and India with population-level data, to demonstrate the importance of cultural and socioeconomic context for understanding global trends in overweight and obesity among older adults. The Indian data demonstrate the importance of social position in shaping dietary patterns and

* Corresponding Author: Gillian H. Ice, Ph.D., M.P.H. 301 Grosvenor Hall, Athens, OH 45701 Phone: 740-593-2128, Email: iceg@ohio.edu

physical activity. Increasing medicalization has led to the belief that health problems associated with overweight are easily addressed with medication. As the prevalence of overweight and obesity increases in India so does chronic disease prevalence. In Kenya, overweight and obesity are closely tied with higher socioeconomic status and perceived as a sign of wealth and health. Data from western Kenya suggest that, at least for some health problems overweight are associated with better health. The complex relationships between socioeconomic status, cultural context and body size present considerable challenges for public health efforts towards curbing the growing obesity pandemic.

Keywords: aging, Africa, India, chronic disease, BMI, public health.

THE GLOBAL PATTERNING OF OBESITY

Food consumption patterns, rates of physical activity and socio-economic growth have undergone a series of changes over the last 30 years and have influenced the incidence and prevalence of non-communicable diseases (NCDs) across the world (Schmidhuber 2005). The sheer pace of dietary change and onset of NCDs have left biomedical and public health practitioners perplexed as disease concentrations have sky rocketed in different areas of the globe. Observations made by food and nutrition practitioners over the last 50 years have shown that 'western diets' are high in saturated fats, sugar and a low in fiber (Stubbs 1998; Smil 2000; Selassie and Sinha 2011; Bray 2004; Cohen 1999; Bury 2000). Additionally, "modern" foods are highly refined and have a very low percentage of leafy vegetables. With 'western lifestyles' being defined by lower levels of physical activity, changes in the patterns of 'new' diseases are reflected in nutritional outcomes, such as changes in average stature, body composition, and morbidity. (Popkin 2004, 1994) attributes this increase to the shift in diet composition, patterns of physical activity and changes in the transport and food technology industry. He collectively terms this the "nutrition transition". He suggests that the global availability of fast food products, modifications of lifestyle and profound changes in household technology have positively increased fat and calorie consumption not only in developed but developing nations as well. As a result, the nutrition transition now occurs at lower levels of the gross national product than previously, and is occurring faster in regions undergoing urbanization (Popkin 1994, 2004).

Global prevalence of leading NCDs such as obesity, heart disease, stroke, type 2 diabetes, chronic respiratory diseases and cancer are at an all-time high and will likely not decrease in the next 20 years (Ulijaszek and Lofink 2006; Schmidhuber 2005; Blaxter 2004). Obesity is a complex condition that affects virtually all age and socioeconomic groups. Obese people have a higher amount of body fat than is healthy or desirable.[15] The spread of obesity across the world has affirmed the disease as a socio-cultural, economic, genetic and environmentally determined phenomenon.

In 1995, the World Health Organization (WHO) projected there to be 200 million obese adults worldwide and an additional 18 million children in the under-five category as overweight. Recent estimations suggest that the number of obese adults in 2000 increased to

[15] Adults with a body mass index (BMI, calculated as weight in kilograms divided by height in meters squared) between 25 kg/m2 and 30 kg/m2 are considered overweight. Adults with a BMI greater than or equal to 30 kg/m2 are considered obese.

over 300 million. According to (Flegal et al. 2010) 47% of the global burden of disease can be attributed to chronic NCDs equating to about 60% of the annual 58 million deaths globally. Eighty percent of chronic NCD deaths now occur in low and middle income countries- an occurrence that is adding more pressure to an already struggling public health system. Given the magnitude of the problem in both developed and developing countries, it is crucial that academic and public health scholarship pay close attention to the various dimensions of the pandemic. Despite the hard work conducted by biomedical practitioners, psychologists, nutritionists and anthropologists, there still remains a knowledge gap concerning the cultural and socioeconomic context of the nutritional transition in relation to the emergence of obesity among many of the world's populations. While the nutrition transition and resulting obesity pandemic are getting more attention, most studies outside of the developed world have focused on urban youth. We know less about the impact of these trends on elders. This chapter combines in-depth anthropological data from field work in Kenya and India with population-level data, to demonstrate the importance of cultural and socioeconomic context for understanding global trends in overweight and obesity among older adults.

Demographic, Epidemiologic and Nutritional Shifts in Global History

The nature of the world's current disease trajectory is an extension of large-scale recurring shifts that occurred over time; though these changes in low-middle income countries appear to have occurred more rapidly (Jamison 2006). Initially, these shifts were limited to higher-income urban populations, however recent research has shown that these trends are much broader and have an impact on all segments of society (Hossain, Kawar, and El 2007; Smith 2006). Demographers and epidemiologists throughout history have emphasized the importance of the demographic and epidemiological transitions in high-income countries. Essential to this argument is Popkin's viewpoint of the nutrition transition which highlights that behaviors associated with food and diet are changing rapidly across cultures. These shifts have a direct influence on the global distributions of obesity. The use of the concept nutrition transition in this chapter draws on two dimensions of immense shifts in diet (mainly makeup) and body size and composition in relation to elderly populous' in low-income regions of the world. Popkin (1994) describes 'transitional societies' as low-income countries who parallel to growing in wealth are experiencing shifts in diet and disease patterns. Countries such as China and a range of South East Asian countries are part of this group as are a number of Latin American, North African, sub-Saharan African and Caribbean societies.

Two very important shifts influenced the increase in obesity patterns in the developed and developing worlds. The first was the demographic transition[16] which brought with it a change from high to low fertility and mortality levels (typical of "modern", industrialized countries). The second shift was the epidemiological transition, which Omran (1971) developed to explain the advances in health care experienced by industrialized countries since the 18th century. This theory details the change in patterns and nature of disease, from a high prevalence of infectious (linked with malnutrition, episodic famine, and poor environmental

[16] The demographic transition is a model that describes population change, or transitions in birth and death rates in industrialized regions over the last two hundred years

sanitation) to an increased occurrence of chronic and degenerative diseases (related with urban–industrial lifestyles). The nutrition transition has traditionally addressed the issue of nutritional diseases among child and adult populations. Minimal attention has been paid to the consequences faced by the elderly, how they function in the presence of disease and assessing their quality of life (Mathias et al. 1997 ; Kolotkin, Meter, and Williams 2001). Research on quality of life in relation to obesity and NCDs over the last 20 years and their antagonistic effects in the US has been more extensive among the elderly (Ulijaszek and Lofink 2006). We know far less about the impact of body size, health and quality of life among elders in developing countries.

Obesity: The Developed vs. the Developing World

The past 20 years in particular have seen a dramatic increase in obesity in the US. The CDC (2010) estimated that more than one-third of adults in the US were obese in 2007-2008. Rates of the disease among adult populations have doubled from 15 to 30 percent, since 1980 while childhood obesity rates have more than tripled (Suzman 2009). At present it is feared that one out of every three Americans suffers from obesity. Obese individuals are at increased risk of diabetes mellitus, cardiovascular disease, hypertension, and certain cancers, among other chronic conditions. Only two states (Colorado and the District of Columbia) in 2009 had an obesity prevalence that was less than 20%. In thirty-three states, prevalence levels equaled to or greater than 25%; nine of these states (Alabama, Arkansas, Kentucky, Louisiana, Mississippi, Missouri, Oklahoma, Tennessee, and West Virginia) had a prevalence of obesity equal to or greater than 30% (CDC 2010).

The National Social Life, Health and Aging Project (NSHAP) is a national probability survey of approximately 3000 Americans, aged 57 to 85 years (Suzman 2009). The study included a wide variety of sociodemographic and health information. Anthropometric assessment was conducted on the majority of the sample; for further details see (Williams 2009). In Table 1, we present BMI data, which shows that approximately 30% of the participants were overweight and close to 40% were obese. The frequency of overweight is higher among the oldest group (80+ years) and the rate of obesity is highest among the youngest group (57-69). The frequency of BMI categories varies across income quintiles, with frequency of overweight increasing with income (Table 2). The variation frequency of overweight and obesity across income quintiles is slight however, and all income groups have high rates of overweight and obesity. The NSHAP project is currently collecting a second wave of data and it will be interesting to see if the rates remain stable. Regardless, these data clearly show that obesity is a problem across the lifespan in the United States.

High obesity prevalence appears to be a direct consequence of countries adopting a Western lifestyle (Hossain, Kawar, and El 2007). Such lifestyle changes are playing a direct role in affecting children in these countries; the prevalence of overweight among them ranges from 10 to 25%, and the prevalence of obesity ranges from 2 to 10% (Cohen 1999). Changes in lifestyle, the growth of an affluent middle economic class and the diverse availability of foods have contributed towards nutrition imbalance. Hyper-urbanisation across the African continent in the form of rural-urban migration has resulted in the birth of new diseases (Ulijaszek and Lofink 2006). Western culinary influences lead to new consumption patterns, which affect dietary habits and even the rhythm of consumption. These new dietary habits have created conditions for chronic diseases like obesity and diabetes to take hold.

Table 1. BMI category by age group in the United States (NSHAP)

Age Group	Underweight (%)	Normal (%)	Overweight (%)	Obese (%)
57-69	0.7	20.0	32.7	46.7
70-79	1.3	24.8	34.6	39.3
80+	1.8	32.6	34.2	31.4

Table 2. BMI category by income quintile in the United States (NSHAP)

Income Quintile	Underweight (%)	Normal (%)	Overweight (%)	Obese (%)
1	1.5	27.6	30.0	40.9
2	0.7	22.8	33.2	43.3
3	0.2	23.9	33.6	42.3
4	1.2	21.3	37.4	40.0
5	0.5	19.6	38.1	41.8

The Middle East, Pacific Islands, Southeast Asia, China and South Africa appear to be particularly vulnerable to nutrition transitions. Traditionally, being 'poor' in a country with a per capita gross national product (GNP) of less than $800 a year has been linked with underweight and malnutrition. In contrast, being 'poor' in a middle-income country (with a per capita GNP of about $3,000 per year) is associated with an increased risk of obesity (Raymond, Leeder, and Greenberg 2006). This picture has become more complex as the relationship between socioeconomic status and obesity is not a simple cause and effect equation. Urban areas in the developing world have higher rates of obesity as they are much further along in the nutrition transition than rural areas. That is not to say that individuals in rural areas are immune, especially women (Ulijaszek and Lofink 2006; Cohen 1999; Bury 2000; Wachira, Simiyu, and Onywera 2009). Though conventionally associated with the developed world and primarily the US obesity has effectively spread itself to the developing world in the last 30 years where it was generally not considered to be a major public health issue. The alarming incidence of obesity in the developing world during this time frame highlights the need for development and health practitioners to study obesity as a multi-factorial and biocultural epidemic (Mokhtar et al. 2001; Brown 1991).

Obesity has multiple causes- some of which are deeply influenced by culture (Smil 2000; WHO 2003). As countries such as those in North Africa and sub-Saharan Africa undergo the nutrition transition, it is imperative that key characteristics such as social attitudes, dietary patterns within these regions influenced by their historic and geographic context are documented. The cause of obesity in North Africa, a region with high rates, is not well understood and very few studies explain its development among women (Mokhtar et al. 2001). Complicating the patterns of obesity in a large majority of Africa are the social attitudes and cultural symbolism associated to the female body that make being overweight seem harmless, if not explicitly attractive (Mokhtar et al. 2001; Batnitzky 2011; Rguibi and Belahsen 2006). Being fat is a sign of social status, a cultural symbol of beauty, fertility and prosperity. In Morocco, results from a national household consumption and expenditure survey in 1984 showed signs of high levels of overweight and obesity among women in urban areas (20% of women with body mass index (BMI) > 28) (IASO 2003). In South Africa, urban women have a significantly higher BMI than their rural counterparts (Steyn et al. 2005). In both groups BMI increases with age. Central obesity (defined by cut-off points for waist:hip ratio of 1.0 and 0.85 for men and women, respectively) was found in 42.2% of women and was most prevalent in urban African and women of mixed ancestry (Martorell et al. 2000).

Cases of force feeding as a mechanism to fulfill a particular body image accepted by society have been reported in a few communities. For instance in certain tribes in Nigeria, women are traditionally fattened up before marriage to make them seem more attractive and healthy to their future husbands (Ba 2000). Mauritania, the Northern African country bordering the North Atlantic Ocean between Senegal and Western Saharan, is labeled as Africa's 'wife fattening farm' due to its force feeding culture of "*gavage*" (Ba 2000). Though various reports from Mauritania suggest that gavage is not practiced as much as it was in the past, the ramifications of the procedure has created a plethora of health calamities, especially for young girls and women. A 2000 government survey of 68,000 women in Mauritania cited in a 2003 WHO report, showed that one in five girls between the ages of 15 and 49 had been purposely fed. Nearly 70% and even more among teenagers said they did not regret it. The same survey estimated that two in five women were overweight (not high by American standards) where government surveys show nearly three in five women are overweight. The process of gavage encourages girls as young as 5 and as old as 19 to consume foods that have a high caloric value. These foods include dates, fat-rich camels or cow's milk daily and couscous which produce a series of silvery stretch marks on their upper arms. Resistance to "crash-feeding" or vomiting as a result of over-eating is countered by often violent disciplinary actions (Brown 1991). Often such instances call for the village weight-gain specialist to intervene who may squeeze a young girl's foot between sticks, pull her ear, pinch her inner thigh, bend her finger backward or force her to drink her own vomit. In extreme cases, girls have died from exhaustion and stroke. Though visible reductions of the cultural phenomenon have been made in urban settlements of Mauritania, the same does not apply for areas in the desert where people continue traditional practices. Increasing evidence illuminates that Mauritanian women have replaced gavage with thoroughly modern prescription drug abuse by consuming dexamethasone tablets (a prescription steroid hormone that can cause sharp weight gain).

Although force-feeding in Mauritania is an extreme case, the attraction towards a large body, predominantly among females is a general trend across North and sub-Saharan Africa. Voluptuous bodies may symbolize female fertility, familial wealth and pride (Martorell et al. 2000; Fantino et al. 1983; Brown 1991; Ba 2000). In fact, the main stream U.S. culture stands out as being an exception to this trend. There are however, minority groups in the U.S. which do value plumpness over thinness (WHO 2005).

CASE STUDY ONE: KENYAN GRANDPARENTS STUDY (KGS)

We have been accustomed in associating developing regions such as sub-Saharan Africa, Latin America and the Indian subcontinent as hotspots of infectious diseases, namely HIV/AIDS, malaria and typhoid. Though these diseases are dominant in the developing world, new waves of NCDs have increased in incidence and prevalence in the region. It has been projected that over 115 million people in the developing world suffer from obesity-related problems (CDC 2010). In South Africa alone, 64% of the black and 50% of the white population are overweight or obese (Steyn et al. 2005). Additionally, one in three men and more than one in two adult women are overweight and obese. These levels bare resemblance to those in the USA. Over the last three decades, sub-Saharan Africa in particular has contended with severely high rates of morbidity and mortality from infectious disease, a situation that is worsening as the prevalence of HIV/AIDS increases. Though under nutrition is manifested most prominently as stunting in children is widely prevalent, cases of obesity are burgeoning in selected regions- namely in urbanized Africa (Ziraba, Fotso, and Ochako 2009).

Kenya is a prime example of these trends. Kenya's positive effects of health gains in the 1980s and 1990s have started to show signs of fatigue, with the country experiencing a general deterioration in health status. The escalation of the HIV/AIDS epidemic is challenging the levels of socio-developmental growth and unsurprisingly questioned the methods in which health and health care has been disseminated in the country. In 2009 UNAIDS stated that Kenya's HIV prevalence had risen to an estimated 7%. Parallel to this is the increasing gap between the rich and the poor due to stark social and economic disparities between both income groups (UNAIDS 2009). This occurrence is very closely tied to the growing affluence of the middle class and high rates of urbanization in Kenya (Wachira, Simiyu, and Onywera 2009; Adamo et al. 2011). The physical activity transition refers to a shift away from the high energy expenditure activities such as farming, herding and gathering to the rise in sedentary based jobs and social activities (Steyn et al. 2011; Furnham, Moutafi, and Baguma 2002).

As trends in obesity incidence and prevalence shift drastically in East Africa, levels of interest in the disease have started to signs of life within the public health world. Having said this, much of the obesity content coming out of Kenya is child and adult focused with limited amounts of attention being paid to elderly adults. In light of this gap, longitudinal research conducted through the Kenyan Grandparents Study (KGS) which elucidates the impact of caregiving on the health of elders and has examined change in body size and composition over four years.

In 2005, elders aged 60 years and older were enrolled for a four year study. While the primary focus of the project was to examine the impact of caring for children orphaned due to the local HIV crisis, both caregivers and non-caregivers were enrolled. In the process of obtaining comprehensive data on their health and well-being, BMI and subjective and objective measures of health were collected. These data demonstrate a small but growing group of elders who are classified as overweight or obese (Table 1). Overall, there was a trend of people getting larger with higher fat reserves. This trend is interesting in that this population is placed in a rural region, generally less touched by the nutrition transition. Socioeconomic status was significantly associated with overweight (Table 3). In the process of conducting this study, elders were educated about their health, including their body size. It proved difficult to convince Kenyans who were overweight that this was unhealthy. This likely stems from the fact that people equate large body size with wealth and health. With this perception in mind, longitudinal data health outcomes were examined relative to body mass index categories. We hypothesized that with respect to chronic disease, overweight and obese status would be associated with poorer health outcomes (elevated glucose and blood pressure). We, however, expected self-perceived health to be positively associated with BMI, such that those who were heavier would perceive their health to be better.

Table 3. Body mass index relative to socioeconomic index (SES) quartile in Kenya

SES quartile	Mean (std error)	P value
1	20.4 (0.40)	0.004
2	20.7 (0.40)	0.02
3	21.0(0.40)	0.06
4	22.0 (0.40)	referent

Data Collection Methods

Sample

In 2005, a longitudinal study was initiated in 18 centers from three districts of Nyanza Province, Kenya (Nyando, Nakach and Kisumu Rural). The centers represented 18 different villages[17] within the three districts; 8 locations (13 sub-locations) were within Nyando district, two were in Nyakach and 1 was in Kisumu rural. The centers were located in a central area within the location, typically at a school, church or chief's camp. Participant recruitment was rolling and included 287 Luo grandparents in 2005, 396 in 2006, 389 in 2007 and 390 in 2009, with a total of 689 elders participating at least one year. Data presented here are from a waves of data collection between 2005 and 2007. Participants were recruited with the assistance of the local chiefs. Approximately half of the grandparents were caregivers and half were noncaregivers. To be considered a caregiver, the participant was over 60, a grandparent and caregiver for at least one orphaned grandchild. Noncaregivers were over 60, grandparents and were not the primary care provider for orphaned grandchildren. Consent to participate in the study was obtained for each of the grandparents by a native speaker of Dholuo following a protocol approved by the Kenya Medical Research Institute (KEMRI) ethics board and the Ohio University Institutional Review Board.

[17] A district is usually divided into several divisions (Nyando has four). Each division is further subdivided into locations (Nyando has a total of 29). The administrative leader of a location is the Chief – appointed by the District Commissioner. Locations are further subdivided into sub-locations, headed by an assistant chief. Sub-locations are divided up into different villages. Villages were chosen to represent a wide range of areas within the four divisions of Nyando District, 2 locations within Nyakach and one division within Kisumu Rural District. At the beginning of the research, Nyakach was a division of Nyando District. In 2009, it became its own district.

Socioeconmic Status

Each grandparent participated in an interview conducted in Dholuo by a trained research assistant. The socioeconomic status scale was based on a scale used in Kenya by the Demographic Health Survey (Wagner et al. 1999). This scale has a series of questions about income and material wealth. For example, participants are asked how many livestock they have, materials with which their houses were made, and ownership of a series of material goods. This scale and similar scales have been widely used in subsistence based economies. Data were collected via PalmPilots® using Entryware® software.

Measures of Health

Numerous measures of health were assessed on each elder. A series of questions were used to assess elders self-perceived or subjective health. Perceived health and functional status of the Luo grandparents were measured via an adapted version of the SF-36 (Wagner et al. 1999; Ware and Sherbourne 1992). The SF-36 (MOS Short-Form 36) is a scale made up of 36 questions asking about perceived health and functioning on a variety of domains in the following subscales: mental health (general mental health including distress and well-being), function (limitations due to physical health problems), role physical (limitations in physical activities due to physical or emotional problems), role social (limitations in social activities due to physical or emotional problems), social functioning (limitations in role activities due to emotional problems), general health (self-rated health), vitality (energy and fatigue) and pain (general pain) (Ware 2007). The SF-36 is used as a measure of health related quality of life and a basic measure of perceived health. It has been used in over 4,000 publications and is currently being used in a large quality of life survey in over 50 countries (Wagner et al. 1999; Wyss et al. 1999). The version used in this project was culturally adapted and validated for use in an African context but retains all subscales of the standard SF-36 (Lohman, Roche, and Martorell 1988). Higher scores on each subscale indicate greater the quality of life or better health/ function. In this analysis we examined only the mental health and general health subscales.

Various objective measures were collected to assess the health and nutritional status of Luo grandparents. These measures include anthropometric measurements, physical examination, blood pressure, and hemoglobin and blood glucose levels.

BMI was calculated using measured height and weight. Height was assessed with a GPM® anthropometer (nearest mm) and weight by an Omeron® scale (nearest kg). Height and weight were used to calculate the body mass index for each participant. Standard measurement procedures were used (Labarthe et al. 1991). Each grandparent participated in a physical exam. The physical exam covered the following systems: cardiovascular, respiratory, gastrointestinal, musculoskeletal, neurological, and integumentary (skin). Participant physical exams were conducted by a local clinical officer and a second year osteopathic medical student. Abnormal (pathological) findings in the physical exam were recorded. For example, rashes or fungal infections were recorded as abnormal findings in the integumentary system. Each abnormal finding was recorded and a system was considered abnormal if at least one sign of pathology was present. The number of abnormal systems were summed for analysis.

Blood pressure was collected with the patient sitting and was taken using a standard blood pressure cuff according to arm size on the patient's right arm. Measurements followed the standardized protocols of the SHEP (Systolic Hypertension in the Elderly Program) study.

A series of three measurements were taken with time between each measurement for the elder to rest. The mean of the three blood pressure measurements were used in analysis.

Sterile, disposable lancets were used to collect blood for hemoglobin and blood glucose assessment using standard universal precautions. These assessments occurred in the morning and the elders were asked to fast the morning of the study. A HemoCue® system was used to assess hemoglobin levels.

Blood glucose levels were assessed using a Freestyle® Glucometer. Although participants were asked to fast, many did not. Thus analysis was conducted on random readings.

Analysis

Data were examined using a mixed effects models. Dependent variables were hemoglobin, glucose, systolic and diastolic blood pressure, self-perceived health and function and clinical history and physical exam results. The primary predictor variable was BMI category, divided into underweight, normal and overweight/obese. Models were adjusted for time and socioeconomic status. Post-hoc comparisons across BMI categories were compared with a Bonferroni adjustment for significance.

Results

Over the four years of the study, there was a small increase in the percentage of participants classified as overweight or obese (Table 4). At the same time, there was a small decrease in those classified as underweight.

In support of our hypotheses, increasing BMI was associated with higher glucose and blood pressure (Table 5).

On the other hand, individuals with higher weight had higher hemoglobin indicating that they were also better nourished.

Additionally, people with higher BMIs were found to have fewer physical exam findings suggesting that overall, they were actually healthier. While participants who were underweight perceived their functional status as being lower, they did not differ from other weight categories in their self-perceived health or number of health complaints during the clinical history portion of the exam (Table 6).

Table 4. BMI frequencies from 2005-2009 in Kenya

BMI category	2005	2006	2007	2009
Chronic energy deficiency (%)	5.3	5.6	5.1	5.6
Under weight (%)	22.6	26.9	20.7	19.7
Normal (%)	61.1	58.7	63	62.1
Over weight (%)	8.1	6.6	9	9
Obese (%)	2.8	2.1	2.1	3.6

Table 5. Objective health outcomes relative to BMI status in Kenya

BMI category	Hemoglobin	Glucose	SBP	DBP	Physical exam
Underweight	11.5 ± 4.8[a]	97.3 ± 47.2[a]	126.5± 47.0[a]	73.8 ± 23.9[a]	6.0 ±3.0[a]
Normal Weight	12.4 ±3.1[b]	97.9 ± 29.7[a]	129.6 ± 30.5[a]	75.9 ± 16.3[b]	5.6 ± 1.8[b]
Overweight/Obese	12.4 ±6.6[b]	104.6 ± 65.8[b]	136.1 ± 66.2[b]	80.0 ± 35.6[c]	5.5 ± 4.3[b]

All means adjusted for time and SES. Different letters indicate significant difference at $p<0.05$

Table 6. Subjective health outcomes relative to BMI status in Kenya

BMI category	Self-perceived health	Function	Health complaints
Underweight	17.6 ± 5.0[a]	19.7 ± 9.2[a]	12.8 ± 5.4[a]
Normal Weight	17.8 ± 3.1[a]	20.5 ± 5.6[b]	12.7 ±3.3[a]
Overweight/Obese	17.7 ± 7.0[a]	19.9 ± 13.0[b]	12.1 ±7.4[a]

All means adjusted for time and SES. Different letters indicate significant difference at $p<0.05$.

Discussion of Kenyan Results

In this analysis we found mixed support for our hypotheses that health perceptions would be associated with higher BMI categories while objective measures of health would be poorer among higher BMI categories. Overweight and obesity were clearly linked with higher glucose rates and blood pressure. On the other hand, the association with hemoglobin and physical exam results suggest that at least by some measures people who are heavier actually are healthier. Additionally, we found that those who were underweight were more likely to perceive lower functional ability even though they did not differ in their overall perception of health. Therefore in this context, the Kenyan perception on weight is not totally inaccurate. Indeed, for the health issues which are most salient in rural Kenya, infectious disease, malnutrition, fatigue and ability to function, to be heavier is to be healthier.

Chronic diseases are far less prevalent among rural Kenyans and they are less likely to be experienced physically until advanced stages. Infectious disease rates namely malaria, HIV/AIDS and tuberculosis have been severe in Kenya over the last 20 years reports the Ministry of Medical Services (CIA 2011). Such diseases pose as a socio-developmental problem in countries like Kenya where the public health system is plagued with infrastructural and staffing limitations. The strong onset of NCDs has pushed the country to face a "double burden" in that it is unable to adequately cope with pre-existing and emerging illnesses. Given the low life expectancy, few people currently experience end stage chronic degenerative disease. Thus, it is easy to understand why they fail to see the importance of these health problems. In fact, the fact that these elders have made it to such an advanced age, living in a country where the life expectancy is 59.5 means by their very existence, they are survivors. Their survival to this advanced age may be in part due to their larger weight, which is likely closely tied with greater wealth. This presents a unique challenge to public health practitioners. How do you offset the start of an epidemic in a context where communicable diseases are far more salient to the population?

Case Study Two: Kolkata, India

India has long been considered one of the poorest countries in the world with some of the highest rates of malnutrition (Garg et al. 2009). More recently, however, economic growth and changes in activity patterns and access to processed foods has led to increasing obesity rates in some groups. In general, obesity rates among women in the middle and upper socioeconomic classes have increased significantly in the last decade (Joshi 2003; Ganguli et al. 2011). To further complicate the health implications of the rising obesity rates in India, several studies have suggested that differences in fat patterning – more tendency toward central fat – or possibly the negative impact of lower birth weights followed by adult weight gain put Indian individuals at a higher risk for obesity-related health disorders at a lower BMI and waste circumference (Lohman, Roche, and Martorell 1988).

In order to better understand the process of aging in middle and lower income countries, the World Health Organization began a longitudinal study of aging (SAGE) in 6 countries. In 2007-2008 data was collected on 7,150 individuals across India age 50 and above as well as a comparative sample of 5348 individuals age 18-49. Households were chosen from a current frame using a stratified, multi-stage cluster design[18] Data collected included a broad range of questions including: demographic information, health history and behaviors, stress and social support, and subjective health. In addition, biological measures such as height, weight, waist circumference and blood pressure were collected in the household. A general overview of the distribution of BMI status by age group is given in Table 7. For the purposes of this chapter, standard BMI categories of underweight (< 18.5), normal (< 25), overweight (<30), obese (>30) were used. While underweight individuals still outnumber overweight and obese individuals in all age groups and the majority of individuals fall in the normal weight category, the frequency of overweight and obese individuals is substantial even in the oldest age group. The significance of these frequencies is further highlighted when you consider that the population of India is over one billion individuals so even a small percentage of the populations still represents a large number of individuals.

Table 7. BMI category by age group in India (SAGE)

Age Group	Underweight	Normal	Overweight	Obese
18-29	34.1	43.9	3.9	18.1
30-39	29.7	50.0	11.0	9.2
40-49	28.0	49.5	12.7	9.9
50-59	27.3	47.5	12.7	12.5
60-69	32.2	45.5	8.5	13.8
70-79	37.8	40.3	7.9	13.9
80+	40.3	32.2	4.6	22.9

[18] For more information on SAGE see the WHO/SAGE website (www.who.int/healthinfo/systems/sage/en/index1.html)

The pattern of distribution of BMI category by income (based on an index derived from wages, assets and material goods) is one that is expected for a rapidly modernizing country; the percentage of underweight individuals decreases with increasing income (Table 8). Prevalence of overweight and obese elders increases with increasing income (Table 8).

Table 8. BMI category by income quintile for adults 50+ in India (SAGE)

Income Quintile	Underweight	Normal	Overweight	Obese
1	50.4	36.2	3.0	10.4
2	41.1	42.6	4.7	11.7
3	33.7	44.2	8.6	13.5
4	24.9	50.5	11.5	13.0
5	16.1	47.5	18.4	18.0

While this large-scale population level data is extremely useful and can offer many insights into the changing pattern of health in India, is does lack the ability to provide deeper understandings into the dietary and health transitions in India. The impact of cultural factors are not represented in these broader population level studies.

Understanding Aging and Culture in Kolkata

Kolkata, India is a city in transition. Although, due to the unique political history and it's extraordinarily high population density, poverty, and level of under-development, the changes in Kolkata have been slower to materialize than in other major Indian cities like Delhi and Mumbai. Diet and activity patterns have been changing, however and economic changes have led to expansion of the middle class, more disposable income for the middle and upper classes, increased availability of foreign and processed foods and higher rates of overweight and obesity. Obesity has become a public health issue in Kolkata with public programs and private companies regularly advertising the benefits of weight loss. Very little research has examined the interaction between the changing cultural context of aging and health. Here we describe some preliminary results from a biocultural study of health of wealthy elderly in Kolkata.

Data Collection Methods

Sample

The sample presented here is not typical for India. Individuals were recruited from a wealthy Kolkata neighborhood from the rolls of an active neighborhood association. These individuals were chosen in order to better understand the cultural context of aging without issues of poor access to health care or other resources. All participants were well educated and relatively wealthy. Data was collected from adults age 55+ (mean = 68.6) and included

33 males and 22 females (mostly husband-wife pairs). In addition, informal interviews were conducted with local health care providers and experts on aging to ascertain their perspectives on aging in Kolkata.

Measures of Health

Both objective and subjective measures of health were collected during structured, at home interviews. Standing and sitting height, circumferences and skinfold thicknesses were taken using standard anthropometric techniques (Hruschka 2009). Weight was taken with a Tanita® scale (nearest ½ kg) and BMI was calculated from measured weight and height. Blood pressure was taken in the seated position on the right arm using a standard cuff and sphygmomanometer. Capillary blood collected using a single finger stick with a disposable BD® lancet was used for determination of hemoglobin levels using a HemoCue® system and cholesterol levels using a Cardiocheck® portable blood chemistry analyzer. Physical function measures included lung function (FEV1/FCV), timed chair stands, grip strength, and modified version of the standard Activities of Daily Living (ADL) questionnaire. Health histories, current medications and demographic information was also collected. Individuals were also asked open-ended questions about their health and their aging experiences, in general, and in relation to those around them.

Analysis

All statistical data analysis was conducted using STATA 11 (Stata Corporation, College Station, TX). Differences between BMI classes were assessed using linear regression models controlling for age and sex.

Results

In this sample of wealthy older adults in Kolkata, there was no significant difference in either subjective or objective measures of health between normal and overweight individuals. Only obese individuals were significantly different from other groups and only in the case of diastolic blood pressure, HDL and hemoglobin levels (Table 9). In the case of hemoglobin levels, obese individuals actually had higher levels and significantly lower rates of anemia (Table 9).

Diastolic blood pressure was also lower in obese individuals, but this was most likely due to the fact that more obese individuals were currently taking anti-hypertensive medications. Measures of physical function and measures of subjective health were not associated with BMI category in this sample (Table 10).

Table 9. Objective health outcomes relative to BMI status in Kolkata sample

BMI	Hemoglobin	HDL	Triglycerides	SBP	DBP	Chair Stand
Normal	11.9± 1.7	61.5±18.4	148.5±71.6	134.8±16.1	80.3±8.4	18.3 ±6.7
Overweight	11.8± 1.5	55.4±18.6	176.4±86.1	135.0±19.5	82.7±10.2	17.0±5.9
Obese	12.9 ± 1.5[ab]	49.5±14.5[a]	174.8±58.3	125.9±18.2	77.3±9.0[b]	15.0±4.8

Different letters indicate significant difference at $p<0.05$.

Table 10. Subjective health outcomes relative to BMI status in Kolkata sample

BMI category	Good self-perceived health	Good Relative Health	Feels Old
Underweight	75.0	68.7	53.3
Normal Weight	77.3	81.8	35.5
Overweight/Obese	86.7	53.3	40.0

Kolkata Results in Context

As expected, this sample did have access to regular health care and visited doctors and clinics regularly. In addition, these individuals are very aware of health issues associated with aging and the risks associated with the development of common chronic diseases such as diabetes and cardiovascular disease but are not healthier than the average older Indians. Despite this knowledge, patterns of hypertension and obesity were more similar to U.S. patterns than patterns found in the general Indian population. These participants were more likely to be taking medication for hypertension and cholesterol. It is likely that obese individuals in this group were more likely to be aware of their health risks than individuals who were not obese.

Family is extremely important in the social lives of Indians; this is true especially older adults. In many ways, the role of the older adult and their status within the family has important implications for the dietary and activity patterns of older adults. The oldest son and daughter-in –law are generally responsible for the care and well-being of the parents. Fatness, is generally thought to be a sign of health. Excessive thinness can result in criticism of the care of older adults, especially for the daughter-in-law. Older adults are often encouraged to eat and rarely encouraged to reduce intake or increase exercise. Further, the cultural role of older adults as head of household obliges them to attend many family and religions events. In Kolkata, this always includes large amounts of food, especially sweets. From participant observation, we know that older adults are expected to consume this food; not to do so would be considered a sign of displeasure at the quality of the food. Wealthy older adults in Kolkata, especially those who had retired, acknowledged their enjoyment of these activities. With diminishing social activity, these outings became important to elders. The food is a large part of this experience. Cultural roles, expectations and pressures contribute to the unhealthy dietary patterns in this population and most likely to the obesity rates as well.

Discussion

Culture or cultural factors are often cited as important factor in understanding population health and health disparities. However, systematic attempts at understanding the mechanisms linking culture and health at more than a local level are rare (Steyn et al. 2011; Ziraba, Fotso, and Ochako 2009) as methods for developing measures of broadly applicable culture models are limited (Brown 1991). 'Culture' is often invoked to explain differences between racial and/or ethnic groups in everything related to dietary preferences, energy expenditure and body image (Ulijaszek 2008; Brown 1991; Ba 2000; Helman 2001). However, the colloquial use of the term 'culture' often masks the complexities of the mechanisms and pathways that link a common pattern of beliefs and preferences to health outcomes. Factors such as food preference, perceptions the body and what it means to be healthy are usually considered to be 'cultural' factors vary across racial and ethnic groups but the importance of these factors and the mechanisms through which they work and even how strongly they are shared within a group are far from well understood. The cultural fabric of countries must be considered when assessing the ways in which NCDs are studied. Cultural norms pre-prescribe how women are represented in society and have been prevalent for centuries. Further, shared belief systems often vary not just by race and ethnic group but also by geographic area and age group. Medical and public health practitioners have to work towards developing policies that tackle local perceptions of body image and obesity and associated behaviors that influence cultural practices.

The case examples provided here provide a preliminary examination of the impact of culture on body image and the impact of the "ideal" body image on health. In the Kenyan case, we know, based on our field studies, that large body size is equated with health and wealth. This is particularly true among the older, rural participants and those who have limited exposure to media and western cultural notions. Our younger field assistants, particularly those who live in Kisumu or access the internet frequently, have a view more consistent with U.S. mainstream media, which portrays thinness with wealth and health. Thus, in examining the impact of culture on obesity, we must keep in mind that culture is dynamic and views of ideal body size and behaviors that people engage in to gain or maintain such an ideal will change over time and across age groups. Perhaps optimistically, Ulijaszek and Lofink (2008) suggest that, "although high cultural valuation of body fatness may contribute to the emergence of obesity, it may possibly cease to be an important contributor in subsequent generations" (p. 350).

With the Kenyan data we were able to demonstrate that the health outcomes associated with heavier body size are mixed. In some cases, larger body size was associated with poorer health and in other cases we found that larger body size was associated with better health. This suggests that there is some biological basis to the perception of large body size being associated with good health. Similarly, a number of studies have demonstrated a J- or U-shaped relationship between BMI and mortality (Ulijaszek and Lofink 2006). Increased morbidity due to infectious diseases have been demonstrated in a number of develop countries, including Kenya. Brown (1991) notes, "American ideals of thinness occur in a setting in which it is easy to become fat, and a preference for plumpness occurs in settings in which it is easy to remain lean." (p. 49). Perhaps these ideals are partially due to cultural perceptions of privilege but the local epidemiology may act enhance cultural perceptions. In western Kenya, where HIV/AIDS is highly prevalent, thinness is seen in extreme cases among the infected. Additionally, child mortality associated with diarrheal diseases and wasting is something that people view every day. Superimposed on the relative distribution of infectious and NCDs in this population is a great deal of food insecurity and underweight. In fact, the range of BMI that we observed was 12.4 to 42.3. Therefore, to change perceptions about health and body image, cultural views and ideals are likely not the only driving force. Interventions need to carefully consider such complexity.

In the Kolkata case, we examined a group of wealthy elders who do not have concerns about food security. While they experience NCD, they are surrounded by less economically advantaged populations who have extremely high rates of food insecurity, under nutrition and infectious disease. There is a clear association between socioeconomic class and body size, reinforcing the notion that large bodies are associated with wealth. Furthermore, the elderly in Kolkata who are heavier perceive their health as being better (Krishnaswami 2000; Garg et al. 2009). This perception is interesting given the fact that they have greater knowledge of the risks and consequences of NCD and better access to healthcare providers than in the Kenyan case. Observations in the field lead us to believe that cultural roles of elder heads of household contribute to the production of obesity in this population. Such cultural roles dictate that they spend a great deal of time attending cultural events in which food is central. Small body size and thinness are seen as a marker of poor care by daughters-in-law. Further, there is a generally held belief that medical intervention will cure any obesity related problems. These cultural ideals and practices have likely contributed to the increasing obesity rates among India's affluent. Some of these views will cut across age groups and socioeconomic status as India goes through a nutrition and epidemiological transition, while others will be unique to higher social classes. Before health practitioners plan interventions, we need to better understand the pathways through which culture influences obesity, including variations in culture across socioeconomic strata, ethnicity, age and gender (Brown 1991). Many obesity interventions have gone awry by using incomplete cultural knowledge (Ulijaszek 2008).

Cultural and socioeconomic influences on obesity are many and varied. Culture and SES can influence body size in many ways. Food insecurity can lead to obesogenic eating patterns, low nutrient intake and cultural habits which may not change when individuals, families and populations become food secure. As discussed in the introduction, as nations industrialize activity patterns and food choices change. The ways in which diet and activity pattern are altered during such transitions are dependent on the cultural context and are likely not going to be experienced in the same ways across or even within cultures. Food use is socially and culturally patterned and these patterns are slow to change as nations become food secure. As Ulijasek and Lofink (2006) note "because of the diverse contexts in which obesity has emerged and the complex environments in which it persists, a ubiquitous reversal in the prevalence of obesity at any state is unlikely in the near future" (p.351). Understanding the pathways through which culture influences food choices and activities are critical to developing appropriate interventions.

REFERENCES

[1] Adamo, K.B., A.W. Sheel, V. Onywera, J. Waudo, M. Boit, and M.S. Tremblay. 2011. Child obesity and fitness levels among Kenyan and Canadian children from urban and rural environments: a KIDS-CAN Research Alliance Study. *International Journal of Pediatric Obesity* 6 (2-2):e225-232.

[2] Ba, M.L. 2000. Obesity in Mauritania: epidemiologic aspects. *La Tunisie Medicale.* 78 (11):671-6.

[3] Batnitzky, A. K. 2011. Cultural constructions of "obesity": Understanding body size, social class and gender in Morocco. *Health and Place.* 17 (1):345-352.

[4] Blaxter, M. 2004. *Health.* Cambridge: Polity.

[5] Bray, G.A. . 2004. How do we get fat? An epidemiologic and metabolic approach. *Clinics in Dermatology.* 22 (4):281-288.

[6] Brown, P. J. 1991. Culture and the evolution of obesity. *Human Nature* 2 (1):31-57.

[7] Bury, M. 2000. *Health and Illness in a Changing Society.* Milton Park: Routledge

[8] CDC. *National Health and Nutrition Examination Survey.* National Center for Health Statistics 2010. Available from http://www.cdc.gov/nchs/nhanes/nhanes_ questionnaires.htm.

[9] CIA. 2011. The World Factbook.: Central Intelligency Agency.

[10] Cohen, M.N. 1999. *Health and the Rise of Civilization.* New Haven and London: Yale University Press.

[11] Fantino, M, F Baigts, M Cabanac, and M Apfelbaum. 1983. Effects of an overfeeding regimen--the affective component of the sweet sensation. *Appetite* 4 (3):155-64.

[12] Flegal, KM, MD Carroll, CL Ogden, and Curtin LR. 2010. Prevalence and trends in obesity among United States adults. *Journal of the American Medical Association* 303:235-41.

[13] Furnham, A, J Moutafi, and P Baguma. 2002. A cross-cultural study on the role of weight and waist-to-hip ratio on female attractiveness. *Personality and Individual Differences* 32 (4):729-745.

[14] Ganguli, D., N. Das, I. Saha, P. Biswas, S. Datta, B. Mukhopadhyay, D. Chaudhuri, S. Ghosh, and S. Dey. 2011. Major dietary patterns and their associations with cardiovascular risk factors among women in West Bengal, India. *British Journal of Nutrition* 105 (10):1520-1529.

[15] Garg, C, SA Khan, SH Ansari, and M Garg. 2009. Prevalence of Obesity in Indian Women. *Obesity Reviews: An official journal of the International Association for the Study of Obesity.* 11:105-108.

[16] Helman, C. 2001. *Health and Illness.* Fourth ed. London: Arnold.

[17] Hossain, P., B. Kawar, and N.M. El. 2007. Obesity and diabetes in the developing world-a growing challenge. *New England Journal of Medicine* 356 (3):213- 215.

[18] Hruschka, D.J. 2009. Culture as an explanation in population health. *Annals of Human Biology* 36 (3):235-247.

[19] IASO. 2003. International Association for the Study of Obesity. http://www.iaso.org_.

[20] Jamison, D.T. 2006. Investing in health. In *Disease Control Priorities in Developing Countries*, edited by D. T. Jamison, J. G. Breman, A. R. Measham, G. Alleyne, M.

Claeson, D. B. Evans, P. Jha, A. Mills and P. Musgrove. New York: Oxford University Press.

[21] Joshi, S.R. 2003. Metabolic syndrome-emerging clusters of the Indian phenotype. *Journal of the Association of Physicians in India* 51:445-446.

[22] Kolotkin, R.L., K. Meter, and G.R. Williams. 2001. Quality of life and obesity. *Obesity Reviews* 2: 219-29.

[23] Krishnaswami, K. 2000. Country profile: India, nutritional disorders - old and challenging. *Lancet* 351:1268-1269.

[24] Labarthe, D.R., M.D. Blaufox, W.M. Smith, C.R. Lacy, H. Schnaper, F. LaBaw, S. Mascioli, J. Davey, and E. Lakatos. 1991. Systolic Hypertension in the Elderly Program (SHEP). Part 5: Baseline blood pressure and pulse rate measurements. *Hypertension* 17 (3 Suppl):1162-76.

[25] Lohman, TG, AF Roche, and R Martorell. 1988. *Anthropometric Standardization Reference Manual*. Champaign: Human Kinetics Books.

[26] Martorell, R.L., K. Khan, M.L. Hughes, and L.M. Grummer-Strawn. 2000. Obesity in women from developing countries. *European Journal of Clinical Nutrition* 54:247-252.

[27] Mathias, S. D., C. L. Williamson, H.H. Colwell, M.G. Cisternas, D.J. Pasta, B.S. Stolshek, and D.L. Patrick. 1997 Assessing health-related quality-of-life and health state preference in persons with obesity. *Quality of Life Research* 6 (4):311-322.

[28] Mokhtar, N., J. Elati, R. Chabir, A. Bour, K. Elkari, N.P. Schlossman, B. Caballero, and H. Aguenaou. 2001. Diet Culture and Obesity in Northern Africa. *Journal of Nutrition* 131:887-892.

[29] Omran, A.R. 1971. The Epidemiologic Transition : A Theory of the Epidemiology of Population Change. *Milbank Memorial Fund Quarterly* 49 (4):509-538.

[30] Popkin, B.M. 1994. The nutrition transition in low-income countries: an emering crisis. *Nutrition Reviews* 52 (9):285-298.

[31] ———. 2004. Nutrition Revolution. The Nutrition Transition: An Overview of World Patterns of Change. (62(7 Pt 2):S):140-3.

[32] Raymond, S.U., S. Leeder, and H.M. Greenberg. 2006. Obesity and cardiovascular disease in developing countries: a growing problem and an economic threat. *Current Opinion in Clinical and Nutrition and Metabolic Care* 9 (2):111-16.

[33] Rguibi, M., and R. Belahsen. 2006. Fattening practices among Moroccan Saharawi women. *Eastern Mediterranean Health Journal* 12 (5):619-24.

[34] Schmidhuber, J. 2005. The growing global obesity problem: some policy options to address it. *Journal of Agricultural and Development Economics* 1 (2):272-290.

[35] Selassie, M., and A.C. Sinha. 2011. The epidemiology and aetiology of obesity: A global challenge. . *Best Practice and Research Clinical Anaesthesiology* 25:1-9.

[36] Smil, V. 2000. *Feeding the world - A challenge for the twenty-first century*. Cambridge, Massachusetts: MIT Press.

[37] Smith, O. . 2006. *NCDs and the Poor*. World Bank. Draft.

[38] Steyn, N.P., D. Labadarios, E. Maunder, J.H. Nel, and C. Lombard. 2005. Secondary anthropometric data analysis of the National Food Consumption Survey in South Africa: the double burden. *Nutrition* 21:4-13.

[39] Steyn, N.P., J.H. Nel, W.A. Paker, R. Ayah, and D. Mbithe. 2011. Dietary, social, and environmental determinants of obesity in Kenyan women. *Scandinavian Journal of Public Health* 39 (1):88-97.

[40] Stubbs, R.J. . 1998. Appetite feeding behavior and energy balance in human subjects. *Nutrition Reviews* 57:1-16.

[41] Suzman, R. 2009. The National Social Life, Health and Aging Project: An Introduction. *Journals of Gerontology* 64B (Supplement 1):i5-i11.

[42] Ulijaszek, S.J, and H. Lofink. 2006. Obesity in Biocultural Perspective. *Annual Review of Anthropology* 35:337-360.

[43] Ulijaszek, S.J. 2008. Seven models of population obesity. *Angiology* 59 (Supplement 2):34S-38S.

[44] UNAIDS. 2009. Report on the Global HIV/AIDS Epidemic. Geneva: UNAIDS.

[45] Wachira, L, N Simiyu, and V Onywera. 2009. Physical Activity Practices among Adults with Diabetes: A Clinical Survey on Management of Diabetes Mellitus at Kenyatta National Hospital, Kenya. *African Journal of Applied Human Sciences* 1 (1):22-30.

[46] Wachira, L., N. Simiyu, and V. Onywera. 2009. Physical Activity Practices among Adults with Diabetes: A Clinical Survey on Management of Diabetes Mellitus at Kenyatta National Hospital, Kenya. *African Journal of Applied Human Sciences* 1 (1): 22-30.

[47] Wagner, A.K., K. Wyss, B. Gandek, P.M. Kilima, S. Lorenz, and D. Whiting. 1999. A Kiswahili version of the SF-36 Health Survey for use in Tanzania: translation and tests of scaling assumptions. *Quality of Life Research* 8:101-110.

[48] Ware, J.E. 2007. SF-36 Helath Survey Update.: Rand.

[49] Ware, J.E., and C.D. Sherbourne. 1992. The MOS 36-item short-form health survey (SF-36). I. COnceptual framework and item selection. *Medical Care* 30 (6):473-483.

[50] WHO. 2003. *Diet, nutrition and the prevention of chronic diseases*. Report of a joint WHO/FAO Expert. Consultation. WHO Technical Report Series 916.

[51] ———. 2005. *The SuRF Report 2. Surveillance of chronic disease Risk Factor. Country-level data and comparable estimates.*

[52] Williams, S.R. 2009. Measures of chronic conditions and diseases associated with aging in the National Social Life, Health and Aging Project. *Journals of Gerontology* 64B (Supplement 1):i67-i75.

[53] Wyss, K., A.K. Wagner, D. Whiting, D.M. Mtasiwa, M. Tanner, B. Gandek, and P.M. Kilima. 1999. Validation of the Kiswahili version of the SF-36 Health Survey in a representative sample of an urban population in Tanzania. *Quality of Life Research* 8 (1-2):111-20.

[54] Ziraba, A.K., J.C. Fotso, and R. Ochako. 2009. Overweight and obesity in urban Africa: A problem of the rich or the poor? . *BMC Public Health* 9:465.

INDEX

B

C

F

I

J

K

L

M

N

O

P

Q

R

S

T

U

V

W

Y